3-A

학년

한국에서 유일한
중학영문법
알짜 3000제

Iam books

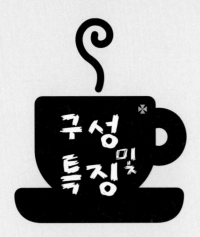

구성 및 특징

1 Grammar Points

사진과 대표 예문만 봐도 쉽게 영문법의 개념을 이해할 수 있는 Visual Approach를 도입하여 문법 설명을 시각화하였습니다. 문법 설명은 머리에 쏙쏙!! 예문과 설명은 한 눈에!! 참신한 예문과 원어민들이 실제로 사용하는 표현을 담았습니다.

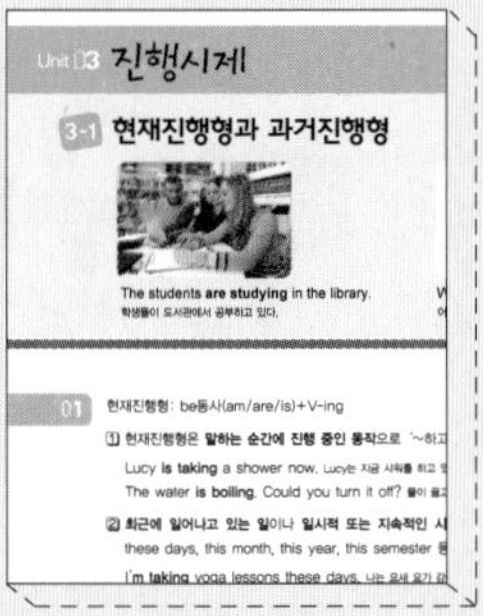

2 서술형 기초다지기

일대일로 대응되는 다양한 문제들을 구성하여 문법 개념을 확실히 이해할 수 있도록 하였습니다. 이를 통해 서술형 문제에 대비할 수 있도록 하였으며 실제 문장 구성 능력을 향상시킬 수 있도록 쓰기 영역을 강화하였습니다. 단순 문법 연습이 아닌 응용·심화 과정을 통해 기초 실력 또한 차곡차곡 쌓을 수 있습니다.

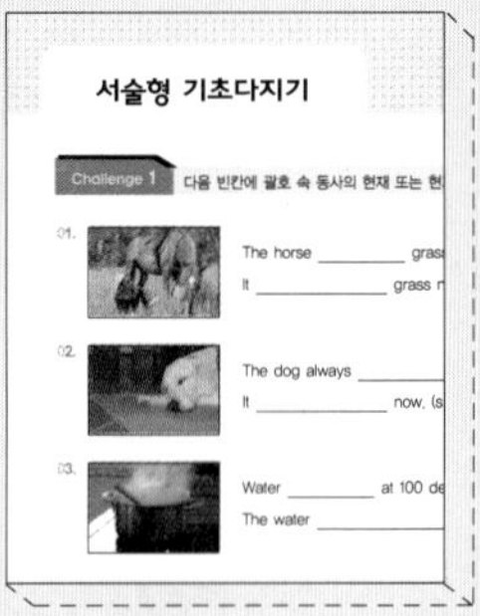

3 이것이 시험에 출제되는 영문법이다!

어떤 문제가 주로 출제되는지를 미리 아는 사람과 막연히 공부를 열심히 한 사람의 성적은 하늘과 땅 차이! 12년간의 내신 만점신화를 이루어낸 저자의 비밀노트를 통해 내신문제를 출제하는 선생님들의 의도와 출제유형, 주관식과 서술형의 출제경향을 정확히 꿰뚫어 보는 눈을 키울 수 있을 것입니다.

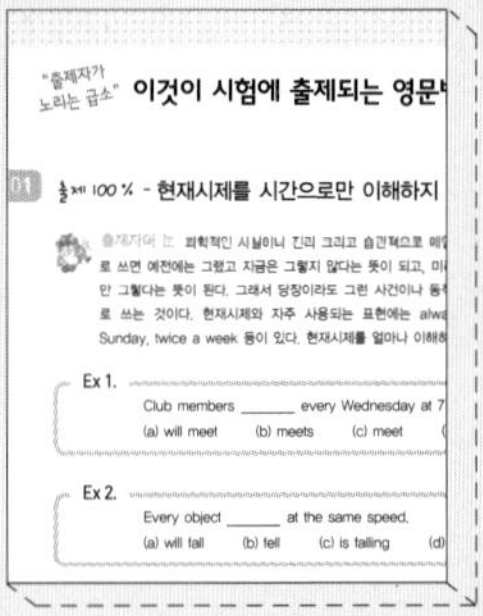

4 기출 응용문제

실제 중학교 내신 시험에서 빈출되는 필수 문법문제와 응용문제를 수록하여 각 chapter에서 배운 문법 사항을 다양한 유형의 문제를 통해 확인하고 연습해 볼 수 있도록 구성하였습니다.

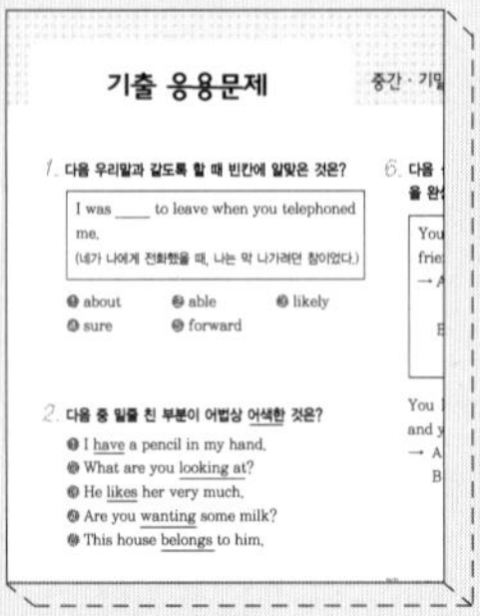

※ 오답 노트 만들기

기출 응용문제 중 틀린 문제를 오답 노트에 정리할 수 있도록 구성하였습니다. 틀린 문제의 문법 개념을 다시 확인하고 해당 문제 유형을 다시는 틀리지 않도록 스스로 공부해 볼 수 있는 코너입니다.

※ 중간 · 기말고사 100점 100승

학교 시험에서 자주 나오는 빈출유형을 분석하여 출제 가능성이 가장 높은 문제를 중심으로 수록하였습니다. 간단한 객관식 문제를 비롯하여 대화문과 독해문, 주관식 문제 등 다양한 문제를 풀면서 자신의 실력을 정확하게 진단해 볼 수 있습니다.

※ 평가대비 단답형 주관식

문법 핵심을 파악하고 어법에 맞는 문장을 직접 쓸 수 있도록 구성하여 학교 단답형 주관식 문제에 철저히 대비할 수 있도록 하였습니다.

※ 실전 서술형 평가문제

교육청 출제경향에 맞춘 서술형 평가대비 문제로, 학생들의 사고력과 창의력을 길러줍니다. 해당 chapter에서 출제될 수 있는 서술형 문항을 개발하여 각 학교의 서술형 평가문제에 철저히 대비할 수 있도록 하였습니다. 단순 암기에서 벗어나 직접 써보고 생각해 볼 수 있는 코너입니다.

chapter 3. 조동사(Modals)

chapter 4. 부정사(Infinitives)

chapter 7. 명사와 관사
(Nouns and Articles)

chapter 8. 대명사(Pronouns)

chapter 9. 형용사(Adjectives)

Chapter 1

시제 I (Tense I)

Unit 01 현재시제

1-1 현재시제의 활용

The Winter Olympics **takes place** every four years.
동계올림픽은 4년에 한 번씩 개최된다.
Figure skating **is** a popular Winter Olympic sport.
피겨스케이팅은 인기 있는 동계올림픽 종목이다.

01 매일 **반복적으로 일어나는 일이나 행동, 지속적인 상태나 성질**을 나타낼 때 현재시제를 쓴다.

Nurses **take** care of patients in hospitals. 간호사는 병원에서 환자들을 돌본다.
We **eat** lunch at one o'clock every day. 우리는 매일 1시에 점심을 먹는다.
Brian **is** angry when he meets his girlfriend. Brian은 여자친구를 만나면 화를 낸다.

02 **과학적, 일반적 사실**을 나타낼 때도 현재시제를 쓴다.

The earth **goes** around the sun. 지구는 태양 주위를 돈다.
Water **freezes** at zero Celsius. 물은 0℃에서 언다.
Jeju-do **is** the largest island in South Korea. 제주도는 한국에서 가장 큰 섬이다.

03 이미 **정해진 일정** 또는 **비행기, 기차, 영화 시간표**와 같이 확실히 정해진 일정에는 현재시제가 미래의 의미를 나타낸다. leave, arrive, start, begin, end, close, open 등이 자주 쓰이는 동사들이다. 단, 개인의 정해진 일정에는 현재시제를 쓰지 않는다.

My plane **arrives** at 7:00 tomorrow evening. 내 비행기는 내일 저녁 7시에 도착한다.
The bus **leaves** at 8:00 tomorrow morning. 그 버스는 내일 아침 8시에 떠난다.
The winter semester **starts** next week. 겨울 학기는 다음 주에 시작된다.

※ Ava **is having** lunch with Jane on Friday. Ava는 금요일에 Jane과 점심 식사를 할 것이다.
▶ 개인의 정해진 일정에는 현재진행형 또는 be going to 사용

04 시간의 부사절(when, before, after, until)과 조건의 부사절(if, unless) 안에서는 **현재시제를 써서 미래를 나타낸다.**

When you **finish** the course, a certificate will be sent to you.
그 과정을 끝마칠 때, 당신에게 자격증이 발송될 것이다.
If another job **comes** along this fall, I will take it. 이번 가을에 다른 일자리가 나타나면 그걸 잡을 것이다.
Until he **apologizes** about the accident, I will not talk to him.
그 사고에 대해 사과할 때까지 나는 그에게 말을 하지 않을 것이다.

서술형 기초다지기

정답 p. 2

Challenge 1 다음 괄호 안의 동사를 이용하여 현재형 문장을 만드세요.

01. Julia _____ (speak) Japanese very well.

02. Kevin _____ (not / drink) coffee very often.

03. The Amazon River _____ (flow) into the Atlantic Ocean.

04. The amusement park _____ (open) at 9:00 and _____ (close) at 6:30 every day.

05. The Olympic Games _____ (take) place every four years.

06. Water _____ (boil) at 100 degrees Celsius.

Challenge 2 다음 단어들을 사용하여 미래의 의미를 지닌 현재시제 문장을 만드세요.

보기	my plane / leave / at 8:00 tomorrow morning. → *My plane leaves at 8:00 tomorrow morning.*

01. the concert / begin / at eight tonight

   → _____

02. the game / start / at one tomorrow afternoon

   → _____

03. the movie / what time / begin / tomorrow

   → _____

Challenge 3 다음 괄호 안의 표현 중 알맞은 것을 고르세요.

01. He (will finish / finishes) the project when he (will return / returns) to Korea.

02. If it (will be / is) warm tomorrow, we (will drive / drive) in the country.

2-1 과거시제의 활용

Yu-na Kim **won** the gold medal in the Ladies' Figure Skating at the Vancouver 2010 Winter Olympic Games.
김연아는 2010 밴쿠버 동계올림픽 여자 피겨스케이팅에서 금메달을 땄다.

01 과거에 시작하여 과거에 끝나서 현재와는 아무런 상관이 없을 때 **과거시제**를 쓴다. 주로 과거의 특정 시간을 나타내는 부사(yesterday, last week, last night, in 1999, in the 1970s 등)와 함께 쓴다.

We **were** impressed with his life story. 우리는 그의 인생에 대한 이야기를 듣고 감명 받았다.
Michael Jordan **was** a great basketball player in the NBA. 마이클 조던은 NBA에서 훌륭한 농구선수였다.
She **went** shopping every Sunday when she **was** young. 그녀가 어렸을 때 매주 일요일마다 쇼핑을 갔다.
Mi-seon first **met** her husband in 2006. 미선은 남편을 2006년에 처음 만났다.

02 **역사적 사실**은 당연히 과거시제를 쓴다.

Dinosaurs **lived** on the earth. 공룡들이 지구상에 살았었다.
King Sejong **invented** the Korean Alphabet, Hangul. 세종대왕이 한글을 만들었다.
The Korean war **broke out** in 1950. 한국전쟁은 1950년에 발발했다.

03 과거시제는 동사원형 뒤에 -ed나 -d를 붙인다.

규칙 변화	look – look**ed**	wash – wash**ed**	visit – visit**ed**
-e로 끝날 때	decide – decide**d**	promise – promise**d**	live – live**d**
자음 + -y로 끝날 때	study – stud**ied**	reply – repl**ied**	worry – worr**ied**
모음 + -y로 끝날 때	enjoy – enjoy**ed**	delay – delay**ed**	destroy – destroy**ed**
「단모음 + 자음」으로 끝날 때	stop – stop**ped**	drop – drop**ped**	plan – plan**ned**
강세가 있는 2음절 동사	visit – visit**ed**	offer – offer**ed**	enter – enter**ed**

04 주의해야 할 동사의 과거형: 불규칙 변화 동사(현재 – 과거 – 과거완료)

cost – cost – cost	spend – spent – spent	hurt – hurt – hurt
leave – left – left	write – wrote – written	hit – hit – hit
put – put – put	build – built – built	cut – cut – cut

서술형 기초다지기

Challenge 1 　다음 빈칸에 괄호 안의 동사를 알맞은 과거시제로 쓰세요.

01. It was warm, so I _____ off my coat. (take)

02. I was very tired, so I _____ to bed early. (go)

03. We went to Kevin's house, but he _____ at home. (be)

04. It was a funny situation, but nobody _____. (laugh)

05. I knew my dad was very busy, so I _____ him. (bother)

06. The film wasn't very good. We _____ it very much. (enjoy)

07. The window was open, and a bird _____ into the room. (fly)

Challenge 2 　〈보기〉와 같이 주어진 표현을 참고하여 의문문과 대답문을 완성하세요.

보기	Pablo Picasso / live / in London　　　→ No / in Paris Q: *Did Pablo Picasso live in London?* A: *No, he didn't. He lived in Paris.*

01. Marie and Pierre Curie / discover / penicillin → No / radium

    Q: _____

    A: _____

02. Marilyn Monroe / come / from France　　　→ No / the United States

    Q: _____

    A: _____

03. Romeo / love / Cleopatra　　　　　　　→ No / Juliet

    Q: _____

    A: _____

2-2 used to

Lucy **used to** play tennis. = Lucy **would** play tennis.
Lucy는 테니스를 치곤 했다.
→ She played tennis regularly for some time in the past, but she doesn't play tennis now.

---

01 used to는 '~하곤 했(었)다'의 의미로 **지금은 하지 않지만 과거에 했던 반복된 행동**을 나타낸다. 「used to+동사원형」으로 쓴다.

Most people **used to**(=would) walk or ride horses. Today they drive cars.
대부분의 사람들은 걸어 다니거나 말을 타고 다니곤 했다. 오늘날 사람들은 차를 운전한다.

Most women **used to**(=would) wash clothes by hand. Today they have washing machines.
대부분의 여자들은 손빨래를 하곤 했다. 오늘날 여자들은 세탁기가 있다.

---

02 실제 원어민조차 규칙적인 것과 불규칙적인 것을 구별하기 애매하기 때문에 **과거의 습관, 특히 행동에 대해서는 used to와 would를 구별 없이 쓰고** 과거의 행위가 아닌 **'상태'인 경우에만 used to**를 사용한다.

There <u>**used to**</u> be four movie theaters in town. 마을에는 극장이 4개 있었다.
　　　→ would (x)

Julia <u>**used to**</u> have very long hair. Julia는 긴 머리를 하고 있었다.
　　　→ would (x)

---

03 used to의 **부정**은 didn't use(d) to 또는 never used to를 쓴다. '예전에는 ~하지 않았지만 지금은 ~한다'라는 의미이다. **의문문은 「Did+주어+use(d) to+동사원형 ~?」**으로 쓴다.

I **didn't use(d) to** play the guitar. 나는 기타를 연주한 적이 없었다. (→ Once I didn't play the guitar, but now I do.)

I **never used to** take a taxi. 나는 택시를 타 본 적이 없었다. (→ Once I didn't take a taxi, but now I do.)

A: **Did** you **use(d) to** work at an insurance company? 보험회사에서 일한 적 있니?

B: Yes, I did. / No, I didn't. 응, 있어. / 아니, 일한 적 없어.

---

04 「be/get used to+V-ing」는 '~하는 데에 익숙하다'의 뜻으로 「be accustomed to+V-ing」도 같은 의미로 사용된다. 「used to+동사원형」과는 의미가 전혀 다르다.

Scott **is used to** using chopsticks, but it was difficult at the beginning.
Scott은 젓가락을 사용하는 데 익숙하지만 처음에는 어려웠다.

I **am used to** living alone. 나는 혼자 사는 것에 익숙하다.

서술형 기초다지기

Challenge 1 다음 빈칸에 used to와 would를 둘 다 쓸 수 있는 경우에는 would를 쓰고, would 를 쓸 수 없는 경우에는 used to를 써서 문장을 완성하세요.

01.

past

Peter _____ (lazy).
Now he's hard-working.

02.

past

Susan _____ (watch) TV all the
time. Now she almost never watches TV.

Challenge 2 다음 문장을 읽고 used to를 이용하여 빈칸을 완성하세요.

01. When I was young, I was shy. Now I'm not shy.

→ I _____ shy, but now I'm not.

02. Now you live in this town. Where did you live before you come here?

→ Where _____ before you come here?

03. When I was a child, I watched cartoons on TV. I don't watch cartoons anymore. Now I
watch news programs. How about you?

→ I _____ cartoons on TV, but I don't anymore.

→ I _____ news programs, but now I do.

→ What _____ on TV when you were a child?

Challenge 3 다음 괄호 안의 동사를 알맞은 형태로 바꾸어 빈칸을 완성하세요.

01. David quit jogging two years ago. He used _____ (jog) four miles a day.

02. I live in the country. I'm not used _____ (live) in the city.

03. This building is now a furniture store. It used _____ (be) a movie theater.

04. It was difficult at first, but Laura is used _____ (eat) Gimchi.

Unit 03 진행시제

3-1 현재진행형과 과거진행형

The students **are studying** in the library.
학생들이 도서관에서 공부하고 있다.

What **were** you **doing** at 10:00 last night?
어젯밤 10시에 무엇을 하고 있었니?

01 현재진행형: be동사(am/are/is)+V-ing

① 현재진행형은 **말하는 순간에 진행 중인 동작**으로 '~하고 있다, ~하는 중이다'의 뜻이다.

Lucy **is taking** a shower now. Lucy는 지금 샤워를 하고 있다.

The water **is boiling**. Could you turn it off? 물이 끓고 있다. 그것 좀 꺼줄래?

② **최근에 일어나고 있는 일**이나 **일시적 또는 지속적인 시간에 걸쳐 진행 중인 동작이나 상태**를 나타내며, these days, this month, this year, this semester 등과 자주 어울려 쓰인다.

I**'m taking** yoga lessons these days. 나는 요새 요가 강습을 받고 있다.

The weather **is becoming** colder and colder. 날씨가 점점 더 추워지고 있다.

Eun-seon **is trying** to improve her Japanese this year.
은선이는 올해 일본어 실력을 향상시키려 노력하고 있다.

③ always와 함께 쓰인 경우 주로 **말하는 사람의 불만이나 비난의 뜻**이 담겨 있다.

Bob **is always complaining**. He's never satisfied. Bob은 항상 불평을 한다. 그는 절대 만족하지 못한다.

You**'re always throwing** your socks everywhere. 너는 항상 양말을 아무데나 던져 놓는구나.

02 과거진행형: be동사의 과거형(was/were)+V-ing

① 과거의 어느 한 시점에 진행되고 있던 동작을 나타내는 것으로 '~하고 있었다'의 뜻이다.

This time last year I **was living** in Singapore. 작년 이맘 때 나는 싱가포르에 살고 있었다.

Nancy **was sleeping** at 10:00 yesterday. Nancy는 어제 10시에 자고 있었다.

② 과거진행형과 과거시제가 함께 쓰일 경우 **먼저 하고 있었던 일은 과거진행으로 쓰고**, 다른 일이 **도중에 끼어들어 짧은 시간 동안 행해진 동작은 과거시제**로 쓴다.

I **was studying** when the electricity **went** off. 전기가 나갔을 때 나는 공부하고 있었다.

As he **was waiting** for his girlfriend, it **began** to rain. 그가 여자친구를 기다리고 있는데 비가 내리기 시작했다.

서술형 기초다지기

Challenge 1 다음 빈칸에 괄호 속 동사의 현재 또는 현재진행형을 쓰세요.

01.

The horse _____ grass every day. (eat)

It _____ grass now. (eat)

02.

The dog always _____ at night. (sleep)

It _____ now. (sleep)

03.

Water _____ at 100 degree Celsius. (boil)

The water _____. Could you turn it off? (boil)

Challenge 2 다음 상황에 맞게 주어진 단어를 활용하여 문장을 완성하세요.

01.

When the e-mail _____, she _____ the coffee.

arrive / drink

02.

While Alice _____ to the bank, the cell phone _____.

ring / drive

03.

Tommy and Nancy _____ in the street when it _____ raining.

walk / start

3-2 미래진행형 / 진행형으로 쓸 수 없는 동사

This soup **tastes** too salty.
이 국은 너무 짠 맛이 난다.
The cook **is tasting** the soup.
그 요리사는 그 국을 맛보고 있다.

01 미래진행형은 **미래의 특정 시점에 진행 중인 일**을 나타낼 때 쓴다. 「will be+V-ing」로 쓰며 '~하고 있는 중일 것이다'로 해석한다.

I**'ll be having** dinner with my friends when you come back home.
네가 집에 돌아올 때쯤이면 나는 친구들과 저녁을 먹고 있는 중일 거야.

Visit me around 2 p.m. I**'ll be waiting** for you. 오후 2시쯤 우리 집에 와. 기다리고 있을게.

Everyone in the family wants to meet you. I**'ll be counting** the minutes till I see you this Friday.
가족 모두가 당신을 만나보고 싶어 해요. 이번 금요일에 만날 시간을 손꼽아 기다리고 있을 거예요.

02 상태동사(state verbs)는 주어가 동작을 나타내지 않고 **어떤 상태로 지속되고 있음을 나타내기 때문에 진행형으로 쓸 수 없다**. 감정, 지각, 소유 등을 나타내는 동사인 like, want, know, believe, think, hear, feel, taste, see, seem, belong, have 등이 이에 해당한다.

I **want** to have a car. 나는 차를 갖고 싶다.
→ I am wanting to have a car. (×)

Sunny **seems** happy. Sunny는 행복해 보인다.
→ Sunny is seeming happy. (×)

03 **상태동사가 상태가 아닌 동작을 나타내는 경우**가 있다. 이때는 동작을 나타내는 진행형을 쓸 수 있다.

I **think** she is crazy.
나는 그녀가 미쳤다고 생각한다.

Susan **looks** angry.
Susan은 화나 보인다.

She **has** two puppies.
그녀는 강아지 두 마리를 갖고 있다.

The milk **smells** odd.
그 우유는 이상한 냄새가 난다.

I**'m thinking** about the problem.
나는 그 문제에 대해 생각 중이다.

What **are** you **looking** at?
너는 무엇을 쳐다보고 있니?

I **was having** dinner when the light went out.
불이 나갔을 때 나는 저녁을 먹고 있었다.

She **is smelling** the flowers.
그녀는 꽃향기를 맡고 있다.

서술형 기초다지기

정답 p. 2

Challenge 1 다음 우리말과 의미가 같도록 빈칸에 알맞은 말을 쓰세요.

01. 어머니는 신문을 읽고 계실 것이다.

→ My mother _____ _____ _____ a newspaper.

02. 내일 아침에 너는 무엇을 하고 있을 거니?

→ What _____ you _____ _____ tomorrow morning?

03. 오늘 오후에는 내가 일을 하고 있을 것이다.

→ I _____ _____ _____ this afternoon.

04. 다음 주 토요일에 나는 Karen과 영화를 보고 있을 것이다.

→ I _____ _____ _____ a movie with Karen next Saturday.

Challenge 2 진행형으로 쓸 수 있는 동사와 쓸 수 없는 동사를 구별하여 빈칸을 완성하세요.

01. A: What are you doing?

B: I _____ (smell) the flowers. They _____ (smell) good.

02. This box _____ (weigh) a lot. I just handed the box to the postal worker.

Right now she _____ (weigh) it to see how much postage it needs.

03. A: What kind of tea do you like?

B: Well, I'm drinking black tea, but I _____ (prefer) green tea.

04. It's night. There's no moon. Kelly is outside. She _____ (look) at the sky.

She _____ (see) more stars than she can count.

4-1 미래를 나타내는 시제 (1)

These shoes are very comfortable. I **will** buy them. 이 신발은 매우 편하다. 이 신발을 살 거야.

I'**m going to** clean my room this evening. 나는 오늘 저녁에 방 청소를 할 거야.

01 미래의 일을 예측 또는 추측하거나 앞으로 일어날 객관적인 사실을 표현할 때 will과 be going to 둘 다 쓸 수 있다.

It **will** rain tomorrow. 내일 비가 올 것 같다.
=It **is going to** rain tomorrow.

02 '~하겠다'라는 의지(willingness)를 나타낼 때나 말하는 순간에 결정한 일을 나타낼 때 will을 쓴다. 의지와 관계없이 생각하거나 믿는 것 또는 자연적 결과를 나타낼 때도 will을 쓴다.

O.K. I **will** be there in 10 minutes. 좋아. 10분 후에 거기로 갈게.
She **will** succeed because she works hard. 그녀는 열심히 일하기 때문에 성공할 것이다.

03 말하기 전부터 이미 마음의 결정을 해 놓은 예정된 계획(prior plans)에 대해 말할 때에는 be going to를 쓴다. 이미 예정된 일에는 will을 쓰지 않는다.

A: What **are** you **going to** do this evening? 오늘 저녁에 뭐 할 거니?
B: I'**m going to** watch a movie with Nancy. Nancy와 함께 영화 보기로 했어.
A: What are your vacation plans? 휴가 계획이 뭐니?
B: We **are going to** spend two weeks on Jeju island. 제주도에서 2주를 보낼 거야.

04 말하는 사람의 마음과 관계없이 뻔히 일어날 상황을 말할 때나 현재의 상황을 근거로 '~할 것이다'라고 예측할 때 be going to를 쓴다.

They'**re going to** get married next week. 그들은 다음 주에 결혼할 거다.
※ They **will** get married. 그들은 결혼할 거다. ▶ 구체적인 정황 없이 막연한 미래 예측

Jane is hungry. She'**s going to** eat the hamburger.
Jane은 배가 고프다. 그녀는 그 햄버거를 먹을 거야. ▶ 현재의 상황을 근거로 추측

서술형 기초다지기

정답 p. 2

Challenge 1 다음 괄호 안의 표현 중 알맞은 것을 고르세요.

01. A: You know that book I lent you? Could I have it back if you're finished with it?

    B: Of course. I (will / be going to) give it to you this afternoon.

02. A: Did you hear? Lucy had a car accident and is in hospital now.

    B: Yes, I know. I (will / am going to) visit her this evening.

03. A: Why are you moving the furniture?

    B: I (will / am going to) clean the floor.

Challenge 2 〈보기〉와 같이 be going to를 이용하여 문장을 완성하세요.

보기

by train

A: Is he going to travel by airplane?
B: *No, he isn't. He is going to travel by train.*

01.

new cell phones

A: Are they going to buy new computers?
B: _____

02.

a horse

A: Is Jennifer going to ride a bicycle?
B: _____

4-2 미래를 나타내는 시제 (2)

Stella **is flying** to New York in two hours.
Stella는 2시간 후에 뉴욕으로 간다.

She **is about to** take a picture.
그녀는 막 사진을 찍으려고 한다.

01 어떤 일을 하기로 **이미 정한 개인의 일정인 경우 현재진행형**으로 **미래**를 나타낼 수 있으며 be going to와 같은 의미로 쓰인다. 단, 기차 시간표나 영화 상영 시간표는 현재시제를 써서 미래를 나타낸다.

She **is meeting** her ex-boyfriend this Sunday. 그녀는 이번 일요일에 예전 남자친구를 만날 예정이다.
▶ 현재진행형이 미래를 대신

She **is meeting** her ex-boyfriend now. 그녀는 예전 남자친구를 만나고 있다. ▶ 미래가 아닌 현재 진행 중인 동작

We're **taking** a trip to Hawaii next year. 우리는 내년에 하와이로 여행을 갈 예정이다. ▶ 현재진행형이 미래를 대신
The next train **leaves** at 6:00 p.m. tomorrow. 다음 기차는 내일 오후 6시에 떠난다. ▶ 현재가 미래를 대신

02 **몇 분 이내에 일어날 아주 가까운 미래**를 표현할 때는 be about to를 쓰고 '막 ~하려고 한다'로 해석한다.

Please don't make a noise! The movie **is about to** start. 조용히 해주세요. 영화가 곧 시작하려고 해요.
I **was about to** leave when she came into the office. 그녀가 사무실로 들어왔을 때 나는 막 나가려던 참이었다.

03 **과거의 시점에서 미래를 표현**할 때 will은 would를 쓰고 be going to는 was/were going to로 쓴다. 미래로 쓰인 현재진행형의 과거는 be동사를 was/were로 바꾸고, be about to도 be동사를 was/were로 바꿔 쓴다.

That bag looked heavy. I **would** help you with it. 저 가방은 무거워 보였다. 나는 너를 도와주려고 했었다.
We **were going to** play tennis yesterday, but it rained all day.
우리는 어제 테니스를 치려고 했었지만 하루 종일 비가 왔다.
I **was meeting** her at the airport. 나는 그녀를 공항에서 만날 예정이었다.
Were you **staying** at this hotel in Hong Kong? 홍콩에서 이 호텔에 머물 예정이었니?
I **was about to** go out when the phone rang. 전화벨이 울렸을 때 나는 막 나가려던 참이었다.

서술형 기초다지기

Challenge 1   다음 주어진 정보를 이용하여 현재진행시제로 미래를 표현해 보세요.

01.

on Saturday / play tennis

Peter _____.

02.

have dinner / with Bob

Lisa _____.

03.

go / to the movies / tonight

Jason _____.

04.

go / to the party

Laura and Kelly _____.

Challenge 2   〈보기〉와 같이 be about to를 이용하여 문장을 완성하세요.

> **보기**   The door is closed. Kelly has her hand on the doorknob.
> → *She is about to open the door.* (open the door).

01. Bob repaired his bicycle. His hands are very dirty. He is holding a bar of soap.

→ _____ (wash his hands)

02. Susan is putting on her coat and heading for the door.

→ _____ (leave outside)

03. Julia has just checked to make sure the doors are locked and turned off the lights in the living room. She is heading toward the bedroom.

→ _____ (go to bed)

이것이 시험에 출제되는 영문법이다!

01 출제 100% - 현재시제를 시간으로만 이해하지 마라.

 출제자의 눈 과학적인 사실이나 진리 그리고 습관적으로 매일 반복되는 일상은 현재시제를 쓴다. 과거로 쓰면 예전에는 그랬고 지금은 그렇지 않다는 뜻이 되고, 미래로 쓰면 지금까지는 그렇지 않고 앞으로만 그렇다는 뜻이 된다. 그래서 당장이라도 그런 사건이나 동작이 발생할 수 있다는 의미는 현재시제로 쓰는 것이다. 현재시제와 자주 사용되는 표현에는 always(빈도부사), every morning, every Sunday, twice a week 등이 있다. 현재시제를 얼마나 이해하는지를 묻는 문제가 출제된다.

Ex 1.

Club members _____ every Wednesday at 7 p.m.

(a) will meet   (b) meets   (c) meet   (d) met

Ex 2.

Every object _____ at the same speed.

(a) will fall   (b) fell   (c) is falling   (d) falls

02 출제 100% - 과거는 현재와는 아무런 관련이 없다.

 출제자의 눈 과거시제는 주로 과거를 표시하는 어구(yesterday, last week, in+과거 연도, ago 등)와 함께 쓰인다. 명백한 과거표시어구와 함께 현재완료시제를 주고 틀린 부분을 고치라는 문제가 출제된다. 또한 과거시제 used to를 이용한 주관식 문제도 자주 나오는데 would를 쓸 수 없는 상황(과거의 동작이 아닌 상태일 때)을 묻는 난이도 있는 문제가 출제되기도 한다. 과거시제의 used to와 '~하는 데 익숙하다'란 뜻의 「be used to+V-ing」를 혼동케 하는 문제가 종종 출제된다. 특히 be used to에서 to 뒤에 동사원형을 쓰게끔 함정을 파놓기도 하는데 이때의 to는 전치사이므로 반드시 동명사(V-ing)를 써야 한다.

Ex 3.

When I was a child, I _____ fishing with my father.

(a) am used to   (b) go   (c) used to go   (d) have gone

Ex 4.

In the summer of 2001, he _____ Korea to participate in a house-building project.

(a) has visited   (b) visited   (c) was visited   (d) would visit

03 출제 100 % - 현재시제가 미래를 나타낸다.

 출제자의 눈 시간의 부사절(when, before, after)이나 조건의 부사절(if, unless) 안에 미래시제인 will을 써놓고 틀렸는지를 판단하는 문제가 나온다. 부사절 안에는 조동사 will을 쓰지 않고 현재시제를 써서 미래를 나타낸다. 또한 대중교통 시간표, 영화, 공연, 운동경기 관람시간과 같이 이미 정해져 있는 일정도 현재시제를 써서 미래를 나타낸다. 하지만 개인의 정해진 일정에는 현재시제를 쓰지 않고 현재진행시제로 미래를 나타내는데 미래를 나타내는 현재진행형은 be going to와 의미가 같다. 미래를 나타내는 현재시제는 be about to, be supposed to, be expected to, be willing to도 있다.

Ex 5.

If it _____ tomorrow, I'm going to go to a movie.

(a) will rain   (b) rain   (c) rained   (d) rains

Ex 6.

The plane _____ Chicago at 10:00 and _____ in Atlanta at 1:30.

(a) is leaving – arrives   (b) leaves – arrives   (c) is leaving – is arriving

04 출제 100 % - 진행시제가 쉽다고 생각하면 큰 오산!

 출제자의 눈 개인의 정해진 일정에는 현재진행시제로 미래를 나타내는데 현재시제와 혼동케 하는 문제가 출제된다. 진행형으로 쓸 수 없는 동사, 즉 감정(dislike, envy, love), 지각(hear, feel, see, smell, taste), 소유(belong, have, own, possess)의 동사들을 기억해 두자. 특히 과거진행형과 과거형을 구별하여 쓸 줄 아는지를 묻는 난이도 있는 문제가 출제된다. 일정 시점 이전에 이미 하고 있었던 동작이나 행위는 과거진행형을 쓰고, 도중에 끼어들어 짧게 행해진 동작은 과거형을 쓰는데 이를 집중적으로 물어볼 수 있다.

Ex 7.

You _____ unhappy. What's wrong with you?

(a) are looking   (b) looks   (c) look   (d) was looking

Ex 8.

While I _____ in the garden, it suddenly began to rain.

(a) sat   (b) is sitting   (c) sit   (d) was sitting

기출 응용문제

중간·기말고사 대비

1. 다음 우리말과 같도록 할 때 빈칸에 알맞은 것은?

> I was _____ to leave when you telephoned me.
> (네가 나에게 전화했을 때, 나는 막 나가려던 참이었다.)

❶ about   ❷ able   ❸ likely
❹ sure   ❺ forward

2. 다음 중 밑줄 친 부분이 어법상 어색한 것은?

❶ I <u>have</u> a pencil in my hand.
❷ What are you <u>looking at</u>?
❸ He <u>likes</u> her very much.
❹ Are you <u>wanting</u> some milk?
❺ This house <u>belongs</u> to him.

3. 다음 빈칸에 들어갈 알맞은 말을 고르시오.

> A: _____ last night?
> B: I went to the Han river.

❶ How are you   ❷ Where are you
❸ What did you do   ❹ What do you do
❺ What were you doing

[4-5] 다음 문장에서 틀린 부분을 바르게 고치시오.

4. I will cancel my departure if it will rain tomorrow.

_____ → _____

5. As the boat was going up the river, I have felt something was lost.

_____ → _____

6. 다음 상황을 읽고 be going to를 사용하여 문장을 완성하시오.

> You have decided to play soccer with your friends this evening.
> → A: What are you going to do this evening?
>   B: I'm going to play soccer with my <u>friends</u>.

You have to call Sunny. It's morning now, and you want to call her tonight.
→ A: Have you called Sunny yet?
    B: _____

7. 다음 밑줄 친 부분의 쓰임이 나머지와 다른 것은?

❶ I'm tired. <u>I'm going to</u> bed now.
    Good night!
❷ Please don't make so much noise.
    <u>I'm working</u>.
❸ The population of the world <u>is rising</u> very fast.
❹ We <u>are leaving</u> for Singapore this evening.
❺ He <u>is taking</u> a shower now.

8. 다음 빈칸에 알맞은 시제를 고르시오.

> A: How did you use to go to school?
> B: I _____ my bicycle to school, but now I take the school bus.

❶ used to ride   ❷ rode
❸ used   ❹ didn't use to ride
❺ am used to riding

오답 노트 만들기

★틀린 문제 : _____   ★다시 공부한 날 : _____

(1) 문제를 왜? 틀렸는지 곰곰이 생각하고 그 이유를 적어본다.

(2) 핵심 개념을 적는다.

(3) 자신이 몰랐던 단어와 숙어 표현이 있으면 정리한다.

(4) 해설집에서 필요한 부분을 골라 풀이 해법을 정리한다.

★틀린 문제 : _____   ★다시 공부한 날 : _____

(1) 문제를 왜? 틀렸는지 곰곰이 생각하고 그 이유를 적어본다.

(2) 핵심 개념을 적는다.

(3) 자신이 몰랐던 단어와 숙어 표현이 있으면 정리한다.

(4) 해설집에서 필요한 부분을 골라 풀이 해법을 정리한다.

★틀린 문제 : _____   ★다시 공부한 날 : _____

(1) 문제를 왜? 틀렸는지 곰곰이 생각하고 그 이유를 적어본다.

(2) 핵심 개념을 적는다.

(3) 자신이 몰랐던 단어와 숙어 표현이 있으면 정리한다.

(4) 해설집에서 필요한 부분을 골라 풀이 해법을 정리한다.

★틀린 문제 : _____   ★다시 공부한 날 : _____

(1) 문제를 왜? 틀렸는지 곰곰이 생각하고 그 이유를 적어본다.

(2) 핵심 개념을 적는다.

(3) 자신이 몰랐던 단어와 숙어 표현이 있으면 정리한다.

(4) 해설집에서 필요한 부분을 골라 풀이 해법을 정리한다.

1. 다음 빈칸에 들어갈 알맞은 시제를 순서대로 나열한 것을 고르시오.

> Tomorrow afternoon we're going to play tennis from 3:00 until 4:30. So at 4:00, we _____ tennis.

❶ play
❷ will play
❸ are going to play
❹ are playing
❺ will be playing

오답노트

2. 다음 빈칸에 들어갈 알맞은 것은?

> Last night firemen _____ to the Seabreeze Hotel and quickly put out a small fire in a bedroom.

❶ hurry
❷ hurried
❸ is hurried
❹ was hurried
❺ hurries

오답노트

[3-4] 다음 글을 읽고 물음에 답하시오.

> Last year I ⓐ <u>went</u> to Africa with my family. It ⓑ <u>was</u> really hot. My dad told me the animals like to swim to keep cool. We ⓒ <u>saw</u> a tall ____ eating leaves from a tree. His neck was so long! Later, we ⓓ <u>had to</u> stay in the car because there ⓔ <u>are</u> a lot of predators close by.

3. ⓐ~ⓔ 중 시제가 틀린 것은?

❶ ⓐ   ❷ ⓑ   ❸ ⓒ   ❹ ⓓ   ❺ ⓔ

4. 빈칸에 들어갈 알맞은 것은?

❶ gorilla
❷ giraffe
❸ leopard
❹ lion
❺ crocodile

오답노트

5. 다음 빈칸에 들어갈 알맞은 말을 쓰시오.

> He went swimming every Sunday last year. But he doesn't now.
> =He _____ ____ go swimming every Sunday last year.

오답노트

6. 다음 빈칸에 들어갈 알맞은 시제를 고르시오.

> A: I ____ visit Mexico. Could you give me any tips?
> B: You'd better not ask for directions in Mexico.
> A: Thanks. I'll keep that in mind.

❶ used to
❷ am about to
❸ will
❹ am going to
❺ was going to

오답노트

[7-8] 다음 빈칸에 들어갈 알맞은 것을 고르시오.

7. The Earth _____ warmer and warmer because of the greenhouse effect.

   ❶ gets   ❷ will get
   ❸ is getting   ❹ is going to get
   ❺ used to get

8. The Pharaohs _____ Egypt for thousands of years.

   ❶ will rule   ❷ rules   ❸ ruled
   ❹ used to rule   ❺ would rule

   오답노트

10. **다음 질문에 알맞은 대답을 쓰시오.**

    Q: Was Pablo Picasso born in London?
    A: _____

    오답노트

11. **다음 빈칸에 들어갈 말로 알맞지 않은 것은?**

    > This ancient temple will be 1,000 years old _____.

    ❶ next year   ❷ next weekend
    ❸ last year   ❹ tomorrow
    ❺ this Sunday

    오답노트

[9-10] 다음 글을 읽고 물음에 답하시오.

> Pablo Picasso was born in Malaga, Spain in 1881. His first word was "lapiz". (spanish for pencil), and he ⓐ learn to draw before he talked. He hated school. He liked to paint pictures. One day, he finished one of his father's paintings. When his father returned, he didn't believe it. It was wonderful! His father never painted again. Pablo was only 13.

9. **밑줄 친 ⓐ를 문맥에 맞게 고칠 때 알맞은 것은?**

   ❶ learns   ❷ used to learn
   ❸ will learn   ❹ was learning
   ❺ learned

   오답노트

[12-13] 다음 글을 읽고 물음에 답하시오.

> Sometimes you want to get in touch with someone you haven't seen for a while. What will you do if he _____ far away? You can write a letter, and he will write back to you. We can do so because we have a very good writing system. We have been using Han-Gul for over five hundred years. It's one of the best writing systems in the world.

12. **윗글에 들어갈 알맞은 동사의 형태를 고르시오.**

    ❶ will live   ❷ lives   ❸ lived
    ❹ living   ❺ used to live

    오답노트

13. 밑줄 친 It이 가리키는 것을 본문에서 찾아 쓰시오.

→ _____

오답노트

❶ could   ❷ would   ❸ didn't use to

❹ was used to   ❺ might

오답노트

14. 다음 빈칸에 들어갈 동사의 알맞은 형태를 고르시오.

> A week ago, I was at home with my mother. I _____ a magazine when I heard a strange sound out of the window.

❶ read   ❷ was reading

❸ have read   ❹ will read

❺ am reading

오답노트

[17-19] 다음 빈칸에 들어갈 알맞은 것을 고르시오.

17. I will finish preparing his favorite food before he _____ back home.

❶ will come   ❷ came

❸ would come   ❹ comes

❺ will be coming

오답노트

15. 밑줄 친 동사를 문맥에 맞게 고치시오.

> Last week, I buy a book about a great man. I started to read the book three days ago, and I have just finished it.

→ _____

오답노트

18. You will notice the same effect if you _____ your eyes, breathe calmly, and manage to relax the next time someone tickles you.

❶ close   ❷ will close

❸ closed   ❹ was closing

❺ are closed

오답노트

16. 다음 빈칸에 들어갈 말로 알맞은 것은?

> · 지금은 거의 아이스크림을 먹지 않지만 어렸을 때는 그것을 먹곤 했다.
> I rarely eat ice cream now, but I _____ eat it when I was a child.

19. After I _____ home yesterday, I drank a cup of tea.

❶ get   ❷ am   ❸ got

❹ will get   ❺ comes

오답노트

30

20. 다음 두 사람의 대화에서 어법상 어색한 것은?

❶ A: What are you doing?
  B: I'm shopping on the Internet.

❷ A: Did you return Pam's phone call?
  B: No, I forgot. Thanks for reminding me. I'll call her right away.

❸ A: Did you see today's top news?
  B: No, not yet.

❹ A: What do you usually do on the Internet?
  B: I just read news and get some pieces of information.

❺ A: What are you going to do this afternoon?
  B: I will work on my report.

오답노트

21. 다음 빈칸에 들어갈 알맞은 말은?

Kevin's wife arranged a surprise birthday party for him. When Kevin _____ home, several people _____ behind the couch or behind doors. All of the light were out, and when Kevin turned them on, everyone shouted "Surprise!"

❶ will be arriving – hid
❷ was arriving – was hiding
❸ arrived – were hiding
❹ has arrived – were hidden
❺ was about to arrive – were about to hide

오답노트

22. 다음 빈칸에 들어갈 알맞은 시제를 고르시오.

Steve loves soccer and tonight there is a big soccer game on TV. He's going to watch it from 7:00 until 9:00 and go to bed at 10:00 this evening. So at 7:30, he _____ the soccer game and at 10:00 will have gone to bed.

❶ will watching
❷ will be watching
❸ is going to watch
❹ watches
❺ watched

오답노트

A. 다음 단어들을 이용하여 과거와 과거진행형 문장을 만드시오.

보기	Jane / wait for / me / when / I / arrive
	→ *Jane was waiting for me when I arrived.*

1. Nancy / watch TV / when / the phone / ring

→ _____

2. it / begin / to rain / while / I / walk / home

→ _____

3. John / take a picture of me / while / I / not look

→ _____

4. I / walk / along the street / when suddenly / I / hear / footsteps behind me

→ _____

B. 다음 〈보기〉의 동사를 이용하여 be going to 형태의 문장을 완성하시오.

보기	walk	buy	wash	eat

1. My hands are very dirty. I _____ them.

2. It's a nice day. I am not going to take the bus. I _____ .

3. I'm hungry. I _____ the sandwich.

4. It's Kelly's birthday next week. We _____ her some gifts.

C. 다음 대화에 들어갈 알맞은 말을 〈보기〉에서 골라 쓰시오.

보 기	· I won't accept his invitation. · I won't let you leave now.	· I'll have the same. · Will you help me?

1. A: What will you have?

B: _____

2. A: He invited you to the party.

B: _____

3. A: _____

B: Sorry, but I've got to. Please.

4. A: _____

B: Sure. I'd be glad to.

D. 〈보기〉와 같이 used to를 이용하여 문장을 완성하시오.

보 기	When Brian was young, he hated school. Now he likes school. → Brian *used to hate school.*

1. When I lived in my hometown, I went to the beach every weekend. Now I don't go to the beach every weekend.

→ I _____, but now I don't.

2. Scott has a new job. He has to wear a suit every day. When he was a student, he always wore blue jeans.

→ Scott _____, but now he doesn't.

3. When Sunny was a child, she often crawled under her bed and put her hands over her ears when she heard thunder.

→ Sunny _____ and _____

when she heard thunder.

실전 서술형 평가문제

출제의도 미래시제를 표현할 수 있는 능력
평가내용 be going to와 현재진행시제를 이해하고 문장 구성하기

A. 다음 사진을 보고 아래 표현들을 이용하여 새 학기 계획을 세워보시오. (be going to와 현재진행형을 사용하여 두 문장씩 영작할 것)

[서술형 유형 : 6점 / 난이도 : 하]

My New Resolutions

〈보기〉 not play computer games
1. go to the gym
2. read a lot of books
3. walk to school

보기	*I'm not going to play computer games.* *I'm not playing computer games.*

1. _____
   _____

2. _____
   _____

3. _____
   _____

출제의도 과거진행형의 이해와 쓰임

평가내용 실생활에서 과거진행형 사용하기

B. 다음은 Sunny가 어제 한 일이다. 사진과 일치하도록 과거진행형으로 문장을 만드시오.

[서술형 유형 : 6점 / 난이도 : 중하]

 6:00~7:00

 8:00~9:00

 11:00~12:00

 2:00~2:30

보기

A: Was she playing the violin at 6:30?

B: No, *she wasn't.*

A: What was she doing?

B: *She was jogging.*

1. A: Was she reading a book at 2:10?

B: No, _____.

A: What was she doing?

B: _____

2. A: Was she singing at 8:30?

B: No, _____.

A: What was she doing?

B: _____

_____

3. A: Was she dancing at 11:30?

B: No, _____.

A: What was she doing?

B: _____

실전 서술형 평가문제

출제의도 과거진행형의 이해와 쓰임
평가내용 실생활에서 과거진행형 사용하기

C. 다음 사진은 모두 과거의 일이다. used to를 사용하여 〈보기〉와 같이 문장을 완성하시오.

[서술형 유형 : 9점 / 난이도 : 중하]

보기

(Christina / not be thin → fat)

Christina didn't use(d) to be thin.

She used to be fat.

1.

(Jane / not have short hair
→ very long hair)

_____

_____

2.

(We / not take a school bus
→ walk to school)

_____

_____

3.

(Bob / not play soccer
→ play basketball)

_____

_____

정답 p. 5

출제의도 실생활에서의 미래 계획 표현하기
평가내용 현재진행시제로 미래를 표현하기

D. 〈보기〉와 같이 Kevin의 다음 주 화요일 일정표를 보고 현재진행시제를 이용하여 미래 계획에 관한 질문과 대답을 완성하시오. [서술형 유형 : 12점 / 난이도 : 중상]

	Tuesday
08:50	Arrive in Hong Kong / Take a taxi to the hotel
10:30	Meet Jason and Lisa at the office
12:00	Have lunch with Jason, Lisa, and the boss
16:00	Return to the office / Work with Jason and Lisa
18:00	Go back to the hotel
19:00	Wait for Lucy in the hotel lobby / Go for dinner
22:00	Return to the hotel / Prepare for the meeting on Wednesday

보기	What time / arrive / in Hong Kong?
	Q : *What time is Kevin arriving in Hong Kong?*
	A : *He is arriving in Hong Kong at 8:50.*

1. Who / meet / at 10:30

Q : _____ ?

A : _____ .

2. What / do / at 12:00

Q : _____ ?

A : _____ .

3. Where / wait / for Lucy

Q : _____ ?

A : _____ .

4. What / do / at 22:00

Q : _____ ?

A : _____ .

실전 서술형 평가문제

출제의도　조건의 의미를 나타내는 if
평가내용　조건의 부사절을 이용하여 미래를 나타내기

E. 주어진 문장을 읽고 조건의 부사절 if를 이용하여 문장을 완성하시오.　　[서술형 유형 : 9점 / 난이도 : 중하]

| 보기 |  | Bob must run very fast and he will win the race.
→ *If Bob runs very fast, he will win the race.* |

1.

The dress may be expensive so Linda may not buy it.

→ _____

2.

Unless you take a subway, you will be late for work.

→ _____

3.

Do you feel tired? You must go to bed.

→ _____

서술형 평가문제	채 점 기 준	배 점	나의 점수
A	표현이 올바르고 문법, 철자가 모두 정확한 경우	2점×3문항＝6점	
B		2점×3문항＝6점	
C		3점×3문항＝9점	
D		3점×4문항＝12점	
E		3점×3문항＝9점	
공통	문법, 철자가 1개씩 틀린 경우	각 문항당 1점씩 감점	
	내용과 전혀 일치하지 않거나 답을 기재하지 못한 경우	0점	

Chapter 2

시제 II (Tense II)

1-1 현재완료 형태와 용법

Julia is looking for her purse. She can't find it.
Julia는 그녀의 지갑을 찾고 있다. 그녀는 그것을 찾을 수가 없다.
She **has lost** her purse.
→ She lost it and she still doesn't have it.
그녀는 지갑을 잃어버렸다.

01 현재완료 「have/has+p.p.(과거분사)」는 '**과거에 ~했다**'와 '**지금은 ~하다**'라는 **의미**를 둘 다 포함하고 있는 시제이다. '현재까지 ~했다'의 뜻으로 **현재가 반드시 포함**되어 있다는 것을 명심하자.

Tom **has lost** his cell phone. He's in trouble now. Tom은 휴대전화를 잃어버려서, 지금 곤란한 상태에 있다.

02 현재완료의 용법: have/has+p.p.

용법	예문	의미
완료	I've already **searched** the Internet but found nothing. 이미 인터넷을 다 찾아봤지만 아무것도 찾을 수 없었다.	과거에 시작하여 방금 전 또는 최근에 완료된 일로, 방금 전은 과거라고 하기엔 현재와 너무 가깝다. (주로 just, already, yet, now, recently와 함께 쓰임)
계속	I **have lived** in this apartment since 2009. 나는 2009년 이후로 줄곧 이 아파트에서 살고 있다.	과거부터 현재까지 계속되는 일 (주로 for, since와 함께 쓰임)
결과	My friend, Lisa, **has left** for Sydney. 내 친구 Lisa는 시드니로 떠났다.	과거의 일이 현재의 어떤 결과를 낳았을 때 (주로 have lost, have gone to 형태로 쓰임)
경험	**Have** you ever **bought** anything on the Internet? 인터넷에서 물건을 산 적이 있니?	과거부터 현재까지의 반복된 일이나 경험 (주로 ever, never, before, once, often과 쓰임)

※ just now는 과거시제와 함께 쓰고, just는 현재완료와 쓴다.
   She returned just now. (과거) / She has just returned. (현재완료)

03 have gone to와 have been to는 형태가 비슷하나 그 뜻이 전혀 다르므로 주의한다.

1 have gone to+장소: ~에 가버렸다(그래서 지금 여기 없다) (결과, 완료)

   She **has gone to** America. So she is not here now. 그녀는 미국으로 가버렸다. 그래서 지금 여기 없다.

2 have been to+장소: ~에 가본 적이 있다(경험), ~에 갔다 왔다(완료)

   Have you ever **been to** the zoo? 동물원에 가본 적 있니? (경험)

서술형 기초다지기

정답 p. 5

Challenge 1 다음 괄호 안의 표현 중 알맞은 것을 고르세요.

01. Have you ever (meet / met) a movie actor?

02. I (have known / knew) her since she was a child.

03. Have you ever (ate / eaten) bulgogi?

04. He has (just / just now) arrived at the station.

Challenge 2 다음 괄호 안의 동사를 이용하여 현재완료 문장을 만드세요.

01. Edward is looking for his key. He can't find it.

→ He _____. (lose)

02. Jane can't walk because her leg is in a cast.

→ She _____. (break)

03. Bob's car was very dirty. Now it is clean.

→ He _____. (wash)

Challenge 3 다음 문장을 괄호 안의 지시대로 완성하세요.

01. She has lost her purse.

→ _____ (의문문)

→ Yes, _____. / No, _____.

02. I have forgotten her name.

→ _____ (never를 이용한 부정문)

03. I have been to Egypt.

→ _____ ever _____? (의문문)

→ Yes, _____. / No, _____.

1-2 현재완료 계속적 용법

I first met Susan in 1999. Susan and I are still good friends.
It is 2011.
→ Susan and I **have been** good friends **since** 1999.
→ Susan and I **have been** good friends **for** 12 years.
나는 Susan을 1999년에 처음 만났다. Susan과 나는 아직도 좋은 친구 사이이다.
2011년이다.
→ Susan과 나는 1999년부터 좋은 친구로 지내고 있다.
→ Susan과 나는 12년 동안 좋은 친구로 지내고 있다.

01 현재완료의 계속적 용법은 '과거부터 지금까지 쭉 ~해왔다'의 뜻으로 'for나 since'와 함께 자주 사용한다. **for(~동안에)는 시간의 길이**(a length of time)를 나타내고 **since(~이래로)는 과거에 시작된 특정한 시점**(a period of time)을 나타낸다.

She started to work in this company in 2005. She still works here.
→ She **has worked** in this company since 2005. 그녀는 2005년부터 이 회사에서 일하고 있다.

I **have lived** here for two years. 나는 여기에서 2년 동안 살고 있다. ▶ 현재완료
=I moved here two years ago, and I still live here.

※ I **lived** in Athens for two years. 나는 아테네에서 2년 동안 살았다. ▶ 과거시제
  =I don't live in Athens now.

02 since 뒤에 「주어+동사」가 함께 올 수 있는데 이때, **동사는 반드시 '과거'**를 쓴다. '~이래로 지금까지'로 해석한다.

I've **studied** English **since** I **was** a high school student. 나는 고등학생 때부터 영어를 공부해 오고 있다.
Alice **has met** many people **since** she **came** here. Alice는 여기에 온 이후부터 많은 사람을 만나고 있다.

03 when은 과거의 한 시점을 나타내므로 **현재완료와 함께 쓰지 않는다.**

Karen **has worked** at the hotel **since** she finished school.
학교를 졸업한 이래로 Karen은 그 호텔에서 일해 왔다. ▶ 지금도 호텔에서 근무하고 있음

Karen **worked** at the hotel **when** she finished school. 학교를 졸업했을 때 Karen은 그 호텔에서 일을 했다.
▶ 지금도 호텔에서 근무하는지 여부는 알 수 없음

04 How long ~?으로 물어보는 현재완료시제의 질문은 과거에 시작해서 지금까지의 어떤 행동이나 상태의 특정한 기간을 물어보므로 for와 since가 있는 **현재완료의 계속적 용법으로 대답**한다.

Q: **How long** have you lived in London? 얼마나 오랫동안 런던에 살았나요?
A: I have lived in London **for** 6 years. 6년 동안 살았어요.

서술형 기초다지기

정답 p. 5

Challenge 1 다음 단어를 활용하여 현재완료시제를 만들고 괄호 안의 표현 중 알맞은 것을 고르세요.

01. I _____ (know) Rachel for [ten years / ten years ago].

02. She _____ (work) here [for / since] 2004.

03. I _____ (meet) her since I [am / was] a freshman in high school.

04. Sue _____ (have) a lot of problems since she [come / came] to this country.

05. My wife and I _____ (know) each other since we [are / were] in elementary school.

06. Our phone bill _____ (rise) since we [buy / bought] a cell phone.

Challenge 2 다음 문장을 How long을 이용한 완료시제로 완성하세요.

01. How long _____ (you / know) Rachel?

   - For almost twenty years.

02. How long _____ (you / study) Spanish?

   - Since I was an elementary school student.

Challenge 3 다음을 〈보기〉와 같이 현재완료 계속적 용법의 문장으로 완성하세요.

보기	I / not see / a movie / two months
	→ *I haven't seen a movie for two months.*

01. Lisa / read / two history books / Monday

   → _____

02. My sisters / not play / beach volleyball / last summer

   → _____

03. Laura / be / photographer / ten years

   → _____

1-3 현재완료시제와 과거시제

She was a news anchor **for** 5 years.
그녀는 5년 동안 뉴스 앵커였다.

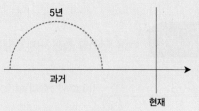

과거에 시작해서 과거에 끝났음.
(지금은 뉴스 앵커가 아님)

She has been a news anchor **for** 5 years.
그녀는 5년 동안 뉴스 앵커를 하고 있다.

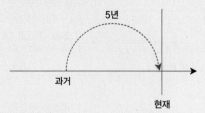

과거에 시작해서 현재도 이어지고 있음.
(5년 전에 시작해 지금도 뉴스 앵커임)

01 과거와 현재완료를 구분 짓는 핵심요소는 과거 사실에 대한 정보인가, 아니면 현재에 대한 정보인가의 여부이다. 즉, **과거는 과거의 특정 시간이 언급되어 현재와는 전혀 무관한 과거의 사실만을 말하는 반면, 현재완료는 특정 시간이 중요하지 않은 가까운 과거에 막 끝난 동작이나 현재까지 지속되고 있는 동작·상태**를 나타낸다.

02 과거시제와 현재완료시제의 비교

과거시제	현재완료
① 과거에 시작한 일이 과거에 끝났으며 현재와는 아무런 관련이 없다. My dad **visited** Singapore when I was 10. 우리 아빠는 내가 10살 때 싱가포르에 다녀오셨다. ② 정확한 과거 시점을 언급할 때는 과거시제를 쓴다. ③ 과거의 특정한 때를 나타내는 부사와 함께 쓴다. **Did** you **see** the news on TV last night? 어젯밤 TV에서 그 뉴스를 봤니? I **didn't play** golf last summer. 나는 지난 여름에 골프를 하지 않았다.	① 현재까지 영향을 미치는 동작이나 상태로, 과거의 특정한 시간을 언급하지 않는다. My dad **has visited** Singapore before. 우리 아빠는 전에 싱가포르에 가보신 적이 있다. ② 과거의 동작을 나타내지만 과거의 특정한 때를 알 수 없다. ③ 현재완료 계속적 용법은 현재까지 지속되고 있는 동작이나 상태를 나타낸다. ④ 과거의 특정한 때를 나타내는 부사와는 함께 쓰지 않는다. I **have** never **played** golf. 나는 한 번도 골프를 해본 적이 없다. **Have** you ever **seen** that movie? 저 영화를 본 적 있니?

서술형 기초다지기

정답 p. 6

Challenge 1 다음 괄호 안의 동사를 알맞은 시제로 바꿔 문장을 완성하세요.

01. Kelly and I are good friends. We _____ (know) each other for 10 years.

02. He _____ (read) the book three hours ago.

03. I have never _____ (eat) such a delicious food.

04. My history teacher told us that the Korean War _____ (break) out in 1950.

05. We _____ (live) in Hong Kong last year.

06. We _____ (live) in Hong Kong since last year.

Challenge 2 다음 괄호 안의 동사를 이용하여 과거 또는 현재완료시제로 문장을 완성하세요.

01. A: Do you and Eric want to go to the movies with us tonight?

    B: No, thanks. We _____ (see, already) it. We _____ (see) it last week.

02. A: Have you ever been in Seattle?

    B: Yes, I _____. I _____ (be) in Seattle several times. In fact, I
       _____ (be) in Seattle last year.

03. A: What Asian countries _____ (you, visit)?

    B: I _____ (visit) Vietnam, Korea, and Japan. I _____ (visit) Vietnam in
       1999. I _____ (be) in Korea and Japan in 2005.

Challenge 3 다음 표현을 이용하여 문장을 완성하세요.

보기	(it / not / snow / this week) → *It hasn't snowed this week.*

01. (Maria / graduate / from high school / in 1999) → _____

02. (I / not / read / a newspaper / yesterday)   → _____

03. (you / take / a vacation / recently?)   → _____

현재완료 진행시제

Bob and Sunny are in their car right now.
They are driving home.
They began to drive two hours ago.
It is now four o'clock.
→ They **have been driving** since two o'clock.
그들은 2시부터 운전하고 있다.
→ They **have been driving** for two hours.
그들은 두 시간 동안 운전하고 있다.
→ How long **have** they **been driving**?
얼마나 오랫동안 운전하고 있니?

01 현재완료 진행(have/has been+V-ing)은 **과거에 시작해서 현재까지 진행 중인 동작을 강조**할 때 쓰며, '계속 ~하고 있다'의 뜻이다.

It started to rain last night. It's still raining.
→ It's **been raining** since last night. 어젯밤부터 비가 내리고 있다.

We started waiting for the bus 20 minutes ago. We're still waiting now.
→ We've **been waiting** for the bus for 20 minutes. 우리는 20분 동안 버스를 기다리고 있다.

02 현재진행형은 말하는 순간의 진행 중인 동작을 의미하나, 현재완료 진행형은 **과거에 시작하여 현재도 진행 중인 동작을 강조**한다.

Look out the window! A strange woman **is standing** under the tree.
창 밖을 봐! 이상한 여자가 나무 아래에 서 있어.

A strange woman **has been standing** under the tree for two hours.
이상한 여자가 나무 아래에 두 시간 동안 서 있다.

03 **When은 과거시제와 함께 쓰고, How long은 완료시제와 함께 쓴다.**

A : **When did** it **start** raining? 비가 언제 내리기 시작했니?

B : It **started** raining an hour ago. 한 시간 전부터 내리기 시작했어.

A : **How long has** it **been raining**? 얼마나 오랫동안 비가 내리고 있니?

B : It's **been raining** for an hour. 한 시간 동안 내리고 있어.

※ 상태를 나타내는 동사(state verbs)들은 현재/과거/미래진행형뿐만 아니라 현재완료 진행형에도 쓰지 않는다.
(Chapter 1의 3-2 참조)

서술형 기초다지기

정답 p. 6

Challenge 1　다음 두 문장을 for와 since를 이용하여 현재완료 진행시제의 문장으로 만드세요.

> 보기
> The snow started two hours ago. It's still snowing now.
> → *It's been snowing for two hours.*

01. Alice is talking with her friend on the phone. Her friend phoned an hour ago.

→ _____

02. I started Korean classes in December. I'm still studying Korean now.

→ _____

03. They started to play soccer three hours ago. They're still playing soccer.

→ _____

Challenge 2　다음 문장을 〈보기〉처럼 When과 How long을 이용한 의문문으로 만드세요.

> 보기
> It's raining.　→ *How long has it been raining?* (How long?)
> 　　　　　　　→ *When did it start raining?* (When?/start)

01. Kevin is using his computer.　→ _____ (How long?)

→ _____ (When?/start)

02. Jane is eating lunch for 2 hours. → _____ (How long?)

→ _____ (When?/start)

Challenge 3　다음 우리말과 뜻이 같도록 빈칸에 알맞은 말을 쓰세요.

01. 우리는 일 년 동안 이 여행을 (계속) 계획하고 있는 중이다.

→ We _____ this trip for a year.

02. 그는 그녀를 두 시간 동안 (계속) 찾고 있는 중이다.

→ He _____ for her for two hours.

1-5 현재완료와 현재완료 진행시제

They **have been washing** the car.
그들은 차를 세차하고 있다. (세차가 끝나지 않고 진행 중임)

They **have washed** the car.
그들은 세차를 했다. (세차가 모두 끝남)

01 **현재완료 진행**은 지금도 계속 되고 있는 동작을 의미하는 반면, **현재완료**는 이미 끝난 동작이나 상태를 나타낸다. 하지만 현재완료도 현재와 연관이 있다.

She **has read** 50 pages so far. 그녀는 지금까지 50페이지를 읽었다.

She **has been reading** a book for two hours. 그녀는 두 시간 동안 책을 읽고 있다. (→ 지금도 책을 읽고 있음)

02 현재완료 진행은 과거에 시작한 일이 현재에도 진행되고 있음을 나타내고, 어떤 **행동의 지속성을 강조**하기 위해 사용한다.

Lisa **has talked** to Jason on the phone many times. Lisa는 자주 Jason과 전화로 얘기한다.

Lisa and Jason **have been talking** on the phone for thirty minutes.
Lisa와 Jason은 30분 동안 전화로 얘기하고 있다. (→ 지금도 전화 통화를 하고 있음)

03 for, since와 함께 쓰이는 현재완료의 계속은 현재 진행 중임을 강조하는 현재진행형과 의미상 큰 차이는 없다. 특히 live, work, teach, rain, snow, study, stay, wear 등과 같은 동사는 현재완료 계속과 현재완료 진행을 구별 없이 쓴다. **단지 차이가 있다면 현재진행형이 현재 진행 중임을 더 강조한다는** 것밖에 없다.

I **have been** here for thirty minutes. 나는 30분 동안 여기에 있다.

=I came here thirty minutes ago, and I'm still here.

I **have been waiting** for you for thirty minutes. 나는 30분 동안 너를 기다리고 있다.

=I have waited for thirty minutes, and I'm still waiting.

I've **lived** in Egypt for 10 years. 나는 10년 동안 이집트에 살고 있다.

=I've **been living** in Egypt for 10 years.

Karen **has worn** glasses since she was an elementary school student.
Karen은 초등학생 때부터 안경을 착용했다.

=Karen **has been wearing** glasses since she was an elementary school student.

서술형 기초다지기

정답 p. 6

Challenge 1 다음 괄호 안의 동사를 현재완료 진행 또는 현재완료로 만들어 빈칸을 완성하세요.

01. My grandfather _____ (paint) for ten years now.

    He _____ (paint) more than fifty paintings.

02. Bob _____ (write) on his computer for an hour.

    He _____ (already, send) five e-mail messages to his friends.

03. Kathy _____ (drive) for three hours now.

    She _____ (drive) almost 200 miles.

Challenge 2 다음 문장을 for나 since를 이용하여 현재완료 진행형으로 만들고 진행형이 불가능한 문장은 현재완료 계속적 용법으로 만드세요.

> 보기　I / know / Sarah / she was ten
> → *I have known Sarah since she was ten.*

01. Nancy / learn / Korean / two years

    → _____

02. we / have / this car / 2006

    → _____

03. Amy and Kevin / be married / twenty years

    → _____

04. we / wait for you / six o'clock this morning

    → _____

1-6 과거완료시제

We went to the movies last night. We got there late.
우리는 어젯밤 영화를 보러 갔다. 우리는 늦게 도착했다.
The movie had already ended.
영화는 이미 끝나 있었다.

01 **과거보다 더 이전에 시작된 일이 과거의 어느 시점까지 영향을 미친 경우** 과거완료(had+p.p)를 쓴다. 현재완료와 마찬가지로 과거완료도 4가지 의미(결과, 완료, 경험, 계속)로 나타낼 수 있다.

When we arrived, the bus **had** already **left**. 우리가 도착했을 때 버스는 이미 떠났다.

She **had** never **taken** an airplane until she was 10 years old.
그녀는 10살 때까지 비행기를 한 번도 타 본 적이 없었다.

She looked great. She **had been** on a diet for three months.
그녀는 멋져 보였다. 그녀는 석 달 동안 다이어트를 해왔었다.

02 두 개의 동작 중 어느 것이 먼저 일어났는지를 시간적으로 구분하고자 할 때 과거완료를 쓴다. **과거보다 더 먼저 일어난 일은 과거완료로 쓰고 나중에 일어난 일은 과거시제로 쓴다.** 흔히 과거완료를 대과거시제라고 부르기도 한다.

Steve <u>had left</u> his apartment when Alice <u>arrived</u>. Alice가 도착했을 때 Steve는 아파트를 떠났다.
→ 과거완료(과거보다 앞선 시제)   → 과거

03 현재완료(have+p.p)는 현재와 관련이 있지만, **과거완료(had+p.p)는 현재와 아무런 관련이 없다.**

We aren't hungry. We've just **had** lunch. 우리는 배가 고프지 않다. 우리는 막 점심을 먹었다.

We weren't hungry. We'd just **had** lunch. 우리는 배가 고프지 않았다. 우리는 막 점심을 먹었었다.

04 과거진행(was/were+V-ing)은 과거 특정한 시간에 진행 중이었던 동작을 나타내는 반면, **과거완료는 과거의 특정한 시간 그 이전에 이미 끝난 동작**을 나타낸다.

I **was eating** lunch when Bob **came**. Bob이 왔을 때 나는 저녁을 먹고 있었다.

I **had eaten** when Bob **came**. Bob이 왔을 때 나는 저녁을 다 먹었다.

※ 일상 영어에서 과거완료는 자주 쓰는 시제가 아니며, before와 after 같이 시간의 앞뒤 순서를 분명하게 알 수 있는 경우에는 과거완료를 쓰지 않고 보통 과거시제를 쓴다.

After I **had finished** my homework, I went out for a walk. 숙제를 끝내고 나는 산책하러 나갔다.
=After I **finished** my homework, I went out for a walk.

서술형 기초다지기

정답 p. 6

Challenge 1 다음 괄호 안의 표현 중 알맞은 것을 고르세요.

01. Peter lost the book that I (have lent / had lent) him.

02. I (have known / had known) nothing about it until you told it to me.

03. Julie and Mike (lived / had lived) together for fifteen years when they got divorced.

04. She (has / had) already left the office before I returned there.

Challenge 2 다음 우리말과 뜻이 같도록 괄호 안의 단어를 이용하여 문장을 완성하세요.

01. 내가 공항에 도착했을 때 비행기는 이륙한 뒤였다. (take off)

　　→ When I arrived at the airport, the plane _____ _____ _____.

02. 그녀는 그를 전에는 본 적이 없다고 말했다. (see)

　　→ She said that she _____ _____ _____ him before.

03. 그녀가 호주에 갔을 때는 5년 동안 영어를 공부해 오고 있었다. (study)

　　→ She _____ _____ English for five years when she went to Australia.

Challenge 3 다음 상황에 맞게 과거완료, 현재완료, 또는 과거진행시제의 문장으로 완성하세요.

보기	You went to the party, but Eric wasn't there. → _He had gone out._ (he / go / out)

01. You went back to your hometown after many years. It wasn't the same as before.

　　→ _____ (it / change / a lot)

02. Last week the bus fare was 80 cents. Now it is 90.

　　→ _____ (the bus fare / go up)

03. Yesterday Kelly and Scott played tennis. They began at 10:00 and finished at 12:00.

　　→ So at 11:00, _____. (they / play / tennis)

1-7 과거완료 진행시제

 →

I hope the bus comes soon.
I've been waiting for 30 minutes.
(→ He is still waiting now.)
나는 버스가 곧 오길 바라고 있다.
나는 30분 동안 버스를 기다리고 있다.

At last the bus came.
I **had been waiting** for 30 minutes.
(→ She isn't waiting now.)
마침내 버스가 왔다.
나는 버스를 30분 동안 기다렸었다.

01 과거완료 진행시제는 「had been+V-ing」로 쓰며, **과거 어느 때까지 계속된 동작을 강조**할 때 쓴다. '~하고 있었다, ~하는 중이었다'로 해석한다. 훨씬 이전에 시작된 동작이 과거 어느 때까지 지속되었음을 나타내기 때문에 **현재와는 아무런 상관이 없다.**

The police **had been** looking for the man. 경찰은 그 남자를 찾고 있었다. ▶ 경찰은 현재 그 남자를 찾고 있지 않음
She **had been working** as a CEO for two years. 그녀는 2년 동안 CEO로 일하고 있었다. ▶ 그녀는 현재 CEO가 아님

02 과거완료 진행은 **과거의 한 동작이 있기 이전에 이미 진행 중이었던 동작을 강조**한다. 일상 영어에서 과거완료 진행시제도 자주 쓰진 않는다.

Steve **had been working** at his office when the light went out.
전기가 나갔을 때 Steve는 그의 사무실에서 일하고 있었다. ▶ Steve가 일하고 있었던 것은 전기가 나간 시점보다 먼저 진행 중이었던 동작임
→ Steve **had been working**. (longer action)
→ The light **went out**. (shorter action)

We **had been playing** tennis for half an hour when it started to rain.
비가 내리기 시작했을 때, 우리는 30분 동안 데니스를 치고 있었다. ▶ 테니스를 치던 동작은 비가 내린 시점보다 먼저 진행 중이었던 동작임
→ We **had been playing** tennis. (longer action)
→ It **started** to rain. (shorter action)

03 과거완료 진행형은 과거에 발생한 어떤 일에 대한 원인을 나타낸다.

She looked tired. She had been working on the computer for hours. 그 여자는 피곤해 보였다.
　　결과　　　　　　　　　　원인　　　　　　　　　　　　　　　　　　몇 시간 동안 컴퓨터로 일을 하고 있었다.

I hadn't been feeling well for a few days, so I went to see the doctor. 나는 며칠동안 몸이 좋지 않았었다.
　　　　　원인　　　　　　　　　　　　　　　　　결과　　　　　그래서 병원에 갔다.

서술형 기초다지기

Challenge 1　다음 괄호 안의 표현을 활용하여 과거완료 진행시제로 문장을 완성하세요.

01. He _____ alone since she left him. (live)

02. She _____ for 3 hours, so her back started to hurt. (sit)

03. I _____ very hard, so I was not tired. (not, work)

04. Sunny didn't show up until 2 o'clock. I _____ for thirty minutes. (wait)

Challenge 2　다음 괄호 안의 표현 중 어법상 알맞은 것을 고르세요.

01. He (catch / caught) a cold because he (has been singing / had been singing) in the rain.

02. I am at the dental clinic now. I (have been waiting / had been waiting) for 45 minutes.

03. We (have been playing / had been playing) tennis for about half an hour when it (starts / started) to rain heavily.

04. I (have been working / had been working) here for two hours when Bob (comes / came) in at 9 o'clock.

Challenge 3　다음 문장을 주어진 단어를 이용하여 과거완료 진행시제 문장으로 만드세요.

보기	She was very tired when she got home. → *She had been working hard all day*. (she / work / hard / all day)

01. There was nobody in the room, but there was a smell of cigarette smoke.

→ _____ (somebody / smoke / in the room)

02. When I got home, my dad was sitting in front of the TV. He had just turned it off.

→ _____ (he / watch / TV)

"출제자가 노리는 급소" 이것이 시험에 출제되는 영문법이다!

01 출제 100% - 현재완료는 반드시 현재와 연관지어 생각하라.

 출제자의 눈 완료시제의 용법(경험, 결과, 계속, 완료)을 묻는 문제는 기본으로 출제되고 있는데, 현재완료에서 주의할 것은 현재와 관련이 있기 때문에 명확한 과거를 나타내는 yesterday, last week(year, night, month), ago, 「in+과거 연도」 등의 부사구와 함께 쓸 수 없다는 점이다. 특히 과거의 한 시점을 의미하는 when은 현재완료와 함께 쓰이지 않는 것에도 주의하자. 또, just now는 현재완료와 함께 쓰지 않지만, just와 now를 따로 쓸 때에는 현재완료와 함께 쓸 수 있다.

Ex 1.

Elizabeth _____ her mother last week.

(a) visited   (b) has visited   (c) had visited   (d) will visit

Ex 2.

Julia _____ her brother since she was a teenager.

(a) hated   (b) has hated   (c) hates   (d) had hated

02 출제 100% - 계속적 용법의 for와 since가 집중적으로 출제된다.

 출제자의 눈 since와 for를 고르는 문제나, since 앞에 과거완료(had+p.p.)처럼 틀린 시제를 주고 잘못된 곳을 찾으라는 문제가 출제된다. since나 for는 '현재까지'의 의미가 내포되어 있으므로 현재완료 또는 현재완료 진행형과 함께 쓸 수 있다. 또 since절 내에 있는 시제는 '시작점'을 나타내므로 반드시 과거시제를 써야 한다. 시험에서 「for+기간」이 등장하면 일단 그 앞에 완료시제가 쓰였는지를 확인하고 for와 during을 혼동시키는 문제인가도 구별해야 한다. for 다음엔 숫자가 포함된 일정한 기간이 나오는 반면, during은 during vacation처럼 막연한 기간이 나온다.

Ex 3.

A: Where have you been?

B: I've been looking for you _____ the last half hour.

(a) since   (b) for   (d) when   (d) during

Ex 4.

It _____ two years since my girlfriend left for Singapore to study English.

(a) had been   (b) was   (c) has been   (d) will be

03 출제 100% - 과거완료는 과거에 이미 끝난 일이다.

 출제자의 눈 과거완료(had+p.p.)는 과거의 일이므로 since와 함께 쓰지 않고 when이나 until과 함께 자주 쓴다. 또, 의미상 과거인데 현재완료를 써 넣고 잘못된 곳을 고르라고 한다. 특히 과거에 일어난 두 개의 사건 중 먼저 일어난 것을 과거완료(대과거)로 쓴다. 일이 발생한 순서를 거꾸로 거슬러 올라갈 경우 반드시 먼저 일어난 일을 과거완료(대과거)로 표현해야 한다.

Ex 5.

Jane _____ Korean when her family moved to Korea.

(a) has never spoken   (b) spoke   (c) had never spoken

Ex 6.

Before he _____ the room, his wife had fallen asleep.

(a) enters   (b) has entered   (c) had entered   (d) entered

04 출제 100% - 과거완료 진행시제도 현재와 관련이 없다.

 출제자의 눈 현재완료 진행형은 since와 함께 쓰지만 과거완료 진행형은 과거에 끝난 일이므로 since와 함께 쓰지 못하고 when절과는 함께 쓸 수 있다. 특히 과거의 어떤 동작이 있기 이전에 이미 진행 중이었던 동작은 과거완료 진행형을 쓴다. 완료시제에서 주관식으로 가장 많이 출제하는 것은 2개의 문장을 주고 적절한 완료시제를 이용해서 하나의 문장으로 만들어 보라는 단답형 문제이다. 따라서 평소에 완료시제를 이용한 단문 영작연습을 꾸준히 해 두어야 한다.

Ex 7.

Kevin has been doing his homework _____ he got home after school.

(a) when   (b) since   (c) for   (d) during

Ex 8.

They _____ in the subway for 10 hours when the National 119 Rescue Services finally appeared.

(a) has been waiting   (b) have waited   (c) had been waiting

1. 다음 질문에 가장 알맞은 대답은?

> Have you ever read 'Romeo and Juliet'?

❶ Yes, I had read it twice.
❷ No, I had never read it.
❸ Yes, I have never read it.
❹ Yes, I have read it twice.
❺ No, I have ever read it.

2. 다음 밑줄 친 부분과 같은 용법으로 쓰인 것은?

> My grandmother has lived here for 55 years.

❶ How long have you been in Canada?
❷ We have proved our strength to the whole world.
❸ He has gone to Paris.
❹ They have just got married.
❺ Have you ever been to the museum?

[3-4] 다음 두 문장을 한 문장으로 바꿀 때 빈칸에 알맞은 말을 쓰시오.

3.

> They began to play basketball an hour ago. They are still playing.
> → They _____ _____ _____ basketball for an hour.

4.

> The concert began at noon. I entered the concert hall at 1 p.m.
> → The concert _____ _____ when I entered the concert hall.

5. 다음 괄호 안의 동사를 알맞게 고친 것은?

> I lost the MP3 player that I (borrow) from her.

❶ borrow   ❷ will have borrowed
❸ had borrowed   ❹ have borrowed
❺ have been borrowing

6. 다음 빈칸에 들어갈 말로 가장 적절한 것은?

> By the time the concert began, many of the girls _____ in a line for six hours.

❶ have stood
❷ have been stood
❸ had stand
❹ have been standing
❺ had been standing

7. 다음 빈칸에 들어갈 가장 알맞은 말은?

> We have all been hearing music ever _____ we were born.

❶ if   ❷ as
❸ when   ❹ since
❺ because

8. 다음 두 문장을 한 문장으로 고칠 때 빈칸에 알맞은 동사의 형태는?

> · I began to learn Spanish two years ago.
> · I still learn Spanish now.
>   = I _____ Spanish for two years.

❶ learn   ❷ will learn
❸ was learning   ❹ had learned
❺ have learned

오답 노트 만들기

★틀린 문제 : _____   ★다시 공부한 날 : _____

(1) 문제를 왜? 틀렸는지 곰곰이 생각하고 그 이유를 적어본다.

(2) 핵심 개념을 적는다.

(3) 자신이 몰랐던 단어와 숙어 표현이 있으면 정리한다.

(4) 해설집에서 필요한 부분을 골라 풀이 해법을 정리한다.

★틀린 문제 : _____   ★다시 공부한 날 : _____

(1) 문제를 왜? 틀렸는지 곰곰이 생각하고 그 이유를 적어본다.

(2) 핵심 개념을 적는다.

(3) 자신이 몰랐던 단어와 숙어 표현이 있으면 정리한다.

(4) 해설집에서 필요한 부분을 골라 풀이 해법을 정리한다.

★틀린 문제 : _____   ★다시 공부한 날 : _____

(1) 문제를 왜? 틀렸는지 곰곰이 생각하고 그 이유를 적어본다.

(2) 핵심 개념을 적는다.

(3) 자신이 몰랐던 단어와 숙어 표현이 있으면 정리한다.

(4) 해설집에서 필요한 부분을 골라 풀이 해법을 정리한다.

★틀린 문제 : _____   ★다시 공부한 날 : _____

(1) 문제를 왜? 틀렸는지 곰곰이 생각하고 그 이유를 적어본다.

(2) 핵심 개념을 적는다.

(3) 자신이 몰랐던 단어와 숙어 표현이 있으면 정리한다.

(4) 해설집에서 필요한 부분을 골라 풀이 해법을 정리한다.

[1-2] 우리말과 같은 뜻이 되도록 다음 빈칸에 알맞은 것을 고르면?

1.

> 이것은 내가 지금까지 본 가장 지루한 영화이다.
> =This is the most boring movie that I
> _____.

❶ have never seen   ❷ never see
❸ am ever seeing   ❹ have ever seen
❺ have ever seeing

오답노트

2.

> Sunny는 내가 그녀에게 주었던 그 반지를 분실했다.
> =Sunny lost the ring which I _____
> to her.

❶ give   ❷ am giving
❸ will give   ❹ have given
❺ had given

오답노트

[3-4] 다음 빈칸에 알맞은 것을 고르시오.

3.

> He _____ here since July.

❶ is working   ❷ will be working
❸ will work   ❹ has been working
❺ had been working

오답노트

4.

> The train _____ the station when we
> got there.

❶ leaves   ❷ will have left
❸ had already left   ❹ had already leave
❺ has already left

오답노트

5. 다음 밑줄 친 부분에 들어갈 말은?

> A: How long has she been living in
>   Egypt?
> B: She _____ in Egypt for ten years.

❶ is living   ❷ has living
❸ had living   ❹ has been living
❺ had been living

오답노트

6. 다음 밑줄 친 동사를 알맞은 형태로 쓰시오.

> A: What are you doing here now?
> B: I am playing the computer game.
> A: When did you start?
> B: This morning. I play since then.

→ _____

오답노트

7. 다음 빈칸에 들어갈 가장 알맞은 말을 고르시오.

I decided to get up early before the ship entered the harbor. But my room was very hot so I couldn't sleep for hours. At last I fell asleep, but I woke up too late. Oh, no! I took my camera and rushed up. But everything was finished. The ship _____ the harbor.

❶ was entering   ❷ has entered
❸ is going to enter   ❹ has already entered
❺ had already entered

오답노트

8. 다음 빈칸에 들어갈 말이 알맞게 짝지어진 것은?

We started studying Japanese two years ago, and we are still studying it.
＝We _____ Japanese _____ two years.

❶ study − since
❷ studied − for
❸ are studying − since
❹ have been studying − for
❺ have studied − since

오답노트

9. 다음 빈칸에 들어갈 말이 알맞게 짝지어진 것은?

· I've _____ eaten French food.
· I've known her _____ three months.
· Have you _____ been to the amusement park?

❶ never − for − ever
❷ ever − since − never
❸ already − never − for
❹ just − ever − since
❺ since − already − just

오답노트

10. 다음 빈칸에 들어갈 말이 바르게 짝지어진 것은?

Two years _____ since you _____ middle school.

❶ passed − entered
❷ passed − have entered
❸ have passed − entered
❹ have passed − have entered
❺ had passed − have entered

오답노트

11. 다음 글을 읽고 어법상 어색한 부분을 찾아 바르게 고치시오.

Since I was little, I was interested in clothes and fashion. My friends say that I will make a good fashion designer. I am not very sure, though. It's true that I like clothes, but that doesn't mean that I have talent in design.

_____ → _____

오답노트

12. 다음 빈칸에 들어갈 말이 바르게 짝지어진 것은?

> · They had been talking _____ over an hour when he arrived.
> · The man has swum in the river _____ 2 o'clock.

❶ for – for ❷ for – since ❸ of – since
❹ since – for ❺ for – from

오답노트

13. 다음 밑줄 친 부분의 용법과 같은 것은?

> <u>Have</u> you ever <u>been</u> to Africa?

❶ She <u>has gone</u> to Hong Kong.
❷ I told my friend I <u>had bought</u> the book.
❸ I <u>had finished</u> my homework when she called me.
❹ Mike <u>has worked</u> here since he finished university.
❺ How many times <u>have</u> you <u>been</u> to America?

오답노트

14. 다음 대화의 밑줄 친 ⓐ, ⓑ를 바르게 고치시오.

> A: Did you get to the rock concert on time?
> B: No, I didn't. By the time I ⓐ <u>had got</u> to the hall, it ⓑ <u>have already started</u>.

ⓐ _____ / ⓑ _____

오답노트

15. 다음 중 어법상 어색한 것을 고르시오.

❶ When have you first met Lucy?
❷ I slept more than 10 hours last night.
❸ Have you ever read a book on Korean history?
❹ Was the weather good when you were on vacation?
❺ The house was dirty. They hadn't cleaned it for weeks.

오답노트

16. 다음 문장의 밑줄 친 부분과 쓰임이 같은 것은?

> How long <u>have</u> Joe and Cathy <u>known</u> each other?

❶ <u>Have</u> you <u>seen</u> Bob today?
❷ I <u>have been</u> to the amusement park twice.
❸ She <u>has</u> already <u>come</u> back to England.
❹ Jacob often <u>had gone</u> fishing before he moved to Seoul.
❺ She <u>has been</u> in hospital since July.

오답노트

17. 다음 밑줄 친 동사의 형태로 알맞은 것은?

> A : What's this?
> B : It's a book about the Korean economy.
>   I read it since last week.

❶ read
❷ would read
❸ had been read
❹ have been reading
❺ am reading

오답노트

18. 다음 두 문장이 같은 뜻이 되도록 빈칸에 알맞은 말을 넣어 문장을 완성하시오.

> Teachers have held the music night for five years.
> → The music night _____ _____ _____ _____ _____ for five years.

오답노트

[19-20] 다음 글을 읽고 물음에 답하시오.

> ⓐ Have you ever heard of Albert Schweitzer? When he was young, he heard that many people in Africa were dying because ⓑ they had no doctors.

19. 위 글의 밑줄 친 ⓐ와 쓰임이 같은 것은?

❶ I have not finished it yet.
❷ He has lost his watch.
❸ I have never been to Europe.
❹ She has gone to Japan.
❺ She has been ill since last week.

오답노트

20. 밑줄 친 ⓑ의 they가 가리키는 것은?

❶ Schweitzer
❷ his friends
❸ African people
❹ Gandhi
❺ Indian people

오답노트

21. 다음 우리말과 같은 뜻이 되도록 괄호 안의 단어를 바르게 배열하시오.

> · 한국어를 공부하신 지 얼마나 되셨나요?
> (long, been, you, studying, how, Korean, have)

→ _____

오답노트

A. 다음 우리말에 맞게 주어진 단어를 알맞게 배열하시오.

1. 그녀는 3년째 이 마을에서 살고 있다.

(lived / in / she / three years / has / for / this town)

→ _____

2. 그는 이틀 동안 아무것도 먹지 못하고 있다.

(has / anything / two days / not / he / for / eaten)

→ _____

3. 그들은 아직 그 도시를 방문하지 못했다.

(have / the city / yet / visited / not / they)

→ _____

B. 다음 문장에서 **틀린** 부분을 찾아 바르게 고쳐 쓰시오.

1. We weren't hungry. We have just eaten lunch.

→ _____

2. Kelly and Sunny went to the movie theater. They were late. The movie already began.

→ _____

3. I invited Susan to the party, but she couldn't come. She had make plans to do something else.

→ _____

4. Last month I went to London. It was my first trip to England. I have never be there before.

→ _____

C. 〈보기〉와 같이 계속의 의미를 지닌 현재완료시제를 이용하여 빈칸을 완성하시오.

보
기

teacher / six years

She *has been a teacher for six years*.

1.

collect stamps / two years

He _____

_____.

2.

work for the company / 1995

Nancy and Tom _____

_____.

3.

rain everywhere / last night

It _____

_____.

D. 다음 괄호 안의 단어들을 이용하여 현재완료와 현재완료 진행형 문장을 하나씩 만드시오.

보
기

Julia is reading a book. She started two hours ago. She is still reading it, and now she is on page 30.

→ *She has been reading for two hours.* (read / for two hours)

→ *She has read 30 pages so far.* (read / 30 pages so far)

1. Seo-yoon is from Korea. She is travelling around Asia at the moment. She began her trip three months ago.

→ _____ (travel / for three months)

→ _____ (visit / three countries so far)

실전 서술형 평가문제

출제의도 have/has＋과거분사
평가내용 현재완료시제를 이용하여 문장 서술하기

A. 아래 Peter의 체크리스트에서는 한 일에는 ∨표시가, 하지 않는 일에는 X표시가 되어 있다. 이 내용을 현재완료 또는 현재완료 부정문으로 완성하시오. (already와 yet을 사용할 것) [서술형 유형 : 8점 / 난이도 : 중하]

Exciting things to do	
ride a horse	∨
try bungee-jumping	X
try scuba diving	∨
travel around Australia	X
taste snake	X
stay in the jungle for a week	∨

보기	*Peter has already ridden a horse.* *Peter has not tried bungee-jumping yet.*

1. _____

2. _____

3. _____

4. _____

출제의도 현재완료 계속적 용법
평가내용 since를 이용하여 현재완료 계속적 용법 만들기

B. 〈보기〉와 같이 현재완료의 계속적 용법을 이용하여 문장을 영작하시오.   [서술형 유형 : 10점 / 난이도 : 중]

보 기	My brother / buy / a new car My brother / not have / any accidents → *My brother hasn't had any accidents since he bought a new car.*

1. Steve / start / working   Steve / travel abroad / many times

→ _____

2. Karen / decide / to study more   Karen / improve / her Spanish

→ _____

3. Sunny / start / going / to the gym   Sunny / lose / ten kilos

→ _____

4. Jim / move / to Scotland   I / not see / Jim

→ _____

5. Nancy / find / a new job   Nancy / not go out with / her friends

→ _____

실전 서술형 평가문제

출제의도 have/has been+V-ing
평가내용 현재완료 진행시제를 이용하여 문장 서술하기

C. for 또는 since를 이용하여 〈보기〉와 같이 현재완료 진행시제를 만드시오.

[서술형 유형 : 9점 / 난이도 : 중]

보기

teach / at Yonsei University / six years

→ *He has been teaching at Yonsei University for six years.*

1.

work for / a newspaper / 2005

_____

_____

2.

jog / in the park / two hours

_____

_____

3.

talk / on the phone / 5 o'clock

_____

_____

출제의도 과거와 과거완료 사용

평가내용 두 가지의 시제를 이용한 시간의 순서 표현하기

D. 괄호 안의 접속사를 이용하여 〈보기〉와 같이 과거시제와 과거완료시제를 활용한 문장으로 완성하시오.

[서술형 유형 : 8점 / 난이도 : 중]

보기	I left the office. Then I realized my briefcase was still on my desk. (after) → *After I had left the office, I realized my briefcase was still on my desk. /* *I realized my briefcase was still on my desk after I had left the office.*

1. The thieves ran away. A while later the police arrived.   (by the time)

→ _____

2. Lucy did the shopping. Then she had coffee with Susan.   (after)

→ _____

3. Sarah finished her assignment. Then she gave it to the teacher.   (when)

→ _____

4. Scott typed up his story. A while later his computer broke down.   (before)

→ _____

실전 서술형 평가문제

 출제의도 과거시제와 과거완료시제의 사용
평가내용 두 가지의 시제를 이용한 시간의 순서 서술하기

E. **다음은 일이 일어난 순서대로 나열한 것이다. 주어진 문장을 참고하여 과거시제 또는 과거완료시제를 이용하여 시간의 순서에 맞게 영작하시오.** [서술형 유형 : 9점 / 난이도 : 중]

1. (1) Somebody broke into our house during the night. (2) My wife and I arrived at home in the morning. (3) We called the police.

→ We arrived at home in the morning and found that somebody _____ into our house during the night. So we _____.

2. (1) My dad came back from vacation a few days ago. (2) I met him the same day. (3) He looked very tired.

→ I _____ a few days ago. He _____ just _____.
He _____.

3. (1) Lucy went out. (2) I tried to phone her this morning. (3) There was no answer.

→ I tried to phone Lucy this morning, but _____ no answer.
She _____ out.

서술형 평가문제	채 점 기 준	배 점	나의 점수
A		2점×4문항=8점	
B		2점×5문항=10점	
C	표현이 올바르고 문법, 철자가 모두 정확한 경우	3점×3문항=9점	
D		2점×4문항=8점	
E		3점×3문항=9점	
공통	문법, 철자가 1개씩 틀린 경우	각 문항당 1점씩 감점	
	내용과 전혀 일치하지 않거나 답을 기재하지 못한 경우	0점	

Chapter 3

조동사 (Modals)

1-1 can, could

Kathy **could** play tennis last year, but she **can't** play tennis now.
Kathy는 작년에 테니스를 칠 수 있었지만, 지금은 칠 수 없다.

01 조동사 can은 **현재와 미래의 능력**을 나타낸다. can의 과거는 could로 **과거에 할 수 있었던 능력**(ability)을 나타내고 부정은 can/could 뒤에 not을 붙인다.

I **can** speak both English and Chinese. 나는 영어와 중국어를 할 수 있다.

Can you speak any foreign languages? 외국어를 할 줄 아니?

Fred **could** play soccer last year, but he **can't** play soccer now.
Fred는 작년에 축구를 할 수 있었지만, 지금은 할 수 없다.

She **couldn't** play the violin when she was seven years old. 그녀는 7살 때 바이올린을 연주할 수 없었다.

02 can이 **허락**(give permission)을 나타낼 때 '~해도 좋다'의 뜻이고, 부정은 can 뒤에 not을 붙여 '~해서는 안 된다'의 뜻이다. **가능성**(possibility)을 나타낼 때는 주로 바람직하지 않은 일이 일어날 수 있음을 내포하기도 한다.

Customers **can** use the computers for free. 고객들은 컴퓨터를 무료로 사용할 수 있습니다. ▶ 허락
You **can't** smoke here. 여기서 담배를 피우면 안 된다. ▶ 허락
Children **can** have cancer. 어린이들도 암에 걸릴 수 있다. ▶ 가능성
Customers' needs **can** change daily. 고객들의 요구는 날마다 바뀔 수 있다. ▶ 가능성
Look at those dark clouds. It **could** start raining any minute.
시커먼 구름 좀 봐. 지금 당장이라고 비가 올 거 같아. ▶ 가능성

03 **능력을 나타내는 can은 be able to와 같은 의미**로 쓰이나, 일상 영어에서는 can을 주로 쓴다. 하지만 can은 쓸 수 없고 be able to만 써야 하는 경우가 있다.

① 미래 조동사(will)와 함께 쓰일 경우
Jane **will be able to** learn Japanese.
Jane은 일본어를 배울 수 있을 거야.

② 완료시제와 함께 쓰일 경우
She **has been able to** drive a car. 그녀는 차를 운전할 수 있었다.

서술형 기초다지기

Challenge 1 다음 괄호 안의 정보를 이용하여 의문문과 대답을 완성하세요.

> **보기**
> A: *Can Seo-yoon speak English?*
> B: *Yes, she can.* (Seo-yoon can speak English.)

01. A: _____
    B: _____ (Kevin can't write with his left hand.)

02. A: _____
    B: _____ (Ron can eat with chopsticks.)

03. A: _____
    B: _____ (I can go shopping with you this afternoon.)

Challenge 2 다음 빈칸에 could 또는 couldn't를 알맞게 써 넣으세요.

01. Kevin _____ play with us yesterday, but now he can.

02. When I was a child, I _____ play the cello, but now I can.

03. My dad was very fast, and he _____ run 100 meters in 12 seconds.

04. Before Seo-yoon came to Canada, she _____ understand much English.
    Now she can understand everything.

Challenge 3 다음 문장의 can/could를 be able to로 바꿔 다시 쓰세요.

01. It's summer now. My friends and I can play tennis outdoors.
    → It's summer now. _____

02. I can't go ice skating now, but I could go ice skating last winter.
    → _____

03. When Sunny comes home, she can help you with your homework.
    → _____

1-2 must be, may, might

They **are** in the hospital. 그들은 병원에 있다. (100% 확신)
They **must be** in the hospital. 그들은 병원에 있는 게 틀림없다. (95% 확신)
They **may(=might) be** in the hospital.
그들은 병원에 있을지도 모른다. (50% 이하 추측)

---

01 100% 현재의 사실이라고 확신할 때는 현재형을 쓰고, 현재 상황에 대한 논리적 이유가 있는 강한 확신 (95%)의 경우에는 'must be(~임에 틀림없다)'를 쓴다.

She **is** warm-hearted like her mother. 그녀는 그녀의 엄마처럼 마음이 따뜻하다. ▶ 100% 확신이나 사실
She **must be** warm-hearted like her mother. 그녀는 그녀의 엄마처럼 마음이 따뜻할 것이 틀림없다. ▶ 95% 확신

---

02 추측(guess)과 가능성(possibility)로 쓰이는 may와 might는 '~일지도 모른다'의 의미이다. may와 might 는 큰 의미 차 없이 둘 다 사용할 수 있다. **추측이나 가능성을 나타낼 때 may와 마찬가지로 might는 과거가 아닌 현재나 미래**를 나타낸다.

It **may** rain today. Take an umbrella with you. 오늘 비가 올지도 모른다. 우산을 가져가.
She **might** not come to the meeting tomorrow. 그녀는 내일 회의에 못 올지도 모른다.

※ may 대신 might만 써야 하는 경우는 가능성이 현저히 떨어지는 가정법(20% 이하)

If I knew her better, I **might** invite her to dinner. 내가 그녀를 더 잘 안다면 저녁식사에 그녀를 초대할지도 모를 텐데.
▶ 그녀를 잘 모르기 때문에 실제로는 그녀를 초대하지 않을 것이라는 뜻이 담겨있는 가정법으로, 여기서는 might 대신 may를 쓸 수 없다.

---

03 can과 마찬가지로 **may 또한 허락(permission)**을 나타내는데 '~해도 좋다'라는 뜻이다.

You **may** use my digital camera if you want. 원한다면 내 디지털 카메라를 써도 좋다.
You **may** come whenever you have time. 시간이 있을 때 언제든 와도 좋다.
You **may** not smoke here. 여기서 담배를 피우면 안 된다.

---

04 may well : '~하는 것이 당연하다', may(=might) as well : '~하는 것이 낫다'

You **may well** be sad to hear the news. 네가 그 소식을 듣고 슬픈 것은 당연하다.
You **might as well** keep it a secret. 너는 그것을 비밀로 하는 것이 낫다.
I **may as well** die as marry such a man. 그런 사람과 결혼하느니 차라리 죽는 게 낫다.

서술형 기초다지기

Challenge 1 다음 괄호 안의 표현과 알맞은 조동사를 이용하여 문장을 완성하세요.

01.

그는 교통경찰관이다. (a traffic policeman)

→ _____

02.

너는 내 차를 써도 좋다. (my car / use)

→ _____

03.

그녀는 피곤한 것이 틀림없다. (tired)

→ _____

04.

그녀는 훌륭한 음악가가 될지도 모른다.
(a great musician / become)

→ _____

Challenge 2 밑줄 친 조동사의 뜻이 가능(possibility)인지 허락(permission)인지를 구별해 보세요.

01. They <u>may</u> take their two grandchildren with them. (possibility / permission)

02. It <u>may</u> be hot and humid all weekend. (possibility / permission)

03. You <u>may</u> not stay up until midnight. Your bedtime is nine o'clock. (possibility / permission)

Challenge 3 다음 빈칸을 may, may well, 또는 may as well을 이용하여 완성하세요.

01. It is natural that she should get angry with him.

= She _____ get angry with him.

02. You would rather plug your nose. Here comes the smelly boy.

= You _____ plug your nose. Here comes the smelly boy.

03. It is possible that she is rich. = She _____ rich.

1-3 정중한 부탁(요청)

May I see your driver's licence?
운전면허증 좀 볼 수 있을까요?

Could you tell me how to get to the airport?
공항에 어떻게 가야 하는지 알려줄 수 있나요?

01 'I'를 주어로 하는 **May I ~?** 또는 **Could/Can I ~?**로 공손하고 정중한 부탁(polite request)을 할 수 있다. May I ~?가 가장 정중한 표현이고 가까운 사이에는 Can/Could I ~?를 많이 쓴다. **여기서 Could는 Can의 과거가 아닌 현재와 미래를 나타내고 please를 쓰기도 한다.**

FORMAL	**May I** (please) use your pencil?	▶ 모르는 사이 (They don't know each other.)
	Could I use your pencil, (please)?	▶ 잘 알지 못하는 사이 (They might or might not know each other.)
INFORMAL	**Can I** use your pencil?	▶ 친한 사이 (They have been speaking together or they know each other.)

02 'you'를 주어로 하는 **Can/Will/Would/Could you ~?**로 정중한 부탁을 할 수 있다. 친구나 가족과 같은 가까운 사이에서는 Can you ~?를 쓰고 please를 덧붙여 쓰기도 한다.

Would you shut the door, please? 문을 좀 닫아주시겠어요?

Could you give me some information about Korea? 한국에 관한 정보를 주실 수 있나요?

Can you marry me? 나와 결혼해 줄래?

03 제안(offering)이나 초대(inviting)를 할 때 **Would you like+(대)명사 ~?** 또는 **Would you like to+V ~?**를 쓴다.

Would you like a cup of coffee? 커피 한잔 하실래요?

- Yes, please. 네, 좋아요.

I'd like a cheeseburger and a Coke. 나는 치즈버거와 콜라를 원해요. ▶ I'd like+명사=I want+명사

Would you like to go to the movies with us Saturday night? 토요일 밤에 우리랑 같이 영화 보러 갈래?

I'd like to try on this jacket, please. 이 자켓을 입어보고 싶어요. ▶ I'd like to+V=I want to+V

Challenge 1　May/Can/Could I ~를 이용하여 다음 빈칸을 완성하세요.

> **보기**
> Student : *May I* hand in my homework tomorrow, please?
> Teacher : No, you may not.

01. Student : _____ have a little more time?

Teacher : No, you may not. The test time is up.

02. Student : _____ borrow your dictionary?

Classmate : Sure.

03. You : _____ speak with Professor Jones?

Secretary : He's not here at the moment. _____ take a message?

Challenge 2　다음 상황을 읽고 Can/Would/Could ~?를 이용한 문장으로 만드세요.

> **보기**
> You are on a bus and you want to ask the person sitting next to you to close the window.
> What do you say? → *Could/Would you close the window (please)?*

01. You want to have a picnic with your friends at the park. Ask your mother for permission.

→ _____

02. Tom wants his father to teach him how to drive a car. What does he say?

→ _____

Challenge 3　다음 상황을 읽고 Would you like ~?를 이용한 문장으로 빈칸을 완성하세요.

01. You're on a subway. You see an old woman standing. Offer her your seat.

→ _____

02. Your friend looks thirsty. Offer her something to drink.

→ _____

1-4 must, have (got) to

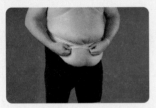

You **must** do exercise for your health.
당신은 건강을 위해서 운동을 해야 한다.

Today is Sunday. 오늘은 일요일이다.
You **don't have to** go to school. 너는 학교에 갈 필요가 없다.

01

must는 필요(necessity)나 확신(95% certainty)을 가지고 **상대방에게 그 일을 꼭 하라는 강한 강조의 의미**를 지닌다. 부정 형태 must not(=mustn't)은 '~해서는 안 된다'라는 강한 금지의 뜻이다.

You **must** eat more fresh vegetables. 너는 신선한 채소를 더 많이 먹어야 한다.
You **must** drive slowly through the school zone. 어린이 보호구역을 통과하는 동안은 천천히 운전해야 한다.
Students **mustn't** tell a lie to their teachers. 학생들은 선생님께 거짓말을 해서는 안 된다.

02

have to도 must와 같은 의미로 '~해야 한다'의 뜻이다. 일상 영어에서는 must보다 have to를 더 많이 쓴다. have got to는 have to의 미국식 표현으로 구어체에서 주로 쓴다.

To get a cheap ticket, you **have to** book in advance. 싼 입장권을 얻기 위해서는 미리 예약을 해야 한다.
It's Saturday, but I **have got to** work. 토요일이지만 나는 일해야 한다.

03

have to의 부정은 don't have to / don't need to / need not으로 모두 '~할 필요가 없다'란 뜻이다. 반면, must not은 「~해서는 안 된다」란 뜻의 강한 금지를 나타낸다.

You **don't have to** wash the car. It is clean. 너는 세차할 필요가 없다. 차는 깨끗하다.
You **don't need to** tell her the story. 너는 그 이야기를 그녀에게 할 필요는 없다.

04

must와 have (got) to는 미래형과 과거형이 없어서 **미래는 will have to, 과거는 had to**로 쓴다.

Next week I'**ll have to** go to Hong Kong. 다음 주에 나는 홍콩에 가야 한다.
I **had to** get up early yesterday. 나는 어제 일찍 일어나야 했다.

※ 논리적 근거를 가지고 추측하는 must be의 부정은 must not을 쓰지 않는다. '~임에 틀림없다'는 must be의 부정은 can't be(=cannot be)로 쓰고 '~일 리가 없다'라는 뜻이다.

She **must be** crazy to get married with that man. 그 남자와 결혼을 하다니 그녀는 미친 것이 틀림없다.
She **can't be** married. She is only 17. 그녀는 결혼을 할 리가 없다. 고작 17살이다.

서술형 기초다지기

다음 사진을 참고하여 must와 mustn't를 이용한 문장을 영작하세요.

01.

you / swim / in the river

→ _____

02.

the man / eat / the hamburger

→ _____

03.

he / smoke / in the museum

→ _____

04.

you / be quiet / in class

→ _____

Challenge 2 다음 문장을 괄호 안의 지시대로 바꾸어 쓰세요.

01. I have to study for my medical school exams. (과거)

→ _____

02. Next week, John must interview five people. (미래)

→ _____

Challenge 3 다음 빈칸에 don't/doesn't have to 또는 mustn't를 넣으세요.

> **보기** You _mustn't_ cross the street when the walker's light is red.

01. The soup is too hot. You _____ eat it yet. Wait for it to cool.

02. Whatever you do, you _____ touch that switch. It's very dangerous.

03. When the phone rings, you _____ answer it. It's up to you.

1-5 should, ought to, had better, would rather

Nancy has got a bad cold.
Nancy는 독감에 걸렸다.
She **should**(=**ought to**) see a doctor.
그녀는 진찰을 받는 게 좋겠다.

01 충고나 제안의 의미로 쓰일 경우 should와 ought to는 같은 의미로 '~해야 한다, ~하는 게 좋겠다'라는 뜻이다. 하지만, 일상 영어에서는 should를 많이 쓴다.

You look tired. You **should** go to bed. 피곤해 보인다. 너는 자러 가는 게 좋겠다.
There's a lot of snow. You **ought to** wear boots. 눈이 많이 왔다. 너는 부츠를 신어야 한다.

02 should의 부정은 should not, ought to의 부정은 ought not to를 쓴다. 각각 shouldn't와 oughtn't to 로 줄여 쓸 수 있다. 하지만 부정문이나 의문문에서는 ought to보다 should를 더 많이 쓴다.

You **shouldn't** believe everything you read in the newspapers.
네가 신문에서 읽는 모든 것을 믿어서는 안 된다.
People **oughtn't to** drink and drive. 음주운전을 하지 말아야 한다.
I broke my friend's CD player. **Should** I buy a new one for him?
나는 친구의 CD 플레이어를 고장 냈다. 새것을 사줘야 하나?

03 「had better+동사원형」은 '~하는 게 좋겠다/낫겠다'의 뜻으로, should와 같이 충고나 조언을 할 때 쓴다. 하지만 의미상 **더 강한 어감이나 경고의 메시지**(strong advice or warning)를 담고 있어 충고를 따르지 않을 때는 어떤 문제가 생길 수 있다는 뜻을 내포하고 있다. 부정은 「had better not+동사원형」을 쓴다.

The movie starts at 8:00. You**'d better** go now, or you'll be late.
영화는 8시에 시작한다. 지금 출발하는 게 좋겠다, 그렇지 않으면 늦는다.
It's raining. You **had better** take an umbrella. 비가 온다. 너는 우산을 가져가는 게 좋겠다.

04 「would rather+동사원형」은 '~하는 것이 더 좋다, ~하고 싶다'의 뜻으로, **어떤 것을 더 선호한다는 의미를** 나타내어 had better와는 차이가 있다. 「would prefer to+동사원형」으로 바꿔 쓸 수 있고 부정은 「would rather not+동사원형」으로 쓴다. 「A보다 차라리 B가 좋다」는 의미의 「would rather B than A」도 유용한 구문이다. 이는 「prefer B to A」로 바꿔 쓸 수 있는데, 이때 A와 B 자리에는 명사나 동명사가 와야 한다.

Would you like to sit on a chair? 의자에 앉으실래요?
– No, thanks. I**'d rather**(=I'd prefer to) sit on the floor. 아니오, 나는 바닥에 앉는 게 좋겠어요.
I **would rather** play soccer than (play) basketball. 나는 농구보다 축구를 하고 싶다.
=I **prefer** playing soccer **to** (playing) basketball.

서술형 기초다지기

정답 p. 10

Challenge 1 다음 괄호 안의 표현 중 알맞은 것을 고르세요.

01. You (should / ought) be more careful when you cross the street.

02. I don't want to go for a walk. I (would / had) rather have a rest.

03. They (ought to not / ought not to) bring any drink into the building.

04. I think you'd (not rather / rather not) go out in this weather.

05. It's cold today. You'd (better / rather) wear a coat when you go out.

Challenge 2 should와 shouldn't를 이용하여 문장을 완성하세요.

> 보기
>
> Julie has got a terrible headache.
> → *She should take an aspirin.* (take / an aspirin)
> → *She shouldn't go to the concert.* (go / to the concert)

01. John can never wake up early in the morning, so he's always late for work.

→ _____. (go to bed / late / at night)

→ _____. (use / an alarm clock)

02. Peter feels very tired.

→ _____. (work / so hard)

→ _____. (take a break)

Challenge 3 다음 빈칸에 들어갈 말을 아래에서 골라 괄호 안의 조동사를 이용하여 완성하세요.

listen	watch TV	be a freelancer

01. It's raining outside. I _____ at home than go to the movies. (would rather)

02. You _____ to his words. (not / had better)

03. I _____ than a company worker. I don't want to work full time. (would rather)

Unit 02 조동사 Ⅱ

2-1 과거 추측(조동사+have+p.p.)

The phone rang but she didn't hear it.

She **was** asleep. 그녀는 자고 있었다. (100% 확신)
She **must have been** asleep. 그녀는 자고 있던 게 분명하다. (95% 확신)
She **might have been** asleep. 그녀는 자고 있었을지도 모른다. (50% 확신)
=She **could have been** asleep.

The light was red, but the car didn't stop.

The driver **didn't see** the red light. 운전자는 적신호를 보지 못했다. (100% 확신)
He **must not have seen** the red light.
그는 적신호를 봤을 리가 없다. (95% 확신)
=He **couldn't have seen** the red light.
=He **can't have seen** the red light.
He **may not have seen** the red light.
그는 적신호를 못 봤을지도 모른다. (50% 확신)
=He **might not have seen** the red light.

---

01 100% 과거의 사실이라고 확신하면 과거형을 쓴다. 「must have+p.p.」는 '~했음에 틀림없다'(95%)라는 뜻으로, 과거 상황에 대한 논리적 이유가 있는 강한 확신이나 추측인 경우에 쓴다. 반면, 「may/might/could have+p.p.」는 '~했을지도 모른다'(50%)는 뜻이다.

She looked so serious. She **might have done** poorly on the exam.
그녀는 아주 심각해 보였어. 시험을 잘 보지 못했나봐.

The ground is wet. It **must have rained** last night. 땅이 젖어 있다. 어젯밤에 틀림없이 비가 왔을 것이다.

02 「can't/couldn't have+p.p.」, 「must not have+p.p.」 모두 '~했을 리가 없다'(95%)의 뜻으로, 50% 이하의 추측을 나타낸다. 「may/might have+과거분사」의 부정은 「may/might not have+과거분사」를 쓰고 '~하지 않았을지도 모른다'의 뜻이다.

She **didn't sing** in front of people. 그녀는 사람들 앞에서 노래를 부르지 않았다.

She **couldn't(=mustn't) have sung** in front of people. 그녀는 사람들 앞에서 노래를 불렀을 리가 없다.

She **might not have sung** in front of people. 그녀는 사람들 앞에서 노래를 부르지 않았을지도 모른다.

He **cannot have done** it. 그가 그것을 했을 리가 없다.

서술형 기초다지기

Challenge 1 다음 괄호 안의 조동사와 동사를 사용하여 빈칸을 완성하세요.

> **보기**
> I have seen him enter his house. He *must be* (must, be) at home now.

01. I saw her leave her house five minutes ago. She _____ (must not, be) at home now.

02. Why didn't Kevin answer his cell phone? He was probably in the shower.
    He _____ (may, be) in the shower.

03. When I woke up this morning, the light was on. I _____ (must, forget) to turn it off when I went to bed.

04. I don't understand how the accident happened. The driver _____ (must not, see) the red light because of heavy rain.

05. A: I was surprised that Sunny wasn't at the meeting.
    B: She _____ (might not, know) about it.

Challenge 2 다음 문장을 괄호 안의 조동사를 이용하여 추측을 나타내는 표현으로 만드세요.

> **보기**
> It is possible that he was in his office. (may)
> → He *may have been in his office.*

01. It is impossible that he knew about it. (can't)
    → He _____.

02. It is possible that Tiffany is in her office. (may)
    → She _____.

03. It is probable that the secretary revealed the secret. (might)
    → She _____.

04. It is almost certain that she has forgotten the promise. (must)
    → She _____.

2-2 과거 추측 must have+p.p. / should have+p.p.

The driver got seriously hurt in a car crash.
그 운전자는 자동차 충돌사고로 심하게 다쳤다.
He **should have fastened** his seat belt.
그는 안전벨트를 맸어야 했는데 (매지 않았다).

01 should의 과거형인 「should have+p.p.」는 '~했어야 했는데 (못했다)'의 의미로, **과거에 했어야 하는 일이나 행동에 대한 후회, 유감**을 나타낸다. 「ought to have+p.p.」로 바꿔 쓸 수 있고 과거의 행위나 동작을 하지 않았음을 내포하고 있다.

The Government **should have done** more to help homeless people.
정부가 노숙자를 돕기 위해 더 많은 것을 했어야 했는데 (하지 않았다).

The bus **ought to have arrived** at 9 p.m. 버스가 9시에 도착했어야 하는데 (하지 않았다).

02 must의 과거형인 「must have+p.p.」는 **과거 사실에 대한 강한 추측**이다. '~이었음에/~했음에 틀림없다'라는 뜻으로, **과거의 행위나 동작을 실제 했음을 내포**하고 있다.

She **must have gone** to Singapore. I haven't seen her for a while.
그녀는 싱가포르로 갔음에 틀림없다. 한동안 그녀를 보지 못했다.

He looks tired. He **must have stayed** up all night.
그는 피곤해 보인다. 그는 밤을 꼬박 새운 것이 틀림없다.

03 부정문인 「should not have+p.p.」는 '~하지 말았어야 했는데 (했다)'의 의미이다. 「ought not to have+p.p.」도 같은 의미로 쓴다.

You **should not have eaten** the food. 너는 그 음식을 먹지 말았어야 했는데 (먹었다).

We went to a movie, but it was a waste of time and money.

→ We **should not have gone** to the movies. 우리는 그 영화를 보러 가지 말았어야 했다.

※ 「need have+p.p.」는 '~할 필요가 있었는데 (하지 않았다)'의 뜻이고 부정은 「need not have+p.p.」로 '~할 필요가 없었는데 (사실은 했다)'의 뜻이다. 이는 영국식 표현으로 미국식 영어에서는 잘 사용하지 않는다.

We **need not have worried** about that.
우리는 그것에 대해 걱정할 필요가 없었다.

서술형 기초다지기

Challenge 1 다음 두 문장이 같은 뜻이 되도록 빈칸에 알맞은 말을 쓰세요.

> 보
> 기
> I am sure that he missed the train.
> =He *must have missed* the train.

01. I didn't listen to my mother, but I regret it.

= I _____ to my mother.

02. It is almost certain that she has forgotten my phone number.

= She _____ my phone number.

03. It is not right that you laughed at his mistakes.

= You _____ at his mistakes.

Challenge 2 다음 우리말과 같은 뜻이 되도록 괄호 안의 동사를 이용하여 빈칸을 완성하세요.

01. 그는 연습을 많이 했음에 틀림없다.

→ He _____ (practice) a lot.

02. Amy는 매일 밤 일기를 썼어야 했다.

→ Amy _____ (write) the diary every night.

Challenge 3 다음 문장을 「ought (not) to have+p.p.」를 이용하여 바꾸어 쓰세요.

> 보
> 기
> She is sorry she gave the child scissors to play with.
> → *She ought not to have given the child scissors to play with.*

01. Jane didn't do well on the test this morning. She's sorry that she went to the party last night.

→ _____

02. There were no free tables in the restaurant. We're sorry we didn't reserve a table.

→ _____

이것이 시험에 출제되는 영문법이다!

01 출제 100% - 조동사의 의미를 정확히 알아두자!

 출제자의 눈 조동사의 기본적인 의미에 따라 우리말에 알맞은 조동사를 고르는 문제가 자주 출제된다. 특히 조동사 can은 그 의미에 따라 적절히 be able to로 활용할 줄 아는지를 묻는 문제가 나온다. 또한 must와 have (got) to의 과거는 had to를 쓴다는 것에도 주의하자. 문제를 푸는 관건은 문맥 속의 상황이 지나간 일인가를 확인하는 것이다.

Ex 1.

다음 밑줄 친 부분과 바꿔 쓸 수 있는 것은?

Christina <u>couldn't</u> go to the movies yesterday.

(a) weren't able to   (b) will be able to

(c) don't have to   (d) wasn't able to

Ex 2.

Sorry I'm late, but _____ go to a bank to get some money out.

(a) have to   (b) had to   (c) must   (d) should

02 출제 100% - 추측의 must be와 not의 위치에 주의하자.

 출제자의 눈 강한 금지를 나타내는 must not과 불필요함을 뜻하는 don't have to, don't need to, need not을 구별해서 쓰는 문제가 출제된다. 특히, 조동사의 부정문에서 not의 위치를 물어보거나 어법상 틀린 부분을 고르는 문제가 오고, '~임에 틀림없다'의 뜻인 must be와 「must+동사원형」을 구별하는 문제도 출제된다. '~일 리가 없다'는 뜻의 「can't+동사원형」을 영작문제로 주거나 may not과 can not을 주고 의미를 구별하는 문제가 출제되기도 한다.

Ex 3.

Her playing was terrible. She _____ a pianist.

(a) may not   (b) must be   (c) cannot be   (d) can't have been

Ex 4.

· 저 남자와 결혼하다니 그녀는 미친 것이 틀림없어.

=She _____ crazy to get married with that man.

(a) may be   (b) must   (c) should be   (d) must be

03 출제 100% - had better와 would rather의 쓰임에 주의하자.

 출제자의 눈 had better와 would rather는 둘 다 '~하는 게 좋겠다'의 표현이지만 had better는 충고(advice)의 의미이고, would rather는 선호(preference)의 의미이다. 이 둘의 의미에 맞는 표현을 영작하거나 고르는 문제가 출제된다. had better와 would rather는 바로 뒤에 동사원형을 써야 하는데 to부정사를 써 놓기도 하고 부정문에서는 not의 위치를 잘못 쓰거나 don't를 주고 헷갈리게 할 수도 있다. 또한 would like와 would like to를 각각 want와 want to로 바꿔 쓸 수 있는지 묻는 문제도 다양한 형태로 출제된다.

Ex 5.

· 오늘 학교에 늦지 않는 것이 좋겠다. 그러니까 당장 일어나.

= You _____ be late for school today, so get up right away.

(a) had not better　(b) would rather not　(c) had better　(d) had better not

Ex 6.

· 밑줄 친 부분과 의미가 같은 것은?

I want to cut this sandwich in half and share it with you.

(a) I would like cut this sandwich in half and share it with you.

(b) I would like to cut this sandwich in half and share it with you.

(c) I had better cut this sandwich in half and share it with you.

04 출제 100% - 현재냐 과거냐 그것이 문제로다.

 출제자의 눈 조동사 뒤에 나타나는 완료형 have+과거분사(p.p.)는 원칙적으로 본동사의 시제보다 하나 더 이전의 과거시제를 의미한다. 따라서 현재에서 과거를 추측할 때는 「조동사+have+p.p.」를 사용한다. 특히 「must have+p.p.」와 「should have+p.p.」를 구별하는 문제가 집중적으로 출제되는데 둘 다 현재에서 과거를 추측할 때 사용된다. 반면, 「must have+p.p.」는 과거에 했던 일에 대한 강한 추측을 나타내고, 「should have+p.p.」는 과거에 하지 못한 일에 대한 후회나 비난을 나타낸다는 것도 기억하자.

Ex 7.

It _____ rained during the night, for the road is wet.

(a) should have　(b) might have　(c) ought not have　(d) must have

1. 다음 표지판의 의미로 알맞은 것을 고르시오.

❶ You may park here.
❷ You must park here.
❸ You must not park here.
❹ You don't have to park here.
❺ You must have parked here.

2. 다음 괄호 안의 단어를 바르게 배열하시오.

> 네 건강이 점점 더 악화되고 있다. 너는 담배를 줄
> 이는 게 좋겠다.
> =Your health is getting worse. You
> _____ on your smoking.
> (cut down, better, had)

3. 다음 문장의 밑줄 친 부분에 들어갈 알맞은 말은?

> You had better _____ English hard.

❶ to study   ❷ studying   ❸ studies
❹ study   ❺ studied

[4-6] 다음 빈칸에 알맞은 단어를 쓰시오.

4. 그녀는 20대임에 틀림없다.
   =She _____ in her twenties.

5. 그는 거짓말쟁이일 리가 없다. 그는 정직한 소년이다.
   =He _____ a liar. He is a very
   honest boy.

6. 너는 여기에서 신발을 벗을 필요가 없다.
   =You _____ take off your shoes
   here.

7. 다음 중 어법상 옳은 문장을 고르시오.

❶ He oughts to see a doctor.
❷ She needs not to do it now.
❸ He should helps her.
❹ She ought go there with her mother.
❺ You shouldn't tell a lie.

8. 다음 빈칸에 알맞은 말을 쓰시오.

> 우리는 집에서 비디오를 시청하느니 차라리 영화
> 를 보러 가겠다.
> =We _____ _____ go to the
> movies _____ watch a video at
> home.

9. 다음 빈칸에 알맞은 조동사를 쓰시오.

> A : Seo-yoon plays the violin very well.
> B : She _____ _____ practiced a
> lot.(그녀는 연습을 많이 했음에 틀림없다.)

10. 다음 빈칸에 들어갈 알맞은 말을 고르시오.

> She _____ me.
> =I am sorry that she didn't tell me.

❶ may tell   ❷ may have told
❸ should have told   ❹ must have told
❺ should told

11. 다음 빈칸에 알맞은 말을 쓰시오.

> 그는 거기에 갔어야 했는데.
> =He _____ _____ _____ there.

오답 노트 만들기

★틀린 문제 : _____   ★다시 공부한 날 : _____

(1) 문제를 왜? 틀렸는지 곰곰이 생각하고 그 이유를 적어본다.

(2) 핵심 개념을 적는다.

(3) 자신이 몰랐던 단어와 숙어 표현이 있으면 정리한다.

(4) 해설집에서 필요한 부분을 골라 풀이 해법을 정리한다.

★틀린 문제 : _____   ★다시 공부한 날 : _____

(1) 문제를 왜? 틀렸는지 곰곰이 생각하고 그 이유를 적어본다.

(2) 핵심 개념을 적는다.

(3) 자신이 몰랐던 단어와 숙어 표현이 있으면 정리한다.

(4) 해설집에서 필요한 부분을 골라 풀이 해법을 정리한다.

★틀린 문제 : _____   ★다시 공부한 날 : _____

(1) 문제를 왜? 틀렸는지 곰곰이 생각하고 그 이유를 적어본다.

(2) 핵심 개념을 적는다.

(3) 자신이 몰랐던 단어와 숙어 표현이 있으면 정리한다.

(4) 해설집에서 필요한 부분을 골라 풀이 해법을 정리한다.

★틀린 문제 : _____   ★다시 공부한 날 : _____

(1) 문제를 왜? 틀렸는지 곰곰이 생각하고 그 이유를 적어본다.

(2) 핵심 개념을 적는다.

(3) 자신이 몰랐던 단어와 숙어 표현이 있으면 정리한다.

(4) 해설집에서 필요한 부분을 골라 풀이 해법을 정리한다.

1. 다음 중 어법상 바르지 <u>않은</u> 것은?

❶ You should not go there.
❷ I would rather not do that.
❸ We ought to not lose this chance.
❹ You must get a regular checkup.
❺ You had better go abroad than stay here.

오답노트

2. 다음 두 문장의 뜻이 같아지도록 빈칸을 채우시오.

You should shave your beard before your job interview.
＝You _____ your beard before your job interview.

오답노트

3. 다음 빈칸에 알맞은 것은?

Kevin walked past me without speaking.
He _____ me.

❶ must see
❷ shouldn't have seen
❸ cannot seen
❹ must not have seen
❺ may not have seen

오답노트

4. 다음 문장의 밑줄 친 부분이 의미하는 것은?

I feel sick. I <u>shouldn't have eaten</u> so much chocolate.

❶ 추측　❷ 허락　❸ 부탁　❹ 후회　❺ 감탄

오답노트

5. 다음 빈칸에 알맞은 말을 고르시오.

We went to a museum yesterday. We enjoyed ourselves till noon. But it was terrible in the afternoon. We didn't listen to the guide, so we were lost! We _____ _____ listened to the guide.

❶ must have
❷ shouldn't have
❸ should have
❹ ought not to have
❺ may have

오답노트

6. 다음 괄호 안에 주어진 단어를 바르게 배열하시오.

· 나는 컴퓨터 게임을 하느니 차라리 친구들을 만나는 게 낫겠다.
　＝I _____
　than play computer games.
　　(my friends, rather, would, meet)

오답노트

7. 다음 문장이 의미하는 바로 알맞은 것은?

> She must have remembered my promise.

❶ I am sure that she remembers my promise.
❷ I am sure that she remembered my promise.
❸ I am not sure that she remembers my promise.
❹ I am not sure that she remembered my promise.
❺ I hope that she can remember my promise.

오답노트

[8-9] 다음 빈칸에 알맞은 것을 고르시오.

8.

> I was very tired yesterday. So I _____ finish my homework.

❶ should ❷ may ❸ mustn't
❹ had to ❺ couldn't

9.

> I can't speak Japanese well, but I _____ speak it well next year.

❶ should ❷ will can
❸ will be able to ❹ can be going to
❺ had

오답노트

10. 다음 중 밑줄 친 단어의 의미가 다른 하나는?

❶ The girl cannot find her MP3 player.
❷ You cannot play the drum, can you?
❸ A year ago I couldn't speak English, but now I can.
❹ They are still alive? It cannot be possible.
❺ She cannot ski down the highest course.

오답노트

11. 다음 빈칸에 공통으로 들어갈 단어를 쓰시오.

> · _____ you like something to eat?
> · Do you want to watch TV?
>   − No, I _____ rather read my book.

오답노트

[12-13] 다음 우리말을 바르게 영작한 것을 고르시오.

12.

> 그들은 어제 줄서서 기다려야만 했다.

❶ They must wait in line yesterday.
❷ They may wait in line yesterday.
❸ They must have waited in line yesterday.
❹ They had to wait in line yesterday.
❺ They were able to wait in line yesterday.

오답노트

13.

> 우리는 그 영화를 보러 가지 말았어야 했다.

❶ We must not have gone to the movie.
❷ We should go to the movie.
❸ We'd rather go to the movie.
❹ We need not have gone to the movie.
❺ We shouldn't have gone to the movie.

오답노트

14. 다음 밑줄 친 말의 쓰임이 나머지와 다른 하나는?

❶ We <u>must</u> wear a school uniform in the school.
❷ You <u>must</u> be quiet in the classroom.
❸ If you fail the exam, you'll <u>have to</u> take it again.
❹ You <u>must</u> register your motorcycle to take part in the race.
❺ He <u>must</u> be happy to see his mother.

오답노트

15. 두 문장의 뜻이 서로 같지 않은 것은?

❶ It is necessary for us to study English.
  =We should study English.
❷ Rainbows can be seen at night.
  =We can see rainbows at night.
❸ You had better obey the safety rules.
  =Why do you obey the safety rules?
❹ I would like a cup of coffee with a piece of chocolate cake.
  =I want a cup of coffee with a piece of chocolate cake.

❺ Since the buses are running late tonight, we don't have to leave early.
  =Since the buses are running late tonight, we don't need to leave early.

오답노트

[16-17] 다음 빈칸에 알맞은 단어를 쓰시오.

16.

> 모든 물고기가 죽었거나 달아났음에 틀림없다.
> =All the fish _____ _____ died or fled.

17.

> 나는 먹을 것을 가져왔어야 했는데.
> =I _____ _____ brought something to eat.

오답노트

18. 다음 밑줄 친 부분과 바꿔 쓸 수 있는 것은?

> You <u>don't have to</u> answer if you don't want to.

❶ need not   ❷ have to   ❸ must not
❹ need   ❺ must

오답노트

19. 다음 두 문장이 같은 뜻이 되도록 빈칸을 채울 때 가장 알맞은 것은?

> It is possible that Julie has done the work by herself.
> =Julie _____ done the work by herself.

❶ might
❷ can't have
❸ should have
❹ must have
❺ may have

오답노트

20. 다음 문장의 밑줄 친 부분과 의미가 같은 것은?

> You <u>may</u> not enter the forbidden areas of the temple.

❶ You <u>may</u> go to the concert next week.
❷ He <u>may</u> not come here tonight.
❸ My parents <u>may</u> still be eating at the restaurant.
❹ She <u>may</u> decide to go camping.
❺ They thought that she <u>might</u> study in the library.

오답노트

21. 다음 빈칸에 들어갈 말로 알맞지 <u>않은</u> 것은?

> Look at the "No Parking" sign. You _____ park your car here.

❶ can't
❷ must not
❸ shouldn't
❹ don't have to
❺ ought not to

오답노트

22. 다음 중 어법상 틀린 문장은?

❶ They all realize that they ought to keep it clean.
❷ You'd better to calm down.
❸ I would like to hear from you soon.
❹ She was able to get a job.
❺ You should have taken my advice.

오답노트

23. 다음 빈칸에 공통으로 들어갈 알맞은 단어를 쓰시오.

> · You _____ not worry about things above your ability.
> · Your score is lowest in the class. You _____ have studied harder.

오답노트

A. 우리말과 일치하도록 빈칸에 알맞은 말을 쓰시오.

1. 축구를 하느니 차라리 컴퓨터 게임을 하겠다.

→ I _____ _____ play computer games _____ play soccer.

2. 너는 그 차를 사지 말았어야 했다.

→ You _____ _____ have bought the car.

3. 나는 어딘가에 휴대폰을 떨어뜨렸음에 틀림없다.

→ I _____ have dropped my cellular phone somewhere.

4. 그녀가 그런 실수를 저질렀을 리가 없다.

→ She _____ have made such a mistake.

B. 다음 문장을 might를 사용하여 〈보기〉와 같이 고쳐 쓰시오.

보 기	It's possible that I'll go to the concert. → *I might go to the concert.*

1. Perhaps she will not sit here.

→ _____

2. Maybe it will snow tomorrow.

→ _____

3. It's not probable that I will travel to India.

→ _____

C. 다음 문장에서 can을 be able to로 바꾸어 다시 쓰시오.

1. Can you speak any foreign languages?

→ _____

2. Most students can't understand what the teacher is saying.

→ _____

3. When I was a child, I could swim in the river.

→ _____

D. 다음 두 문장이 같은 뜻이 되도록 알맞은 말을 넣으시오.

1. I should return this to the owner.

→ I _____ _____ return this to the owner.

2. You don't have to come to the meeting.

→ You _____ _____ come to the meeting.

3. I want to talk with her.

→ I _____ _____ to talk with her.

4. Keep quiet during the exam.

→ You _____ _____ quiet during the exam.

E. 다음 우리말에 맞게 괄호 안의 동사를 이용하여 빈칸을 채우시오.

1. 너는 그 장면을 보지 말았어야 했는데.

→ You _____ the scene. (see)

2. 나는 그녀를 같은 장소에서 만났을지도 모른다.

→ I _____ her at the same place. (meet)

3. 너는 그의 말을 듣지 않는 게 좋겠다.

→ You _____ to his words. (listen)

출제의도 상대방에게 강력한 충고하기
평가내용 조동사 must를 활용한 실생활의 표현 능력

A. 다음 사진을 참고하여 학교에서 해야 할 일과 하지 말아야 할 일을 must 또는 must not을 이용하여 영어로 쓰시오.

[서술형 유형 : 8점 / 난이도 : 하]

1.

run in the hallway

_____

2.

listen to the teacher

_____

3.

talk with your friend

_____

4.

sleep in class

_____

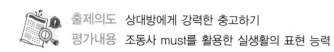

출제의도 상대방에게 강력한 충고하기

평가내용 조동사 must를 활용한 실생활의 표현 능력

B. 아래 호텔 규칙(Hotel Rules)을 읽고, must 또는 mustn't를 이용하여 문장을 완성하시오.

[서술형 유형 : 10점 / 난이도 : 하]

Hotel Rules

〈보기〉 *Do not smoke in your room.*

1. Do not take food into your room.
2. Pay for your room on the day you arrive.
3. Return to the hotel by 10:00 p.m. every night.
4. Leave your key at the reception desk when you go out.
5. Leave your room at 9:00 a.m. on the day you leave.

보기	*You mustn't smoke* in your room.

1. _____ food into your room.

2. _____ for your room on the day you arrive.

3. _____ to the hotel by 10:00 p.m. every night.

4. _____ your key at the reception desk when you go out.

5. _____ your room at 9:00 a.m. on the day you leave.

출제의도 had better+동사원형, should have+과거분사(p.p.)
평가내용 상대방에게 충고나 조언하기

C. 다음 사진을 참고하여 주어진 표현과 had better, should 또는 shouldn't have+p.p.를 이용하여 문장을 영작하시오.

[서술형 유형 : 12점 / 난이도 : 중하]

보기		(start / go / to the gym) (eat / chocolate)	Lucy wants to lose weight. → *She should (=had better) start going to the gym.* → *She shouldn't (=had better not) eat chocolate.*

1.

(call / the police)

(leave / her handbag / open)

Kelly lost her purse.

→ _____

→ _____

2.

(study / more)

(stop / watch / so much TV)

Bob isn't a very good student.

→ _____

→ _____

3.

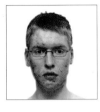

(put / some cream on)

(stay / in the sun / so long)

Brian got sunburnt.

→ _____

→ _____

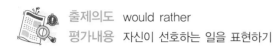

출제의도 would rather

평가내용 자신이 선호하는 일을 표현하기

D. 다음 표현 중에서 자신이 선호하는 것을 골라 would rather ~ than을 이용하여 영작하시오.

[서술형 유형 : 12점 / 난이도 : 중상]

> 보 기
>
> Which would you prefer to play soccer or tennis?
>
> → *I'd rather play tennis than soccer. / I'd rather play soccer than tennis.*

1. Which would you prefer to be a journalist or a school teacher?

→ _____

2. Where would you prefer to live in a big city or in a country?

→ _____

3. Which would you prefer to have tuna salad or chicken salad?

→ _____

4. What would you prefer to study English or Japanese?

→ _____

서술형 평가문제	채 점 기 준	배 점	나의 점수
A		2점×4문항=8점	
B		2점×5문항=10점	
C	표현이 올바르고 문법, 철자가 모두 정확한 경우	4점×3문항=12점	
D		3점×4문항=12점	
E		3점×6문항=18점	
공통	문법, 철자가 1개씩 틀린 경우	각 문항당 1점씩 감점	
	내용과 전혀 일치하지 않거나 답을 기재하지 못한 경우	0점	

출제의도 should have+과거분사(p.p.) / 정중한 부탁
평가내용 과거의 일에 대해 후회하는 문장 만들기 / 상대방에게 정중한 부탁하기

E. 1~3번은 괄호 안의 말을 이용하여 〈보기〉와 같이 과거의 일에 대해 후회하는 문장을, 4~6번은 주어진 글을 읽고 「조동사＋I/you ~?」를 이용한 부탁의 표현을 완성하시오. [서술형 유형 : 18점 / 난이도 : 중상]

보 기	A: The movie was very boring. B: *We shouldn't have gone to the movie.* (not / go)

1. A: It's raining outside, but we don't have any umbrella.

　　B: _____ (bring)

2. A: We didn't do well on the test because we didn't study for it last night.

　　B: _____ (study)

3. A: Hurry up. We are late for the meeting again.

　　B: _____ (get up earlier)

보 기	You want to borrow your friend's calculator. What do you say? → *May[Can, Could] I borrow your calculator?*

4. You want your brother to help you with your homework. What do you say?

　　→ _____

5. Jason wants his father to teach him how to drive a car. What does he say?

　　→ _____

6. Your best friend is having a party. Offer to help him clean up when the party is over.

　　→ _____

Chapter 4

부정사 (Infinitives)

Unit 01 명사적 용법

1-1 주어와 보어로 쓰이는 to부정사

To exercise everyday is not easy.
→ **It** is not easy **to exercise everyday**.
매일 운동하는 것은 쉽지 않다.

01 주어 자리에는 명사나 대명사를 주로 쓰지만 **동작이나 행동을 주어로 표현할 때는 부정사를** 쓴다. '~하는 것, ~하기'의 뜻이 된다.

Junk food is not a healthy food at all.
인스턴트 음식은 전혀 건강에 좋은 음식이 아니다. ▶ 명사 주어는 동작을 표현할 수 없음

To eat junk food is not good for children.
인스턴트 음식을 먹는 것은 아이들에게 좋지 않다. ▶ 부정사 주어는 주어의 동작을 표현할 수 있음

02 주어 자리에 오는 부정사는 대부분 그 자리에 가주어 **It을 쓰고 to부정사를 뒤로 보낸다.** 이것을 가주어·진주어 구문이라고 한다. 가주어는 해석하지 않고 진주어인 to부정사만 주어처럼 해석한다.

To visit my parents once a month is a joy in my life. 한 달에 한 번 부모님을 방문하는 것은 삶의 즐거움이다.
→ **It** is a joy in my life **to visit** my parents once a month.

To travel faster than the speed of light is impossible. 빛의 속도보다 더 빠르게 이동하는 것은 불가능하다.
→ **It** is impossible **to travel** faster than the speed of light.

※ to부정사가 문장 맨 앞의 주어로 오는 경우는 주로 속담이나 문학작품과 같은 문어체 문장에서 볼 수 있다.
To see is **to believe**. 보는 것이 믿는 것이다.
To love and **to be loved** is the greatest happiness. 사랑하는 것과 사랑받는 것은 가장 큰 행복이다.

03 주격 보어 자리에는 (대)명사, 형용사를 쓰지만 **동작이나 행동을 보어로 표현할 때는 부정사를** 쓴다. '~하는 것, ~하기'의 뜻이 된다.

The function of the heart is **to pump** blood. 심장의 기능은 혈액을 뿜는 것이다.
My dream is **to speak** five languages. 내 꿈은 5개국어를 말하는 것이다.

서술형 기초다지기

정답 p. 13

Challenge 1 〈보기〉와 같이 부정사를 이용하여 문장을 완성하세요.

| 보기 | (learn / a foreign language) | → *To learn a foreign language* is very important. |

01. (live / in a foreign country)   → _____ isn't easy.

02. (reach / a decision)   → The goal of the meeting is _____.

Challenge 2 다음 문장을 It ~ to부정사(가주어·진주어 구문)의 문장으로 바꾸어 쓰세요.

01. To spend so much time playing computer games is not good.

→ _____

02. To camp alone in the woods is very dangerous.

→ _____

Challenge 3 주어진 표현을 이용하여 문장을 완성하세요.

| 보기 | | Monica is an English teacher.
Her job *is to teach English*. (teach English) |

01.

Jane has bad eyesight.

Her wish _____. (see things clearly)

02.

Nancy likes to take trips a lot.

Her plane for the next vacation _____. (go to Egypt)

1-2 목적어로 쓰이는 to부정사

She loves **to watch** a horror movie.
그녀는 공포영화 보는 것을 좋아한다.

Can you show me **how to use** this washing machine? 이 세탁기를 어떻게 사용하는지 가르쳐 줄래?

01 타동사의 목적어로 명사와 대명사를 쓰지만 **동작의 내용을 목적어로 표현할 때는 to부정사**를 목적어로 쓴다. '~하는 것(을)'의 뜻이 된다.

Jane likes the flowers. Jane은 그 꽃들을 좋아한다. ▶ the flowers는 동작을 표현하지 못함
Jane wants **to buy** the flowers. Jane는 그 꽃들을 사기를 원한다.
We decided **not to go** out because of the weather. 우리는 날씨 때문에 밖에 나가지 않기로 했다.

02 부정사는 **'앞으로 해야 할 일'이라는 미래의 의미가 내포**되어 있다. 따라서 다음의 동사들은 앞으로 하고자 하는 행위를 표현하기 때문에 뒤에는 의미상 부정사를 쓰게 된다.

decide	hope	promise	plan	want
refuse	offer	learn	agree	wish
pretend	would like	manage	afford	mean

She **tried to give** him his medicine, but he refused to open his mouth.
그녀는 그에게 약을 먹이려 했지만 그는 입을 열려고 하지 않았다.
I **promised not to be** late for the meeting. 나는 회의에 늦지 않기로 약속했다.
Susan and Mark have **decided to get** married next month. Susan과 Mark는 다음 날에 결혼하기로 결정했다.

03 to부정사가 의문사와 함께 쓰일 때는 '어떻게 ~할지'(how to부정사), '무엇을 ~할지'(what to부정사), '어디서 ~할지'(where to부정사), '언제 ~할지'(when to부정사), '어느 것을 ~할지'(which to부정사)를 나타낸다. 이들은 문장에서 **명사처럼 쓰여 '주어, 목적어, 보어'** 역할만 한다. 단, why는 이런 식으로 부정사와 함께 쓰지 않는다.

Please tell me **how to get** to the police station. 경찰서에 어떻게 가는지 좀 알려주세요.
I don't know **what to give** her for a birthday present. 그녀에게 생일 선물로 무엇을 줘야 할지 모르겠다.
She hasn't decided **where to stay** during her trip. 그녀는 여행하는 동안 어디서 머물지 결정하지 않았다.

※「의문사+to부정사」는「의문사+주어+should+동사원형」으로 바꿔 쓸 수 있다.
I don't know **what to do** next.=I don't know **what I should do** next.

서술형 기초다지기

정답 p. 13

Challenge 1 다음 괄호 안의 동사를 이용하여 문장을 완성하세요.

01. It was a gorgeous day, so we decided _____ for a walk. (go)

02. There was a lot of traffic, but we managed _____ to the airport in time. (get)

03. I'm planning _____ Chicago next week. (visit)

04. Jack promised not _____ late for the meeting. (be)

Challenge 2 괄호 안의 동사를 이용하여 「의문사＋to부정사」로 빈칸을 완성하세요.

> **보기**
> 이 복사기 사용하는 법을 좀 알려주겠니? (use)
> → Can you show me *how to use* this duplicator?

01. 너무 충격적이어서 나는 무슨 말을 해야 할지 몰랐다. (say)

    → It was really shocked, so I didn't know _____.

02. 나는 티켓을 어디에서 구해야 하는지 잊어 버렸다. (get)

    → I forgot _____ a ticket.

03. 누구에게 그 편지를 보내야 하는지 제게 말씀해 주세요. (send)

    → Please tell me _____ the letter to.

Challenge 3 다음 대화를 읽고 〈보기〉와 같이 부정사를 이용한 문장으로 완성하세요.

> **보기**
> A: Please buy me a new PC.
> B: OK, fine.
> → My father promised *to buy a new PC for me*.

01. A: Will we get married?

    B: Yes.

    → They decided _____

    _____.

02. A: What's your name?

    B: I'm not going to tell you.

    → She refused _____

    _____.

1-3 목적격 보어로 쓰이는 to부정사

She told me **to shut up** at once.
그녀는 나에게 바로 입을 다물라고 말했다.

I saw Jane **get** into her car and **drive** away.
나는 Jane이 차를 타고 몰고 가는 것을 봤다.

01 목적어가 **동작이나 행동을 해야 할 경우** 「동사+목적어+to부정사」를 쓴다. 5형식 문장에서 목적격 보어는 명사나 형용사를 쓰지만 동작을 표현하려면 부정사를 써야 한다. 이때 부정사에는 **'앞으로 해야 할 현재나 미래'의 의미**가 내포되어 있다.

They called me **a fool** in front of my girlfriend. 그들은 내 여자 친구 앞에서 나를 바보라고 불렀다.
▶ 목적격 보어인 명사 a fool은 동작을 표현하지 못함

The doctor advised me **to eat** more vegetables. 의사는 나에게 더 많은 야채를 먹으라고 충고했다.
▶ 목적격 보어인 to부정사는 목적어의 동작을 표현함

02 사역동사(make, have, let)는 '(목적어에게) ~하도록 시키다/허락하다'의 의미로 **목적어가 동작을 해야 할 때 목적격 보어 자리에 'to' 없이 '동사원형'**으로만 쓴다.

The police officer **made** Kathy **open** her bag. 경찰관은 Kathy에게 가방을 열게 했다.
She **had** me **wait** outside the store. 그녀는 내가 가게 밖에서 기다리게 했다.
My friend **let** me **use** his cell phone. 내 친구는 내가 그의 휴대전화를 쓰도록 허락했다.

03 지각동사(see, watch, hear, feel, listen to, look at, notice) 또한 **목적어가 동작을 해야 할 때 목적격 보어 자리에 'to' 없이 '동사원형'**으로만 쓴다. 단, 진행 중인 상황을 나타낼 때는 현재분사(V-ing)를 쓴다.

Did you **feel** the house **shake** just now? 너는 집이 지금 흔들리는 것을 느꼈니?
The neighbor **saw** a thief **breaking** into a house. 그 이웃은 도둑이 집 안으로 침입하는 것을 봤다.
I **heard** some strange sound **coming** out of the room. 나는 그 방에서 이상한 소리가 나는 것을 들었다.

04 사역동사 get은 목적격 보어 자리에 to부정사를 쓰고, help는 '동사원형' 또는 'to부정사' 둘 다 쓸 수 있다. help는 목적어를 생략했을 때 (목적어가 상대방과 서로 알만한 경우 또는 people, they, we, you 등의 일반인일 때 생략 가능) 동사 두 개가 연이어 나올 수 있다.

Bob doesn't smoke anymore. Lisa **got** him **to give up** that habit last year.
Bob은 더 이상 담배를 피우지 않아. Lisa는 작년에 그가 그 습관을 버리게 했어.

Can you **help** me (to) **find** my cell phone? 내가 휴대전화 찾는 것을 도와주겠니?

Doing meditation **helps** (to) **calm** us down. 명상하는 것은 우리의 마음을 진정시키는 데 도움을 준다.

서술형 기초다지기

정답 p. 13

Challenge 1   다음 괄호 안의 표현 중 알맞은 것을 고르세요.

01. She advised me not (tell / to tell) a lie.

02. The teacher made the boy (clean / to clean) the classroom.

03. We watched the full moon (rise / to rise) yesterday.

04. My dog smelled something (burning / to burn) in the kitchen.

05. The police watched something (move / to move) in the house.

06. My mother wanted me (finish / to finish) my homework.

07. Good teachers help their students (learn / learning) good manners.

Challenge 2   다음 우리말과 뜻이 같도록 괄호 안의 말을 이용하여 문장을 완성하세요.

01. Lisa는 어제 그녀의 남편에게 창문을 수리하게 했다. (repair, the window, her husband)

   → Lisa had _____ yesterday.

02. 그의 아버지는 그가 자전거를 사는 것을 허락해 주셨다. (a bicycle, buy)

   → His father _____ .

03. 경찰은 군중들에게 그 건물을 즉시 떠나라고 강요했다. (leave, the building, the crowd)

   → The police forced _____ immediately.

Challenge 3   〈보기〉와 같이 주어진 단어를 이용하여 대화를 요약하세요.

> **보기**
> Maria : Mom, can I borrow the car?
> Mom : Only if you drive your brother to soccer practice.
> → Maria's mother _made Maria drive_ her brother to soccer practice. (make, drive)

01. Students : Can we use our dictionaries during the test?

   Teacher : No. You should be able to guess the meaning of the words from the context.

   → The teacher _____ their dictionaries. (not let, use)

Unit 02 형용사적 용법

2-1 형용사처럼 쓰이는 to부정사

He is the first man **to fall** in love with me.
그는 나와 사랑에 빠진 첫 번째 남자이다.

If you **are to** succeed, you must study hard.
네가 성공하길 원하면 열심히 공부해야 한다.

01 '돕다, 읽다, 먹다' 등의 동사가 to부정사가 되어 '도울 (친구), 읽을 (책), 먹을 (음식)'과 같이 명사를 꾸며 주며 '~(해야) 할'의 뜻이 되는데 이렇게 to부정사는 **명사 바로 뒤에서 명사를 꾸며 주는 형용사 역할**을 한다.

I have a lot of friends **to advise** me. 나는 나에게 충고를 해줄 친구가 많다.
People have a right **to enjoy** a happy life. 사람들은 행복한 삶을 즐길 권리가 있다.

02 수식을 받는 명사가 전치사의 목적어인 경우 「to부정사+전치사」로 쓴다. 이때도 역시 to부정사가 명사 바로 뒤에 위치하고 '~(해야) 할'로 해석한다.

The old couple don't have a house **to live in**. 그 노부부는 살 집이 없다.
　　　　　　　　　　　　　　　　　　(~ live in a house → a house to live in)
She needs someone **to talk with**. 그녀는 이야기를 나눌 사람이 필요하다.
　　　　　　　　　　　　　　　(~ talk with someone → someone to talk with)

03 something, anything, everything, nothing과 같이 -thing으로 끝나는 대명사는 반드시 형용사가 뒤에서 꾸미고, 이를 다시 **to부정사가 수식**하면 「-thing+형용사+to부정사」의 어순이 된다.

We need to buy **something cold to drink**. 우리는 마실 시원한 것 좀 사야 한다.
I have **something important to show** you. 나는 너에게 보여줄 중요한 것이 있다.

04 be동사의 보어로 형용사를 쓰듯이, to부정사 역시 형용사처럼 주어를 서술하는 역할을 한다. 이를 「be to 용법」이라 하고 예정(be going to), 의도(want to, intend to), 의무(should), 가능(can), 운명(be doomed to), 의무(must) 등이 있다.

The meeting **is to** be held **tomorrow**. 회의는 내일 열릴 예정이다. ▶ 예정
If you **are to** succeed, you should work hard. 네가 성공하고자 한다면 열심히 일해야 한다. ▶ 의도
The camera **was not** to be found. 그 카메라를 찾을 수가 없었다. ▶ 가능
She **was never to** see her home again. 그녀는 두 번 다시 고향에는 돌아오지 못할 운명이었다. ▶ 운명
The rules **are to** be observed. 규칙들은 지켜져야만 한다. ▶ 의무

서술형 기초다지기

Challenge 1 다음 문장을 〈보기〉와 같이 to부정사를 이용한 문장으로 바꿔 쓰세요.

> 보기
> I don't have a pencil. + I will write with it.
> → *I don't have a pencil to write with.*

01. They're looking for an apartment. + They want to live in the apartment.

    → _____

02. Bring me several pieces of paper. + I need to write on them.

    → _____

03. She needs a friend. + She wants to talk with the friend.

    → _____

Challenge 2 다음 빈칸에 알맞은 「be+to부정사」를 쓰고 그 용법을 쓰세요.

> 보기
> The conference is going to be held in Moscow next week.
> → The conference *is to be held* in Moscow next week. (*예정*)

01. If you intend to gain trust, you must show a fine example.

    → If you _____, you must show a fine example. (   )

02. Not a star could be seen in the sky.

    → Not a star _____ in the sky. (   )

03. The President is going to speak on TV tonight.

    → The President _____ on TV tonight. (   )

04. They were destined to work together for life.

    → They _____ together for life. (   )

부사적 용법

3-1 목적을 나타내는 to부정사

Why did you go to the library?
- I went to the library because I wanted to borrow some books.
- I went to the library **in order to** borrow some books.
- I went to the library **to borrow** some books.
- I went to the library **for** some books.
- I went to the library **so that I could** borrow some books.

너는 도서관에 왜 갔니? 나는 몇 권의 책을 빌리고 싶었기 때문에 도서관에 갔다.
나는 몇 권의 책을 빌리기 위하여 도서관에 갔다.

---

01 행위에 대한 **이유나 목적**을 정확하게 나타내기 위해 「in order to+동사원형」를 쓴다. '~하기 위하여'의 뜻으로, 일상 영어에서는 in order를 생략하고 주로 to부정사만 쓴다.

We went to the cafeteria (**in order**) **to have** lunch. 우리는 점심을 먹기 위하여 구내식당에 갔다.
He turned on the TV (**in order**) **to watch** the news. 그는 뉴스를 보기 위하여 TV를 켰다.

※ so as to 또한 '~하기 위하여'란 뜻으로 'in order to'와 마찬가지로 격식을 갖춘 표현에만 사용한다.

02 목적을 나타내는 to부정사는 **긍정문일 경우** 「so that+주어+can/could」로, **부정문일 경우** 「so that+주어+won't/wouldn't」로 바꿔 쓸 수 있다. 부정사의 부정은 부정사 바로 앞에 'not'을 붙이면 된다.

She arrived early **to finish** the given work. 그녀는 주어진 일을 끝내기 위하여 일찍 도착했다.
→ She arrived early **so that** she **could** finish the given work.

We wear coats in the winter **to keep** warm. 우리는 몸을 따뜻하게 하기 위하여 겨울에 코트를 입는다.
→ We wear coats in the winter **so that** we **can** keep warm.

I hurried (**in order**) **not to be** late for school. 나는 지각하지 않기 위해 서둘렀다.
→ I hurried **so that** I **wouldn't** be late for school.

03 목적과 의도를 나타내고자 할 때 to부정사 대신 「for+명사/동명사」로 나타낼 수도 있다. for는 전치사이므로 뒤에 명사 또는 동명사를 써야 한다.

I'm going to Australia **to take** English language program. 나는 어학연수를 하러 호주에 갈 예정이다.
→ I'm going to Australia **for** English language program.

Let's go to the cafe **to have** coffee. 커피 마시러 그 카페에 가자.
→ Let's go to the cafe **for** coffee.

This knife is only **to cut** bread. 이 칼은 빵을 자르기 위한 것이다.
→ This knife is only **for** cutting bread.

서술형 기초다지기

정답 p. 13

Challenge 1   다음 빈칸에 to 또는 for 중 알맞은 것을 써 넣으세요.

01. Some people need English _____ get a better job.

02. We need a dictionary _____ vocabulary.

03. I sometimes use my computer _____ do homework.

04. I play tennis twice a week _____ exercise and relaxation.

Challenge 2   〈보기〉와 같이 주어진 표현을 이용하여 문장을 완성하세요.

보기	watch the news + turn on the TV → After he got home from work, Bob *turned on the TV (in order) to watch the news*.

01. let in some fresh air + open the bedroom windows

→ Every night I _____.

02. ask them for some money + write a letter to his parents

→ Sometimes Peter _____.

03. listen to a soccer game + have the radio on

→ Some afternoons at work, my co-workers _____.

Challenge 3   다음 두 문장을 'so that ~ can/could/wouldn't'를 사용한 문장으로 만드세요.

보기	She hurried. She didn't want to miss the bus. → *She hurried so that she wouldn't miss the bus.*

01. The teacher spoke very slowly. She wanted us to understand what she said.

→ _____

02. I'm going to go to the nursing home. I want to take part in volunteer work.

→ _____

3-2 결과, 원인, 조건, 판단을 나타내는 to부정사

Do you think this water is safe **to drink**?
이 물이 마시기에 안전하다고 생각하니?

She was shocked **to hear** the news that he died.
그녀는 그가 사망했다는 소식을 듣고서 충격을 받았다.

01 to부정사가 **형용사 뒤에 위치**하여 형용사를 꾸밀 때 '∼하기에'의 뜻이 된다. 단, 감정을 나타내는 형용사 (happy, glad, sad, sorry, pleased, surprised, excited, disappointed)를 꾸밀 때는 '∼해서, ∼하게 되어서'의 뜻으로 감정의 원인을 나타낸다.

This novel is difficult **to understand**. 이 소설은 이해하기가 어렵다.

Some of these words are not easy **to pronounce**. 이 단어들 중 몇 개는 발음하기에 쉽지 않다.

Kelly was pleased **to meet** Susan. Kelly는 Susan을 만나서 기뻤다.

I am sorry **to hear** that your mother is sick. 너의 엄마가 편찮으시다는 말을 들어서 유감스럽다.

02 to부정사는 **동사의 결과**를 나타내기도 하는데 이때는 '∼해서 (결국) ∼되다'의 뜻이다. 주로 grow, awake, live 등의 동사와 함께 쓴다. 'only to부정사, never to부정사'도 결과를 나타낸다.

At midnight I awoke **to see** a woman standing near the door.
나는 한밤중에 깨어나서 문 옆에 서 있는 여자를 보았다.

She grew up **to be** a famous judo player. 그녀는 커서 유명한 유도선수가 되었다.

We hurried to the airport **only to miss** the plane. 우리는 서둘러 공항에 갔지만 그만 비행기를 놓쳤다.

He went to the haunted house, **never to come** back. 그는 흉가에 가서 결코 돌아오지 못했다.

03 to부정사는 **must be, cannot be, 감탄문**과 함께 쓰여 '∼하다니, ∼하는 것을 보니'란 뜻의 **판단의 근거나 이유**를 나타낸다. 조동사 will 또는 would와 함께 쓰여 '∼한다면'이란 조건(if의 의미)을 나타내기도 한다.

They must be crazy **to let** him drive their car. 그가 차를 몰도록 하다니 그들은 미쳤음에 틀림없다.

He cannot be a gentleman **to say** such a rude thing. 그렇게 무례한 말을 하다니 그는 신사일 리가 없다.

You would be foolish **to miss** the opportunity again. 네가 그 기회를 다시 놓친다면 어리석은 일일 것이다.

To hear him talk, you would think him a doctor. 그 사람 말하는 것을 들으면 의사라는 생각이 들 거다.

04 **문장 맨 앞에 to부정사로 시작하고 뒤이어 「주어＋동사」**가 나올 때, 문장 맨 앞에 있는 부정사는 '∼하기 위하여'란 뜻의 목적을 나타낸다.

To lose weight, you had better take up some sport. 살을 빼기 위하여 너는 운동을 시작하는 것이 좋다.

서술형 기초다지기

Challenge 1
다음 빈칸에 들어갈 말을 〈보기〉에서 골라 알맞은 형태로 쓰세요.

fail	come	believe	hear	see

01. Steve was sorry _____ the bad news.

02. I studied very hard only _____ the examination.

03. She must be foolish _____ what he told her.

04. He went to Singapore in 1999, never _____ back.

Challenge 2
다음을 to부정사를 이용한 문장으로 고쳐 쓰세요.

> **보기**
> She was surprised. + She got a letter.
> → *She was surprised to get a letter.*

01. Are you happy? + You will go to the party.

→ _____

02. I was excited. + I ate such delicious food.

→ _____

03. She grew up. She became the greatest leader in history.

→ _____

Challenge 3
다음 우리말과 뜻이 같도록 괄호 안의 표현을 이용하여 문장을 완성하세요.

01. 그녀는 커서 치과의사가 되었다.

→ She _____ _____ _____ _____ a dentist.

02. 컴퓨터를 고친다면 나는 숙제를 할 수 있다.

→ I can do my homework _____ _____ the computer. (fix)

03. 그녀는 2005년에 이집트에 가서 결코 돌아오지 않았다.

→ She went to Egypt in 2005, _____ _____ _____ _____. (come back)

3-3 too ~ to / enough to

Tiffany isn't old **enough to** go to school.
Tiffany는 학교에 갈 정도로 나이가 들지 않았다.
Tiffany is **too** young **to** go to school.
Tiffany는 학교에 가기에는 너무 어리다.

01 「too+형용사/부사+to부정사」는 '~하기에는 너무 ~하다'의 뜻으로, **too를 형용사나 부사 앞**에 쓴다. 「too ~ to부정사」를 「so+형용사/부사+that+주어+can't/couldn't」로 바꿔 쓸 수 있다.

I'm **too** busy **to** attend the meeting. 나는 회의에 참석하기에는 너무 바빴다.

She is **too** weak **to** lift that heavy box. 그녀는 저 무거운 상자를 들기에는 너무 약했다.
=She is **so** weak **that** she **can't** lift that heavy box.

The building was **too** old **to** be remodeled again. 그 건물은 다시 리모델링하기에는 너무 오래되었다.
=The building was **so** old **that** it **couldn't** be remodeled again.

02 「형용사/부사+enough to부정사」는 '~할 정도로 ~하다'의 뜻으로, 형용사/부사를 enough 앞에 쓴다. 「so+형용사/부사+that+주어+can/could」로 바꿔 쓸 수 있다.

She is old **enough to** watch this movie. 그녀는 이 영화를 볼 나이가 된다.
My dad is strong **enough to** endure the difficult situation. 아빠는 그 어려운 상황을 견딜 정도로 강하다.
=My dad is **so** strong **that** he **can** endure the difficult situation.

Kelly studied hard **enough to** enter the university. Kelly는 그 대학에 들어갈 정도로 열심히 공부했다.
=Kelly studied **so** hard **that** she **could** enter the university.

03 「enough to부정사」를 '충분히'로 해석하는 경향이 있는데, '~할 정도로'의 의미가 더 정확하다. **'충분히'란 뜻으로 쓸 때의 enough는 형용사로 명사 앞**에 써야 한다.

I had **enough time** to study TOEIC during the vacation. 나는 방학 동안 토익을 공부할 충분한 시간이 있었다.
She has **enough money** to buy a car. 그녀는 차를 살 만큼 충분한 돈을 가지고 있다.

서술형 기초다지기

정답 p. 14

Challenge 1 다음 문장을 too ~ to 또는 enough to를 이용한 문장으로 바꾸어 쓰세요.

01. You are so strong that you can carry the heavy box.

→ _____

02. The smart phone is so expensive that I can't buy it.

→ _____

03. This MP3 player is so small that it can fit in my pocket.

→ _____

04. The water was so cold that I couldn't swim in it.

→ _____

05. He has enough money, so he can travel around the world.

→ _____

06. There is enough room in the car, so we can get on it.

→ _____

Challenge 2 다음 문장을 so ~ that을 이용한 문장으로 다시 쓰세요.

01. This coffee is too hot for me to drink.

→ _____

02. The wind was strong enough to break windows.

→ _____

03. Jane was too young to get married.

→ _____

04. Jessica is kind enough to help the poor people.

→ _____

05. My father was too sleepy to watch the movie on TV.

→ _____

Unit 04 반드시 알아야 할 용법

4-1 부정사의 시제 / 부정사의 의미상 주어

I am sorry **to have been** absent yesterday.
어제 결석해서 죄송합니다.
(= I am sorry that I **was** absent yesterday.)
You should study hard.
너는 열심히 공부해야 한다.
→ It is important **for you** to study hard.
　　네가 열심히 공부하는 것이 중요하다.

01
to부정사도 현재 또는 과거와 같은 시제를 표현할 수 있다. to부정사의 동작이 **문장 전체의 시제와 동일한 때
에 일어나거나 미래를 나타낼 때는** 「to+동사원형」을 쓴다.

It **seemed** that the children **were** happy.
= The children seemed **to be** happy. 그 아이들은 행복한 것처럼 보였다.

The owner of a baseball team always **expects** the team **to win** every game.
= The owner of a baseball team always expects that the team **will win** every game.
　야구팀의 구단주는 항상 팀이 모든 경기에서 승리하기를 기대한다.

02
말하는 시점보다 더 이전에 있었던 to부정사의 동작은 「to have+p.p」로 쓴다.

It **seems** that she **forgot** what to do. 그녀는 무엇을 해야 할지를 잊어버렸던 것 같다.
= She seems **to have forgotten** what to do. ▶ 잊어버린 사실은 말하는 시점보다 먼저 일어난 일

It **seemed** that the girl **had cried** all day long. 그 소녀는 하루 종일 울었던 것 같았다.
= The girl seemed **to have cried** all day long. ▶ 운 것은 말하는 시점보다 먼저 일어난 일

03
모든 동작은 그 행위의 주체에 해당하는 주어를 가진다. 부정사의 주어가 문장의 주어나 목적어와 일치하거
나 일반인일 때 따로 의미상 주어를 쓸 필요가 없지만 **동작의 주인이 다른 경우 부정사 앞에** 「for/of+명사/
목적격 대명사」를 반드시 써 준다.

He decided to ask her out on a date. 그는 그녀에게 데이트 신청하기로 결정했다.
　　　　　　　　　　　　　　　　▶ ask 동작의 주체(의미상 주어)는 문장 전체의 주어인 He

I want **you** to do the work. 나는 네가 그 일을 하길 원한다. ▶ do 동작의 주체(의미상 주어)는 목적어 you

To learn English is important. 영어를 배우는 것은 중요하다. ▶ 일반인 we, you, people 등의 의미상 주어 → 생략

It's impossible **for him** to climb the mountain. 그가 그 산을 오르는 것은 불가능하다.
The chair is too heavy **for her** to move. 그녀가 의자를 옮기기에는 너무 무겁다.

※ 사람을 칭찬하거나 비난하는 형용사(kind, nice, silly, (im)polite, stupid, careful, careless, generous, mean) 뒤에
　는 for 대신에 「of+명사/목적격 대명사」를 쓴다.
It was stupid **of her** to believe him. 그녀가 그를 믿은 것은 어리석었다.

서술형 기초다지기

Challenge 1 다음 괄호 안의 표현 중 알맞은 것을 고르세요.

01. He appears (to be / to have been) rich before.

02. It was difficult (for / of) me to understand what she was saying.

03. The accident seems (to happen / to have happened) when I was young.

04. It is very careless (for / of) you to leave the door open.

Challenge 2 다음 문장을 부정사를 이용하여 다시 쓰세요.

보 기	It appears that she bought a nice dress yesterday. → *She appears to have bought a nice dress yesterday.*

01. It seems that Susan enjoys writing on her blog.

    → _____

02. It seems that they worked together in the past.

    → _____

03. It appeared that she had stopped smoking.

    → _____

Challenge 3 다음 문장을 의미상 주어(for/of+명사)를 이용하여 〈보기〉와 같이 완성하세요.

보 기	Students should do their homework. → It's important *for students to do their homework*.

01. A child usually can't sit still for a long time.

    → It's difficult _____.

02. She gave up her new job although it is hard to get another job.

    → It was stupid _____.

4-2 대부정사 / 독립부정사

I asked her to play the violin, but she did not **want to**. 나는 그녀에게 바이올린을 연주해 달라고 했으나, 그녀는 그러고 싶지 않았다.

To make matters worse, it began to rain hard. 설상가상으로 비가 많이 내리기 시작했다.

01 같은 내용의 부정사를 피하기 위하여 to부정사의 to만 쓰는 것을 대부정사라고 하는데 to 뒤에 나올 동사를 서로 알고 있을 경우에 쓴다.

I've never eaten Gimchi, but I'd like **to** (eat Gimchi). 나는 김치를 먹어본 적이 없지만 그러고 싶다.

She wanted to go to the concert, but Scott told her not **to** (go to the concert).
그녀는 콘서트에 가고 싶었지만 Scott이 그녀에게 가지 말라고 했다.

A : Would you like to have some coffee? 커피 좀 드실래요?

B : Yes, I'd like **to** (have some coffee). 네, 그러고 싶네요.

02 부정사가 숙어(idiom)처럼 굳어진 표현으로, 문장 전체를 꾸며 주는 **독립부정사**가 있다. 중요 표현은 암기해 두는 것이 좋다.

to be frank with you	솔직히 말하면	so to speak	말하자면, 소위
to begin with	우선, 먼저, 무엇보다도	strange to say	말하기에 이상하지만
not to mention	~은 말할 필요도 없이	needless to say	말할 필요도 없이
to make a long story short	간단히 말하면	to make matters worse	설상가상으로

To tell the truth, I have never been to Europe. 솔직히 말하면, 나는 유럽에 가본 적이 없다.

Strange to say, I saw a ghost under the tree. 이상한 얘기이지만 내가 나무 아래에서 귀신을 봤어.

To be frank with you, she is not honest. 솔직히 말하면, 그녀는 정직하지 않다.

Needless to say, you should keep the secret. 말할 필요도 없이, 당신은 비밀을 지켜야 한다.

He is, **so to speak**, a bookworm. 그는 말하자면 책벌레이다.

서술형 기초다지기

정답 p. 14

Challenge 1   다음 괄호 안의 단어를 이용해 대부정사 형태의 문장을 완성하세요.

> **보기**
> A: Is she going to go out for dinner?
> B: No, she *is not going to*. (not, go)

01. A: Do you want to go to the movies with us tonight?

B: I _____. (would love)

02. A: Why didn't you dance with Bob?

B: Because he _____. (not, ask me)

Challenge 2   우리말과 같은 뜻이 되도록 괄호 안의 말과 대부정사를 이용하여 문장을 완성하세요.

01. 원한다면 그 차를 가져도 된다. (want)

→ You may have the car if you _____ _____.

02. 그가 키스하려고 했을 때 그녀는 허락하려고 하지 않았다. (offered)

→ She wouldn't let him kiss her when he _____ _____.

03. 나는 그 소설을 읽고 싶지만 읽을 시간이 없다. (have time, not)

→ I'd like to read the novel, but I _____ _____ _____ _____.

Challenge 3   다음 우리말과 같은 뜻이 되도록 빈칸에 알맞은 독립부정사를 쓰세요.

01. 솔직히 말하면, 그녀는 예쁘지 않았어.

→ _____, she wasn't pretty.

02. 설상가상으로 그녀는 내가 없는 동안 아팠다.

→ _____, she got sick while I was gone.

03. 우선 제 소개를 하겠습니다.

→ _____, let me introduce myself.

"출제자가 노리는 급소" 이것이 시험에 출제되는 영문법이다!

01 출제 100% - 「의문사+to부정사」는 영작문제로 출제한다.

 출제자의 눈 주어로 쓰인 부정사는 단수 취급하여 단수 동사를 써야 한다. 특히 it을 이용한 가주어·진주어 구문으로 고칠 줄 아는지를 물어보는 문제나 가주어 it을 다른 대명사로 바꿔 놓거나 to 없이 동사원형만 놓고 혼동시키는 문제가 출제된다. 목적어로 「의문사+to부정사」를 넣는 영작문제나 알맞은 의문사를 고르는 문제가 출제될 수도 있다. 명사를 수식하는 경우 부정사의 농작이 '자동사'인 경우에는 부정사 뒤에 반드시 전치사를 써야 한다.

> **Ex 1.**
> 다음 우리말을 영어로 옮기시오.
> · 나는 그 파티에 무엇을 입고 가야 할지 모르겠다.
> → I _____ . (to the party, wear)

02 출제 100% - 목적어나 목적격 보어 자리에 오는 to부정사나 원형부정사를 구별하라.

 출제자의 눈 부정사는 '앞으로 해야 할 현재나 미래'를 내포하고 있다. 따라서 전에 있었던 일이나 경험을 말하지 않고 앞으로의 일을 말할 때 목적어 자리와 목적격 보어 자리에 to부정사를 쓰게 되는데 이것을 사역동사나 지각동사와 함께 혼동시켜 자주 출제한다. 사역동사(have, make, let)와 지각동사(see, hear)는 목적격 보어로 동사원형을 쓰는데 이를 집중적으로 출제한다. 그외 get은 목적격 보어 자리에 'to부정사'를 쓰고 help는 'to'를 써도 되고 안 써도 된다.

> **Ex 2.**
> My mother told me never _____ there again.
> (a) go　　　(b) to go　　　(c) going　　　(d) gone

> **Ex 3.**
> My mother then made me _____ the numbers.
> (a) memorizing　　　(b) to memorize　　　(c) memorized　　　(d) memorize

> **Ex 4.**
> I saw a boy in the gym _____ basketball.
> (a) to play　　　(b) playing　　　(c) played　　　(d) plays

03 출제 100% - enough to와 too ~ to는 영작문제로 출제한다.

 출제자의 눈 enough to는 enough 앞에 형용사/부사를 쓰고 too ~ to는 too 뒤에 형용사/부사를 쓰는데, 어순을 틀리게 해놓고 고칠 수 있는지를 묻는 객관식 문제가 나온다. 이 둘을 각각 so ~ that+주어+can/can't로 문장 전환할 줄 아는지를 묻는 주관식 문제나 서술형 문제도 출제된다. 의미상 주어를 밝히는 경우 「for/of+명사」를 써서 표현하는데 이 둘을 고르는 문제가 내신의 단골손님이다. 어떤 사람의 성질이나 성격, 상태의 형용사를 쓸 때, '(누구누구)의' 성질을 표현해야 하므로 전치사 of를 쓸 수밖에 없다. kind, silly, generous, nice, stupid, careful, careless (im)polite, clever, foolish, cruel, considerate(사려 깊은) 등이 그러한 형용사의 예이다.

Ex 5.

다음 문장을 enough to부정사를 이용하여 다시 써 보시오.

The woman is so strong that she can kill an alligator.

=The woman is _____.

Ex 6.

두 문장이 같은 뜻이 되도록 의미상 주어를 이용하여 빈칸을 완성하시오.

He left without saying goodbye.

=It is impolite _____.

04 출제 100% - 부정사도 시제를 나타낼 수 있다.

 출제자의 눈 「to+동사원형」는 문장의 동사와 같은 시제(현재면 현재, 과거면 과거)임을 나타내고, 「to have+p.p」는 문장의 동사보다 '더 과거'임을 나타낸다. expect, hope, wish 등과 같은 동사 뒤에 오는 「to+동사원형」은 그 동사의 시제보다 미래임을 내포하고 있다. 「It seems/appears ~ that ~」 구문을 주고 「to+동사원형」 또는 「to have+p.p」를 골라 영작하거나, 서로 문장 전환하는 문제가 집중적으로 출제된다.

Ex 7.

두 문장의 의미가 같도록 빈칸을 완성하시오.

It seems that students feel tired these days.

=Students _____ these days.

1. **다음 빈칸에 알맞은 것은?**

> It was difficult ＿＿＿＿ me to find the post office.

❶ of　❷ at　❸ in　❹ for　❺ on

2. **다음 빈칸을 채우시오.**

> Jessica said to Bob, "How can I use this machine?"
> → Jessica asked Bob ＿＿＿＿ ＿＿＿＿ ＿＿＿＿ this machine.

3. **밑줄 친 부분의 쓰임이 다른 하나는?**

❶ I have something to show you.
❷ He is the only one to save mankind.
❸ There are famous sights to see in Seoul.
❹ Sunny has a lot of friends to help her.
❺ I'm here to help you do your homework.

4. **다음 빈칸에 알맞은 것은?**

> A: Your brother looks angry.
> B: Well, he says he's all right now, but he still seems ＿＿＿＿ angry.

❶ to being　❷ that he was
❸ that he is　❹ to have been
❺ to be

5. **다음 괄호 안의 단어들을 바르게 배열한 것은?**

> (to, forget, enough, healthy)
> We are ＿＿＿＿＿＿＿＿＿＿ yesterday for the fresh start of tomorrow. New Year's Day is always the day we start our new life filled with hope.

❶ healthy enough to forget
❷ forget to healthy enough
❸ to forget healthy enough
❹ healthy enough forget to
❺ enough healthy to forget

6. **다음 빈칸에 알맞은 말을 쓰시오.**

> I asked her what I should do.
> =I asked her ＿＿＿＿ ＿＿＿ ＿＿＿.

7. **다음 빈칸에 들어갈 알맞은 말을 쓰시오.**

> It took two hours ＿＿＿＿＿＿＿＿＿ a letter. (내가 편지 쓰는 데 2시간 걸렸다.)

8. **다음 두 문장의 의미가 같도록 알맞게 바꿔 쓴 것은?**

> It seems that she was very sick.
> = ＿＿＿＿＿＿＿＿＿＿＿.

❶ She seems to be very sick.
❷ She seems to have been very sick.
❸ She seemed to be very sick.
❹ She seemed to have been very sick.
❺ It seems to have been very sick.

오답 노트 만들기

* 틀린 문제에는 빨간색으로 V표시를 한다.
* 두세 번 정도 반복해서 복습하고 완전히 알 때에만 O표를 한다.

★틀린 문제 : _____   ★다시 공부한 날 : _____

(1) 문제를 왜? 틀렸는지 곰곰이 생각하고 그 이유를 적어본다.

(2) 핵심 개념을 적는다.

(3) 자신이 몰랐던 단어와 숙어 표현이 있으면 정리한다.

(4) 해설집에서 필요한 부분을 골라 풀이 해법을 정리한다.

★틀린 문제 : _____   ★다시 공부한 날 : _____

(1) 문제를 왜? 틀렸는지 곰곰이 생각하고 그 이유를 적어본다.

(2) 핵심 개념을 적는다.

(3) 자신이 몰랐던 단어와 숙어 표현이 있으면 정리한다.

(4) 해설집에서 필요한 부분을 골라 풀이 해법을 정리한다.

★틀린 문제 : _____   ★다시 공부한 날 : _____

(1) 문제를 왜? 틀렸는지 곰곰이 생각하고 그 이유를 적어본다.

(2) 핵심 개념을 적는다.

(3) 자신이 몰랐던 단어와 숙어 표현이 있으면 정리한다.

(4) 해설집에서 필요한 부분을 골라 풀이 해법을 정리한다.

★틀린 문제 : _____   ★다시 공부한 날 : _____

(1) 문제를 왜? 틀렸는지 곰곰이 생각하고 그 이유를 적어본다.

(2) 핵심 개념을 적는다.

(3) 자신이 몰랐던 단어와 숙어 표현이 있으면 정리한다.

(4) 해설집에서 필요한 부분을 골라 풀이 해법을 정리한다.

1. 다음 빈칸에 들어갈 단어가 바르게 짝지어진 것은?

> It was too cold for us to play tennis.
> =It was _____ cold that we _____ play tennis.

❶ so - could   ❷ too - can't

❸ so - can't   ❹ too - could

❺ so - couldn't

오답노트

2. 다음 빈칸에 알맞은 말을 쓰시오.

> You're supposed to teach me how I should ride a bicycle tonight.
> =You're supposed to teach me _____ _____ _____ a bicycle tonight.

오답노트

[3-4] 두 문장의 뜻이 같도록 빈칸에 알맞은 말을 쓰시오.

3. This MP3 is small. So the children can carry it.
   =This MP3 is _____ _____ for children to carry.

4. It seems that he fixes the bicycle.
   =He _____ _____ _____ the bicycle.

오답노트

5. 다음 문장의 의미와 같은 것은?

> To play reggae music is very hard.

❶ It is very hard to play reggae music.

❷ It is very hard playing reggae music.

❸ It is very hard to playing reggae music.

❹ It is to play reggae music very hard.

❺ It is playing reggae music very hard.

오답노트

6. 다음 빈칸에 들어갈 말로 알맞지 않은 것은? (2개)

> I don't know _____ to do it.

❶ when   ❷ where   ❸ that

❹ how   ❺ why

오답노트

7. 다음 밑줄 친 부분의 쓰임이 다른 하나는?

❶ She wants somebody <u>to love</u>.

❷ Give me a chair <u>to sit on</u>.

❸ I have a lot of work <u>to do</u> today.

❹ I want a pen <u>to write with</u>.

❺ He cannot be a gentleman <u>to say</u> such rude things.

오답노트

8. 다음 중 빈칸에 들어갈 말이 다른 하나는?

❶ It's difficult ____ you to find his house at night.

❷ The box is too heavy ____ her to move.

❸ It is selfish ____ you not to help her homework.

❹ The book is not easy ____ you to read.

❺ It is important ____ me to make money.

오답노트

[9-10] 다음 빈칸에 알맞은 말을 쓰시오.

9. I believe him to be honest.
   =I believe that _____.

10. She is so kind that she can help me.
    =She is kind _____ _____ help me.

오답노트

11. 다음 중 be to의 용법이 다른 하나는?

❶ We are to meet here at six this morning.

❷ If you are to succeed, you must work hard.

❸ Lisa is to come back here by 9 o'clock.

❹ We are to get a 10 percent wage increase in January.

❺ The conference is to be held in Seoul next Monday.

오답노트

[12-13] 다음 우리말과 같은 뜻이 되도록 괄호 안의 말을 이용하여 문장을 완성하시오.

12.
당신을 한 시간 동안이나 기다리게 해서 미안합니다. (keep)
=I'm sorry _____ _____ _____ you waiting for an hour.

13.
그는 그 소설을 읽어 본 적이 있는 척한다. (read)
=He pretends _____ _____ _____ the novel.

오답노트

14. 다음 빈칸에 알맞은 말을 쓰시오.

It seemed that you were disappointed.
=You seemed _____ be disappointed.

[15-16] 다음 중 어법상 어색한 것을 고르시오.

15.
People are the only creatures that
❶ consume without ❷ producing. They don't give milk and don't lay eggs. They are too weak ❸ to pull the plough. They ❹ cannot run ❺ enough fast to catch rabbits. Yet they are lord of all the animals.

오답노트

16.

Advertisers use ❶ many methods to get us ❷ to buy their products. One of their most successful methods ❸ is to make us ❹ to feel dissatisfied with ourselves and our ❺ imperfect lives.

오답노트

17. 다음 우리말을 바르게 영작한 것은?

선생님은 우리에게 떠들지 말라고 하셨다.

❶ The teacher told us to make some noise.
❷ The teacher told we not to make a noise.
❸ The teacher told us not make any noise.
❹ The teacher told us not to make any noise.
❺ The teacher told us not to making any noise.

오답노트

18. 다음 문장의 밑줄 친 부분과 쓰임이 같은 것은?

It is pleasant to meet an old friend.

❶ It is time to work.
❷ It is getting warmer.
❸ It is not easy to break a bad habit.
❹ It is not my book.
❺ It is the age of the computer.

오답노트

19. 다음 빈칸에 알맞지 않은 것은?

A: Do you think the girl is pretty?
B: Yeah, she is very beautiful, but, _____, she isn't kind.

❶ to be sure   ❷ needless to say
❸ so to speak   ❹ to be frank with you
❺ to be honest

오답노트

20. 문맥상 빈칸에 들어갈 알맞은 독립부정사는?

There are many reasons why I don't like her. _____, she often tells lies. Also she is very selfish.

❶ That is to say   ❷ Strange to say
❸ Needless to say   ❹ To begin with
❺ To make matters worse

오답노트

21. 다음 빈칸에 들어갈 알맞은 것을 고르시오.

Jessica collects information and writes articles for several newspapers. She _____ a journalist.

❶ seem to be   ❷ seemed to be
❸ seems   ❹ seems to be
❺ seems to have been

오답노트

22. 다음 중 어법상 **틀린** 문장은?

❶ The skirt is too short for me to wear.
❷ It is hard to change jobs after twenty years.
❸ She let him to carry the bag.
❹ Her voice made him hide in the bushes.
❺ It is thoughtful of you to help the poor and needy.

오답노트

23. 다음 중 문장 전환이 **잘못된** 것을 고르시오.

❶ We were too tired to walk any longer.
   =We were so tired that we couldn't walk any longer.
❷ This hat is too small for him to wear.
   =This hat is so small that he can't wear it.
❸ My father was old enough to stay at home alone.
   =My father was so old that he couldn't stay at home alone.
❹ Sunny was too selfish to help others.
   =Sunny was so selfish that she couldn't help others.
❺ The woman is wealthy enough to travel around the world.
   =The woman is so wealthy that she can travel around the world.

오답노트

24. 우리말과 같은 뜻이 되도록 괄호 안에 있는 단어를 알맞게 배열하시오.

> 그의 친구 중 한 명이 그에게 가지 말라고 충고했다.
> = A friend of his _____
> _____.
>   (not, advised, go, to, him)

오답노트

25. 두 문장이 같은 뜻이 되도록 알맞은 단어를 쓰시오.

> The Romans were so strong that they could rule many countries.
> =The Romans were _____
> _____ many countries.

오답노트

26. 다음 주어진 문장과 같은 의미를 가진 것은?

> It seems that you had a strange dream.

❶ You seems to have a strange dream.
❷ It seems to have a strange dream.
❸ I believe you to have a strange dream.
❹ You seem to have had a strange dream.
❺ You seemed to have had a strange dream.

오답노트

A. 우리말과 같은 뜻이 되도록 괄호 안의 말을 이용하여 문장을 완성하시오.

1. 나는 거기에서 귀신들을 만날 것을 기대했다. (expect)

→ I _____ _____ _____ ghosts there.

2. Jane은 나에게 무엇을 먼저 읽어야 할지 조언해 주었다. (read)

→ Jane advised me _____ _____ _____ first.

3. 그녀는 2008년에 홍콩으로 가서 결코 돌아오지 않았다. (come)

→ She went to Hong Kong in 2008, _____ _____ _____ _____.

B. 다음 우리말에 맞도록 빈칸에 알맞은 말을 쓰시오.

보 기	나는 이른 아침에 공부하는 것이 힘들다. → It is hard *for me to study* early in the morning. (I, study)

1. 나에게 그 책을 빌려주다니 그녀는 매우 친절하다.

→ It is very kind _____ me the book. (she, lend)

2. 그들이 그 문제들을 해결하는 것은 어렵지 않다.

→ It's not difficult _____ the problems. (they, solve)

C. 다음 문장과 의미가 같도록 빈칸에 알맞은 어구를 쓰시오.

1. The general was shocked when he heard the news of a revolt.

= The general was shocked _____ _____ the news of a revolt.

2. She was so tired that she couldn't speak.

= She was too tired _____ _____.

3. She was so stupid that she married such a man.

= How stupid she was _____ _____ such a man.

D. 다음 문장에서 어법상 <u>틀린</u> 것을 골라 바르게 고치시오.

1. Would you kindly let me to know it as soon as possible? _____ → _____

2. My mom told me to not play soccer there. _____ → _____

3. We heard the orchestra to play at Carnegie Hall last year. _____ → _____

4. I will get him finish the work in a week. _____ → _____

E. 다음 문장과 의미가 같아지도록 괄호 안의 표현을 이용하여 바꿔 쓰시오.

1. You are too short to ride this rollercoaster. (so ~ that ~)

= _____

2. She stayed up late to study for the final exam. (in order to)

= _____

F. 다음 괄호 안의 단어를 가지고 too ~ to와 enough to 구문을 이용한 문장을 각각 1개씩 만드시오.

보기	I have a tight schedule tomorrow, so I can't go to the party. → I don't have *enough time to go* to the party. (time) → I'm *too busy to go* to the party. (busy)

1. This tea is very hot. I need to wait a while until I can drink it.

→ This tea is _____ to drink. (hot)

→ This tea isn't _____ to drink. (cool)

2. I'm pretty short. I can't touch the ceiling.

→ I'm not _____ the ceiling. (tall)

→ I'm _____ the ceiling. (short)

실전 서술형 평가문제

출제의도 부정사의 부사적 용법
평가내용 일상 생활 속에서 to부정사의 부사적 용법(목적) 활용하기

A. 다음 각 내용의 이유에 해당하는 것을 찾아 in order to를 이용한 문장으로 완성하시오.

[서술형 유형 : 10점 / 난이도 : 중하]

행동	이유
〈보기〉 She's studying hard	pass the test
1. She's exercising	get there by tomorrow
2. She turned up the volume	keep in shape
3. She must drive all night	hear the news better
4. She must save money	study for the test
5. She's going to the library	buy a new motorcycle

보기	*She's studying hard in order to pass the test.*

1. _____

2. _____

3. _____

4. _____

5. _____

출제의도 동사＋목적어＋to부정사

평가내용 목적어의 행동을 나타내는 문장 완성하기

B. 다음 두 사람의 대화 상황을 5형식 문장을 이용하여 아래와 같이 서술하시오. [서술형 유형 : 8점 / 난이도 : 중]

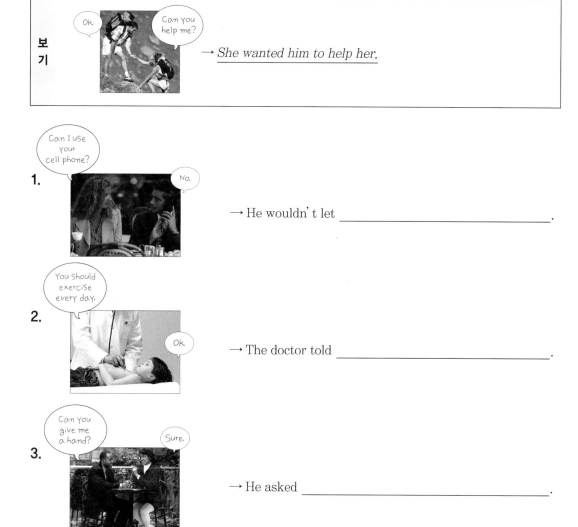

1. → He wouldn't let ＿＿＿＿＿＿＿＿＿＿＿＿＿.

2. → The doctor told ＿＿＿＿＿＿＿＿＿＿＿＿＿.

3. → He asked ＿＿＿＿＿＿＿＿＿＿＿＿＿＿＿.

4. → She warned ＿＿＿＿＿＿＿＿＿＿＿＿＿＿.

실전 서술형 평가문제

출제의도 too ~ to와 enough to
평가내용 부정사의 부사적 용법 활용하기

C. 주어진 표현을 이용하여 **too ~ to** 또는 **enough to** 문장으로 영작하시오.　[서술형 유형 : 9점 / 난이도 : 중상]

보기

Would you like to go out tonight?

tired / go out tonight

→ Jessica *is too tired to go out tonight.*

1.

Dad, can I drive this car?

old / drive this car

Jeff _____

_____ .

2.

Kelly should take part in the math competition.

good / take part in the math competition

Kelly _____

_____ .

3.

It's warm today. We can jump in the water.

warm / jump in the water

It _____

_____ .

출제의도 make, have, let
평가내용 5형식 동사를 이용하여 목적어의 동작 표현하기

D. 〈보기〉와 같이 괄호 안의 단어를 이용하여 대화를 요약하시오.　　　　　[서술형 유형 : 15점 / 난이도 : 중상]

보기	Kevin ：Mom, can I get a puppy? Mother：No, of course you can't get a puppy! 　　→ Kevin's mother *didn't let him get a puppy*. (let, not)

1. Steve ：Can I borrow your camcorder for our class trip to the zoo?

　　Jane ：Sure. I know you will take good care of it.

　　　→ Jane ＿＿＿＿＿＿＿＿＿＿＿＿＿＿＿＿＿＿＿＿＿. (let)

2. Bob ：Can we watch TV now?

　　Mom ：I'm sorry, but you have to finish your homework first.

　　　→ Their mother ＿＿＿＿＿＿＿＿＿＿＿＿＿＿＿＿＿. (allow, not)

3. Nancy：Google is a search engine. Just type *orca* in that space and hit "Return."

　　Peter ：Wow! Look at all that information!

　　　→ Nancy ＿＿＿＿＿＿＿＿＿＿＿＿＿＿＿＿＿ about orcas. (help)

4. Maria ：Mom, can I borrow the car?

　　Mom ：Only if you drive your sister to soccer practice.

　　　→ Maria's mother ＿＿＿＿＿＿＿＿＿＿＿＿＿＿＿. (have)

5. Officer(Woman) ：Show me your licence, sir.

　　Dan ：Here it is, officer. What's the problem?

　　　→ The officer ＿＿＿＿＿＿＿＿＿＿＿＿＿＿＿＿＿. (make)

실전 서술형 평가문제

출제의도 지각동사＋목적어＋동사원형
평가내용 지각동사를 이용하여 사진 묘사하기

E. 아래 사진은 Bob과 Susan이 보거나 들은 광경이다. 사진의 내용과 일치하는 문장을 지각동사를 이용하여 서술하시오.

[서술형 유형 : 9점 / 난이도 : 중]

| 보기 |  | "Look! Steve is waiting for a bus."
→ *We saw Steve waiting for a bus.* (see) |

1.

"Look! Peter and Julia are playing badminton."

→ We _____. (see)

2.

"Listen! Laura is playing the drum."

→ We _____. (hear)

3.

"Look! The girls are walking along the street."

→ We _____. (watch)

서술형 평가문제	채 점 기 준	배 점	나의 점수
A	표현이 올바르고 문법, 철자가 모두 정확한 경우	2점×5문항＝10점	
B		2점×4문항＝8점	
C		3점×3문항＝9점	
D		3점×5문항＝15점	
E		3점×3문항＝9점	
공통	문법, 철자가 1개씩 틀린 경우	각 문항당 1점씩 감점	
	내용과 전혀 일치하지 않거나 답을 기재하지 못한 경우	0점	

Chapter 5

동명사 (Gerunds)

Unit 01 동명사의 용법

1-1 명사처럼 쓰이는 동명사

Eating too much is bad for health.
너무 많이 먹는 것은 건강에 좋지 않다.
Your problem is **eating** too much.
너의 문제는 너무 많이 먹는다는 것이다.

01 동명사는 명사 역할만 있다. 부정사처럼 '~하는 것, ~하기'의 표현을 늘리기 위해 만든 것으로 **주어가 동작을 나타낼 때 (대)명사 대신 동명사**를 쓴다.

English is necessary in many fields. 여러 분야에서 영어는 없어서는 안 된다. ▶ 명사 English는 동작을 표현하지 못함
Speaking in English is hard at first. 영어로 말하는 것은 처음에는 어렵다. ▶ 주어 speaking이 행위를 표현하고 있음
=**It** is hard at first **to speak** in English.

※ 동명사는 가주어 it을 쓰고 진주어인 동명사를 뒤로 잘 보내지 않는다. 주어로 동명사를 그대로 쓰는 것이 보통이다.

02 명사가 오는 **보어 자리에도 동명사**를 써서 동작을 나타낼 수 있다.

My hobby **is reading** novels. 내 취미는 소설을 읽는 것이다.
What I like best **is listening** to good music. 내가 가장 좋아하는 것은 훌륭한 음악을 듣는 것이다.
Loving **is giving** and **taking**. 사랑하는 것은 주고 받는 것이다.

03 **목적어가 동작을 나타낼 때**는 (대)명사 대신 **동명사**를 쓴다. 특히 동명사만 좋아하는 동사들이 있다.

enjoy	finish	give up	avoid	quit
deny	put off	mind	stop	dislike
consider	admit	suggest	practice	keep

Seo-yoon enjoys **jogging** with her father. 서윤이는 그녀의 아빠와 조깅하는 것을 즐긴다.
As long as we live, our heart never stops **beating**. 우리가 살아있는 한 심장은 결코 멈추지 않는다.
Nancy suggested **going** to the movies. Nancy는 영화 보러 가자고 제안했다.

※ 동명사의 부정은 동명사 바로 앞에 not 또는 never를 쓴다.
Would you mind **not turning** the TV on? TV를 켜지 않아도 괜찮겠어요?
She regrets **not playing** the game more seriously. 그녀는 경기를 보다 진지하게 하지 않은 걸 후회한다.
He enjoyed **not being** disturbed at home. 그는 집에서 혼자 방해받지 않는 걸 즐겼다.
I'm proud of **never being** late for school. 나는 단 한 번도 지각하지 않은 걸 자랑스러워한다.

서술형 기초다지기

정답 p. 17

Challenge 1 다음 빈칸에 괄호 안의 말을 알맞게 배열하여 문장을 완성하세요.

01. My favorite activity _____. (doing, yoga, is)

02. _____ a good exercise. (taking, is, a walk)

03. _____ children how to write clearly. (teaches, a diary, keeping)

04. I regret _____ today. (bringing, my camera, not)

Challenge 2 다음 문장을 동명사가 주어인 문장으로 바꾸세요.

> **보기**
> It is bad for your mental health to hide your feeling.
> → *Hiding your feeling is bad for your mental health.*

01. It's very interesting to learn new languages.

→ _____

02. It's bad for your eyes to watch TV for too long.

→ _____

Challenge 3 다음 표현 중 알맞은 것을 골라 빈칸을 완성하세요.

have a picnic	talk to her	sit on the floor	break down	laugh

01. It was a gorgeous day, so I suggested _____.

02. It was very funny. I couldn't stop _____.

03. She's a very interesting person. I always enjoy _____.

04. My car isn't very reliable. It keeps _____.

05. I'm afraid there aren't any chairs. I hope you don't mind _____.

1-2 전치사의 목적어로 쓰이는 동명사 / go+동명사

I don't feel like **having** dinner now.
나는 지금 저녁을 먹고 싶지 않다.

Did you **go shopping** yesterday?
어제 쇼핑하러 갔었니?

01 전치사 뒤에는 목적어로 (대)명사를 쓰지만 **동작을 나타낼 때는 동명사**를 쓴다. 전치사 뒤에는 반드시 명사 형태를 써야 하므로 부정사를 쓸 수 없고 명사 역할을 하는 동명사를 써야 한다.

동사+전치사	apologize for, insist on, succeed in, believe in, think about, care about, worry about, approve of, thank for, plan on, feel like 등

I apologize for **being** late. 지각한 것을 사과드립니다.
Kevin left without **finishing** his lunch. Kevin은 점심 식사를 끝내지 않고 떠났다.
Thank you for **inviting** me to the party. 파티에 초대해 주셔서 감사합니다.
Jason has succeeded in **finding** a good job. Jason은 좋은 일자리를 찾는 데 성공했다.

형용사+전치사	interested in, excited about, fond of, tired of, good at, pleased about, sad about, capable of, afraid of, nervous about, responsible for, ashamed of, satisfied with

I was ashamed of **being** scolded in front of my friends. 나는 친구들 앞에서 혼난 것이 부끄러웠다.
Are you interested in **working** with us? 우리랑 함께 일하는 것에 관심 있나요?
I'm not very good at **playing** tennis. 나는 테니스를 잘 치지 못한다.

02 「go+동명사」는 '~하러 가다'의 뜻으로 주로 운동이나 레저에 많이 쓴다. 다음은 「go+동명사」의 형태로 자주 쓰는 표현들이다.

go dancing	go jogging	go fishing	go shopping
go sightseeing	go skiing	go swimming	go (ice)skating
go hiking	go camping	go (water)skiing	go bowling

In the summer we **go swimming**. 여름에 우리는 수영하러 간다.
Bob hasn't **gone fishing** in years. Bob은 몇 년간 낚시하러 가지 않았다.
She likes to **go hiking**. 그녀는 하이킹 하러 가는 것을 좋아한다.

서술형 기초다지기

Challenge 1 〈보기〉와 같이 괄호 안의 전치사를 이용하여 문장을 완성하세요.

> **보기**
> Thank you + open the door (for)
> → *Thank you for opening the door.*

01. I'm worried + be late for the concert (about)

→ _____

02. Are you interested + go to the zoo with us (in)

→ _____

03. She apologized + be so rude to me (for)

→ _____

04. Are you afraid + fly in small planes (of)

→ _____

05. Bob insisted + pay the restaurant bill (on)

→ _____

Challenge 2 다음 문장을 「go+동명사」의 형태로 바꾸어 쓰세요.

> **보기**
> I love to jog. Last night, my dad and I jogged for hours.
> → Last night, my dad and I *went jogging*.

01. It was hot enough for us to swim. We went to the beach and jumped in the water.

→ We _____.

02. I love to put up a small tent by a stream, make a fire, and listen to the sounds of the forest during the night.

→ I love to _____.

03. Yesterday, Karen visited many stores and bought some clothes and makeup.

→ Yesterday, Karen _____.

Unit 02 동명사와 부정사

2-1 목적어로 쓰이는 동명사와 부정사

Lucy hopes **to be** the queen at the party.
Lucy는 파티에서 여왕이 되길 희망한다.

Betty practices **playing** the piano after school.
Betty는 방과 후에 피아노 연습을 한다.

01 동명사는 기본적으로 과거의 의미를 담고 있다. 과거에 경험했거나 기억하고 있는 일, 또는 그 전에 한 일이나 이미 하고 있는 일이라는 과거의 의미를 내포하고 있기 때문에 **아래의 동사들은 동명사를 목적어로 쓸 수밖에 없다.**

enjoy	mind	finish	deny	avoid
quit	give up	put off	admit	practice
keep	suggest	dislike	consider	stop

They denied **stealing** the money. 그들은 그 돈을 훔쳤다는 걸 부인했다.
She enjoys **traveling** by plane. 그녀는 비행기로 여행하는 것을 즐긴다.
Many people have stopped **smoking**. 많은 사람들이 담배를 끊었다.

02 반면, **부정사는 기본적으로 미래의 의미를 담고 있다.** 앞으로 할 일이나 의무 또는 책무라는 의미를 내포하고 있기 때문에 **아래 동사들은 부정사를 목적어로 쓸 수밖에 없다.**

expect	want	hope	decide	plan	offer
promise	refuse	wish	agree	afford	choose

She wants **to travel** by plane. 그녀는 비행기로 여행하길 원한다.
My father promised **to buy** me the iPhone. 아빠는 내게 아이폰을 사주겠다고 약속했다.

03 아래의 동사들은 동명사와 to부정사를 모두 목적어로 가질 수 있으며 **의미에 큰 차이가 없다.**

like	hate	love	start	begin	intend	continue	can't stand	prefer

He loves **waterskiing**. = He loves **to waterski**. 그는 수상스키 타는 것을 좋아한다.
Jane hates **doing** her homework. = Jane hates **to do** her homework. Jane은 숙제하는 것을 싫어한다.
It began **raining**. = It began **to rain**. 비가 내리기 시작했다.

서술형 기초다지기

정답 p. 17

Challenge 1 다음 괄호 안의 동사를 알맞은 형태로 바꾸어 쓰세요.

01. Sunny gave up _____ the ugly boy. (date)

02. Bob and Sally have decided _____ married. (get)

03. Have you ever considered _____ abroad? (study)

04. I promised _____ that again. (not, do)

05. My roommate offered _____ me with my English. (help)

06. I don't mind _____ with four roommates. (live)

07. My boss refused _____ me a raise, so I quit. (give)

08. His family hopes _____ to Singapore this summer. (travel)

09. I stopped _____ Kevin. He was rude to me. (help)

10. I think you should avoid _____ high-fat food. (eat)

Challenge 2 괄호 안의 동사를 동명사와 부정사로 구분하여 쓰고 둘 다 가능한 경우 모두 쓰세요.

01. Why do you keep _____ me the same question over and over again? (ask)

02. The water started _____. (boil)

03. Prices will continue _____ higher. (rise)

04. The children hope _____ to McDonald's for lunch. (go)

05. Steve quit _____ to lose weight. (drink)

06. I began _____ baseball last week. (play)

07. She loves _____ Chinese food with her family. (eat)

2-2 동명사와 to부정사를 모두 목적어로 쓰는 동사

I remembered **to call** him.
나는 그에게 전화해야 하는 걸 기억해냈다.
I remembered **calling** him.
나는 그에게 전화했던 사실을 기억해냈다.

01 **부정사와 동명사를 모두 목적어로 취하지만 뜻이 달라지는 경우**가 있다. 동명사는 과거의 의미, to부정사는 현재나 미래의 의미임을 기억해 두자.

과거(이전)에 했던 경험이나 행동		앞으로 해야 할 일, 의무, 책임
remember+V-ing : ~했던 것을 기억하다		remember+to V : ~할 것을 기억하다
try+V-ing : 한번 ~해보다	VS.	try+to V : ~하려고 노력하다
forget+V-ing : ~했던 것을 잊다		forget+to V : ~할 것을 잊어버리다
stop+V-ing : ~하는 것을 멈추다		stop+to V : ~하기 위하여 멈추다
regret+V-ing : ~했던 것을 후회하다		regret+to V : ~하게 되어 유감이다

I can't forget **meeting** her at the beach. 해변에서 그녀를 만났던 일을 잊을 수 없어. ▶ 과거
Please don't forget **to meet** Mr. Kevin. Kevin씨 만나는 것을 잊지 마. ▶ 미래

I tried **calling** Nancy last night. 나는 어젯밤 Nancy에게 전화를 해봤다.
I tried **to call** Nancy last night. 나는 어젯밤 Nancy에게 전화하려고 노력했다.

We regret **buying** a used car. 우리는 중고차를 산 것을 후회한다. ▶ 과거 행동에 대한 후회
We regret **to inform** you that we are unable to offer you the job.
당신을 고용할 수 없게 된 것을 알려드리게 되어 유감입니다.

02 need+동명사: ~되어져야 할 필요가 있다(수동의 의미), need+to부정사: ~할 필요가 있다

My digital camera needs **repairing**. 내 디지털 카메라는 수리되어야 한다.
=My digital camera needs **to be repaired**.
I need **to repair** my digital camera. 나는 내 디지털 카메라를 수리해야 한다.

03 help+부정사: ~하는 것을 돕다, can't help+동명사: ~하지 않을 수 없다

Everybody helped **(to) clean up** after the party. 모든 사람들이 파티가 끝난 후에 청소하는 것을 도왔다.
She tried to be serious, but she couldn't help **laughing**. 그녀는 진지해지려고 노력했지만 웃지 않을 수가 없었다.
=she couldn't stop herself from laughing

서술형 기초다지기

정답 p. 17

Challenge 1 다음 괄호 안의 동사를 알맞은 형태로 바꾸어 쓰세요.

01. Don't forget _____ the light when you leave. (turn off)

02. I'll never forget _____ the Queen last year. (meet)

03. I was very tired. I tried _____ my eyes open, but I couldn't. (keep)

04. Have you tried _____ your hair color? (change)

05. Please remember _____ the door when you go out. (lock)

06. She can remember _____ in the hospital when she was five. (be)

07. Do you think my jacket needs _____? (wash)

08. He looks so funny. Whenever I see him, I can't help _____. (laugh)

Challenge 2 〈보기〉와 같이 괄호 안의 단어를 활용하여 두 문장의 뜻이 같아지도록 영작하세요.

> **보기** My dad didn't forget that he met a ghost. (forget)
> → My dad didn't forget *meeting a ghost*.

01. I remember that I watched the accident last year. (watch)

→ I remember _____.

02. I'm sorry but I have to say that you aren't on the list. (say)

→ I regret _____.

03. I try not to use the bicycle when I can walk somewhere. (avoid)

→ I try _____.

04. Susan doesn't go to yoga class any more because she has broken her arm. (go)

→ Susan (has) stopped _____.

3-1 동명사의 의미상 주어

Would you mind turning on the TV?
TV를 좀 켜 주시겠습니까?
Would you mind **my** turning on the TV?
제가 TV를 켜도 될까요?

01

동사 이외에도 동작을 나타내는 모든 부정사와 동명사 표현에는 그에 맞는 주어가 있어야 한다. 부정사와 마찬가지로 동명사도 의미상 주어를 가질 수 있다. 하지만 일반인이 동명사의 의미상 주어이거나, 문장의 주어와 동명사의 의미상 주어가 같은 경우 의미상 주어를 따로 쓰지 않는다.

Smoking cigarettes is bad for health. 담배를 피우는 것은 건강에 좋지 않다. ▶ smoking의 의미상 주어는 일반인
Learning a foreign language takes a lot of time.
외국어를 배우는 것은 시간이 많이 걸린다. ▶ learning의 의미상 주어는 일반인

I love **eating** bananas but dislike **shelling** them.
나는 바나나 먹는 것은 좋아하지만 껍질을 벗기는 것은 싫어한다. ▶ 동명사 eating과 shelling의 의미상 주어는 문장 전체의 주어인 I
Do **you** mind **closing** the window? 창문을 좀 닫아 주겠니? ▶ 동명사 closing의 의미상 주어는 문장 전체의 주어인 you

※ 목적어가 동명사의 의미상 주어가 될 때도 있다.
I thanked **Sunny** for **teaching** me English.
나는 Sunny가 나에게 영어를 가르쳐 준 것에 감사했다. ▶ 동명사 teaching의 의미상 주어는 문장 전체의 목적어인 Sunny

02

주어와 일치하지 않고 동명사 행위에 대한 주어를 별도로 표시해 줄 때는 **동명사 바로 앞에 소유격**을 쓴다.

Do you mind **my closing** the window? 내가 창문을 닫아도 되겠습니까? ▶ my가 closing의 의미상 주어
I can't stand **his shouting** when he is angry.
나는 그가 화가 나 있을 때 소리치는 것을 참을 수 없다. ▶ his가 shouting의 의미상 주어

03

의미상 주어로 소유격을 쓰는 것은 다소 딱딱한 표현이어서 일상 영어에서는 **목적격을 많이 쓴다.** 특히, 사람의 이름은 소유격(Mary's)보다 **그냥 이름(Mary)을 동명사 앞에 쓰는 경우가 많다.**

Kevin insisted on **my coming** to the meeting. Kevin은 내가 모임에 와야 한다고 주장했다. ▶ formal
=Kevin insisted on **me coming** to the meeting. ▶ informal
I'm sorry about **Jessica's falling** in love with him. 제시카가 그 남자와 사귄다니 안됐다. ▶ formal
=I'm sorry about **Jessica falling** in love with him. ▶ informal

서술형 기초다지기

정답 p. 17

Challenge 1 〈보기〉와 같이 동명사를 이용한 문장으로 바꾸어 완성하세요.

> **보기**
> They were surprised. He came to the party.
> → They were surprised at *his[him] coming* to the party.

01. I am late. Please forgive it.

→ Please forgive _____ _____ late.

02. They insisted that I stay with her.

→ They insisted on _____ _____ with her.

03. I remember that she sang a song on the stage.

→ I remember _____ _____ a song on the stage.

04. Her daughter leaves for Hong Kong. She will call you before it.

→ She will call you before her _____ _____ for Hong Kong.

05. I want to smoke here. Is it okay?

→ Would you mind _____ _____ here?

06. Karen was angry at Lisa. Lisa lied to her.

→ Karen was angry at _____ _____ to her.

Challenge 2 다음 우리말과 같은 뜻이 되도록 괄호 안의 단어를 이용하여 빈칸을 완성하세요.

01. 나는 그녀가 나를 때린 것을 절대 잊지 않을 것이다. (hit)

→ I'll never forget _____ me.

02. 언니는 내가 그녀의 자전거 타는 것을 싫어한다. (ride)

→ My sister doesn't like _____ her bicycle.

03. 아빠는 우리가 집에 늦게 온 것에 대해 걱정했다. (come)

→ My father worried about _____ home late.

3-2 동명사 없이는 못 사는 표현들

I'm **looking forward to** meeting you again.
나는 너를 다시 만날 것을 기대한다.

She **spent** too much money (**on**) buy**ing** her clothes.
그녀는 옷을 사는 데에 너무 많은 돈을 썼다.

01
look forward to+V-ing : ～할 것을 학수고대하다

The children are **looking forward to** hav**ing** a Christmas party.
아이들은 크리스마스 파티하길 학수고대하고 있다.

02
have difficulty[trouble, a hard time, a difficult time]+V-ing : ～하는 데 어려움을 겪다

Do you **have** much **trouble** solv**ing** the problem? 문제를 해결하는 데 어려움이 많나요?

03
be (not) worth+V-ing : ～할 가치가 있다(없다) (=It is worthwhile to+V)

This book **is worth** read**ing**. (=It is worthwhile to read this book.) 이 책은 읽을 가치가 있다.

04
On+V-ing : ～하자마자 / In+V-ing : ～할 때, ～함에 있어 / by+V-ing : ～함으로써

On see**ing** me, she ran away. 나를 보자마자 그녀는 도망을 쳤다.
By recycl**ing** paper and bottles, we can protect the environment.
종이와 병들을 재활용함으로써, 우리는 환경을 보호할 수 있다.

05
prevent/keep+목적어+from+V-ing : ～가 ～하는 것을 막다, ～때문에 ～하지 못하다

The snow **kept** us **from** climb**ing** the mountain. 눈 때문에 우리는 산에 오르지 못했다.

06
not/never ～ without+V-ing : ～하면 반드시 ～하다

She **never** goes out **without** los**ing** her umbrella. 그녀는 외출만 하면 우산을 잊어버린다.

07
far from+V-ing : 전혀 ～아닌 / above+V-ing : 결코 ～하지 않는

She is **far from** be**ing** interested in sports. 그녀는 스포츠에 전혀 관심이 없다.
She is **above** ask**ing** questions about me. 그녀는 나에 대한 질문을 결코 하지 않는다.

08
object to+V-ing : ～에 반대하다 / It is no use[good]+V-ing : ～해도 소용없다

They **object to** chang**ing** the plans. 그들은 계획을 바꾸는 것에 반대한다.
It is no use try**ing** to excuse yourself. 변명하려 해봤자 소용없는 짓이다.

서술형 기초다지기

정답 p. 17

Challenge 1 다음 두 문장이 같은 의미가 되도록 괄호 안의 말을 이용하여 빈칸을 완성하세요.

보 기	This news is never true. → This news is *far from being true*. (far from)

01. I couldn't enjoy the holiday because of a cold.

→ A cold _____ the holiday. (prevent)

02. It is worthwhile to read a newspaper everyday.

→ A newspaper _____ everyday. (be worth)

03. Whenever I see your face, I always smile.

→ I _____. (never ~ without)

04. Once you get the disease, it is useless to take medicine.

→ Once you get the disease, _____. (it is no use ~)

05. The moment I saw him, I fell in love with him.

→ _____, I fell in love with him. (on+V-ing)

Challenge 2 다음 우리말과 의미가 같도록 빈칸에 알맞은 말을 쓰세요.

01. 나는 이름을 기억하는 데 어려움이 있다.

→ I _____ _____ _____ names.

02. 그 영화는 볼 가치가 있다.

→ The movie is _____ _____.

03. 아무것도 귀신이 돌아오는 것을 막을 수 없다.

→ Nothing can _____ the ghost _____ _____ back.

04. 나는 곧 당신과 같이 일하기를 기대한다.

→ I _____ _____ _____ _____ with you soon.

"출제자가 노리는 급소" 이것이 시험에 출제되는 영문법이다!

01 출제 100 % - 동명사가 주어로 쓰일 때 동사는 반드시 단수를 쓴다.

 출제자의 눈 동명사 주어는 단수 취급하여 동사를 단수형으로 써야 한다. 가장 기본적으로 동명사의 용법을 물어보거나, be동사 뒤에 있는 -ing를 진행형과 동명사 중 어디에 해당하는지 구분하는 문제가 출제되었다. 특히 접속사 and 앞뒤에 같은 품사로 동명사가 와야 하는데 이를 틀리게 해놓거나 전치사 to 또는 like 뒤에 동명사를 써야 하는데 동사원형이나 부정사로 유인하는 문제도 자주 출제된다.

Ex 1.

Playing computer games without eating anything _____ you sick.

(a) makes   (b) make   (c) to make   (d) making

Ex 2.

In business, competition controls the market by _____ companies develop new ideas to ensure survival.

(a) made   (b) to make   (c) making   (d) be making

02 출제 100 % - 동명사냐 부정사냐 그것이 문제로다!

 출제자의 눈 기본적으로 동명사는 과거의 의미를, 부정사는 미래의 의미를 가지고 있음을 기억해 두자. 이를 이용한 문제나 목적어 자리에 부정사와 동명사를 서로 틀리게 써넣고 고르는 문제가 집중적으로 출제된다. 예를 들어, would like와 would love는 to부정사만을 목적어로 쓰며 feel like에서는 like가 전치사이므로 동명사를 쓰고 can't(couldn't) help 뒤에도 반드시 동명사를 쓴다. 이를 부정사와 동명사를 혼동케 하는 문제로 출제할 수 있다.

Ex 3.

It was late, so we decided _____ a taxi home.

(a) taking   (b) takes   (c) will take   (d) to take

Ex 4.

I can't help _____ every time I watch "Friends" on TV.

(a) to laugh   (b) laughing   (c) laugh   (d) to laughing

03 출제 100% - 의미에 따라 동명사와 부정사를 구별해서 쓰는 동사를 조심하라!

 출제자의 눈 remember, stop, try와 같은 동사들은 문맥 전체를 보고 과거의 경험이나 일은 동명사를 쓰고, 앞으로 해야 할 일은 부정사를 쓰는데, 이를 묻는 문제가 가장 많이 출제된다. 단답형 주관식으로 동명사와 부정사를 구별하여 쓰는 문제가 나올 수 있다.

Ex 5.

I remembered _____ the door when I left, but I forgot to shut the windows.

(a) locking   (b) that lock   (c) to lock   (d) locked

Ex 6.

She tried _____ the sofa, and found it was not heavy.

(a) to move   (b) moving   (c) moves   (d) move

04 출제 100% - 동명사와 함께 쓰이는 표현을 암기해 두자!

 출제자의 눈 mind는 '~을 꺼리다'의 의미로 동명사가 아닌 부정사를 목적어로 써놓거나, 또는 전치사 'to'로 끝나는 표현을 주고 부정사로 착각하게끔 하는 문제가 자주 나온다. 한 예로 look forward to, be used to에서 to는 전치사이므로 동명사를 써야 한다. be busy+V-ing, be worth+V-ing, have trouble/difficulty+V-ing의 표현이 시험에서 자주 등장한다. 이와 함께 '~하느라(-ing) 시간을 쓰다(spend)'에서 처럼 spend도 동명사와 함께 짝을 이룬다는 것을 기억해 두자.

Ex 7.

She had no trouble _____.

(a) communicating   (b) to communicate   (c) communicated

Ex 8.

We're all looking forward to _____ you again.

(a) see   (b) seeing   (c) saw   (d) do saw

Ex 9.

Seo-yoon's been living in Japan for 5 years, so she's now used to _____ on the left.

(a) drive   (b) driving   (c) drove   (d) do drive

1. 빈칸에 들어갈 말로 알맞지 <u>않은</u> 것은?

> She _____ watching a horror movie.

❶ enjoyed　　❷ hated　　❸ stopped
❹ liked　　❺ wished

2. 다음 우리말과 일치하도록 괄호 안에 주어진 단어를 올바른 순서대로 배열하시오.

> · 그런 상황에서 나를 비난하지 않은 것에 대해 고마워. (blaming, not, me)
> → Thank you for _____ in that kind of situation.

3. 다음 대화의 빈칸에 들어갈 가장 알맞은 것은?

> A : All the fish and even the plants are dying in the river.
> B : Unless people stop _____, they won't see them any more.

❶ throw trash there
❷ throwing trash there
❸ to throw trash there
❹ throw not trash there
❺ don't throw trash there

4. 다음 밑줄 친 부분이 바르게 쓰인 것을 고르시오.

❶ I remember <u>to see</u> her yesterday.
❷ He continued <u>searching</u> for the herb.
❸ Would you mind <u>tell</u> me again?
❹ She wants <u>speaking</u> Chinese very well.
❺ They enjoyed <u>to eat</u> sandwiches and had a good time.

5. 다음 밑줄 친 부분의 쓰임이 <u>다른</u> 하나는?

❶ <u>Getting up</u> early in the morning is hard.
❷ Ellen started <u>talking</u> about her problem.
❸ Thank you for <u>inviting</u> me.
❹ They are <u>walking</u> to the park.
❺ Students practice written English by <u>writing</u> compositions.

6. 다음 중 어법상 잘못된 부분을 고르시오.

> I <u>could not</u> help <u>be worried</u> about
> 　　　❶　　　　　　　❷
> <u>the young</u> <u>people</u> <u>in this</u> country.
> 　　❸　　　　❹　　　　❺

7. 다음 문장에서 <u>틀린</u> 곳을 찾아 바르게 고치시오.

> Many Korean people are interested in to make friends with Americans. However, they often find this difficult. The language barrier is one difficulty, but there are other problems, such as knowing which subjects to talk about and which subjects to avoid.

> _____ → _____

8. 다음 대화의 내용을 읽고 빈칸에 알맞은 것을 고르시오.

> A : You lent me some money a few months ago.
> B : Are you sure? I don't remember _____ you any money.

❶ lending　　　　❷ to lent
❸ to lend　　　　❹ to lending
❺ lent

오답 노트 만들기

★틀린 문제 : _____   ★다시 공부한 날 : _____

(1) 문제를 왜? 틀렸는지 곰곰이 생각하고 그 이유를 적어본다.

(2) 핵심 개념을 적는다.

(3) 자신이 몰랐던 단어와 숙어 표현이 있으면 정리한다.

(4) 해설집에서 필요한 부분을 골라 풀이 해법을 정리한다.

★틀린 문제 : _____   ★다시 공부한 날 : _____

(1) 문제를 왜? 틀렸는지 곰곰이 생각하고 그 이유를 적어본다.

(2) 핵심 개념을 적는다.

(3) 자신이 몰랐던 단어와 숙어 표현이 있으면 정리한다.

(4) 해설집에서 필요한 부분을 골라 풀이 해법을 정리한다.

★틀린 문제 : _____   ★다시 공부한 날 : _____

(1) 문제를 왜? 틀렸는지 곰곰이 생각하고 그 이유를 적어본다.

(2) 핵심 개념을 적는다.

(3) 자신이 몰랐던 단어와 숙어 표현이 있으면 정리한다.

(4) 해설집에서 필요한 부분을 골라 풀이 해법을 정리한다.

★틀린 문제 : _____   ★다시 공부한 날 : _____

(1) 문제를 왜? 틀렸는지 곰곰이 생각하고 그 이유를 적어본다.

(2) 핵심 개념을 적는다.

(3) 자신이 몰랐던 단어와 숙어 표현이 있으면 정리한다.

(4) 해설집에서 필요한 부분을 골라 풀이 해법을 정리한다.

1. **다음 우리말과 같도록 빈칸을 완성하시오.**

> A: What would you like to do this
>   weekend?
> B: I feel _____ _____ to the
>   movies. (나는 영화 보러 가고 싶어.)

오답노트

2. **다음 밑줄 친 부분과 쓰임이 같은 것은?**

> I like traveling around Eastern Europe
> very much.

❶ Who is the lady standing in front of the
   door?
❷ I was surprised at her passing the exam.
❸ She came running to me.
❹ I heard her screaming in the dark room.
❺ They were listening to music.

오답노트

3. **다음 우리말을 바르게 영작한 것을 고르시오.**

> 나는 이번 주에 소풍 가는 것을 기대하고 있다.

❶ I am looking forward to going on a picnic
   this weekend.
❷ I am looking forward to go on a picnic
   this weekend.
❸ I am looking forward to went on a picnic
   this weekend.

❹ I am looking forward go on a picnic this
   weekend.
❺ I am looking forward to be going on a
   picnic this weekend.

오답노트

4. **다음 문장과 뜻이 같은 것을 고르시오.**

> I distinctly remember locking the door.

❶ I distinctly remember that I locked the
   door.
❷ I distinctly remember that I should lock
   the door.
❸ I distinctly remember to lock the door.
❹ I distinctly remembered to lock the door.
❺ I distinctly remember that I'll lock the
   door.

오답노트

[5-6] 다음 괄호 안의 말을 알맞게 배열하시오.

5. 밤에 혼자 걸어 다니는 것은 위험하다.
→ _____ is dangerous.
        (night, at, alone, walking)

6. Kelly는 그가 그녀에게 정직하지 않았다고 불평했다.
→ Kelly complained about _____
   _____ with her.
        (honest, him, being, not)

오답노트

150

7. 다음 빈칸에 들어갈 말로 알맞게 짝지어진 것은?

· I look forward _____ from you soon.
· He devoted his life _____ the sick.

❶ to hear − to help
❷ to hearing − to helping
❸ hearing − helping
❹ to hearing − to help
❺ to hear − to helping

오답노트

8. 다음 ⓐ와 ⓑ에 들어갈 단어가 바르게 짝지어진 것은?

A : Bill, tell us the difference between these: I tried ⓐ _____ the mountain and I tried ⓑ _____ the mountain.
B : Yes, ma'am. The first one means I climbed it to see what it was like at the top and The second may be followed by 'but I couldn't.'
A : That's right, Bill.

	ⓐ	ⓑ
❶	to climb	to climb
❷	climbing	climbing
❸	to climb	climbing
❹	climbing	to climb
❺	climb	climb

오답노트

9. 다음 빈칸에 들어갈 말이 바르게 짝지어진 것은?

· She will call you before _____ leaving for London.
· I can't understand _____ loving her.

❶ she − he   ❷ her − he
❸ her − him   ❹ she − his
❺ hers − his

오답노트

10. 다음 중 밑줄 친 부분의 쓰임이 다른 하나는?

❶ My family and I are going to Canada for a vacation.
❷ They will be landing in 10 minutes.
❸ The population of the world is rising very fast.
❹ They are wearing their new T-shirts.
❺ Min-ji asked her mother about going to Canada.

오답노트

11. 다음 빈칸에 알맞은 동사의 형태를 쓰시오.

· 나는 우리나라의 십대들에 대해서 걱정하지 않을 수 없었다.
  I could not help _____ worried about teenagers in this country.

❶ be   ❷ being   ❸ was   ❹ is   ❺ am

오답노트

12. 다음 중 어법상 올바른 것은?

❶ Would you mind to open the window for me?
❷ I finished to write the report.
❸ After Mike finished working, he went bowling with his friends.
❹ Kate and Ben can't afford going on vacation this year.
❺ Why did you decide becoming a chef?

오답노트

[13-14] 다음 두 문장을 한 문장으로 쓸 때 빈칸에 알맞은 말을 쓰시오.

13.

> Yesterday she screamed in the dark room. I couldn't understand it.

→ I couldn't understand _____ _____ in the dark room yesterday.

오답노트

14.

> My mom insisted that I get married to Peter.

→ My mom insisted on _____ _____ married to Peter.

오답노트

15. 다음 중 어법상 어색한 곳을 찾아 번호를 쓰고 바르게 고치시오.

> I remember ❶ taking a watch to pieces when I ❷ was a child. I spent hours in ❸ to try to put it back together again. In the end, I ❹ had to have it done by ❺ a watchmaker.

_____ → _____

오답노트

16. 다음 빈칸에 들어갈 말이 바르게 짝지어진 것은?

> · I remember _____ her at a party once.
> · She tries to avoid _____ shopping on Sundays.

❶ to see − going
❷ to see − to go
❸ seeing − going
❹ seeing − to go
❺ having seen − to go

오답노트

17. 다음 빈칸에 알맞은 말을 쓰시오.

> · 많은 비 때문에 우리는 어제 테니스를 치지 못했다.
> → The heavy rain _____ us from _____ tennis yesterday.

오답노트

18. 다음 빈칸에 알맞은 말을 쓰시오.

> As it was snowing heavily, airplanes couldn't leave on time.
> =The heavy snow _____
>   airplanes _____ leaving on time.

오답노트

19. 빈칸에 들어갈 말이 바르게 짝지어진 것은?

> · Kathy spent too much money _____ her hair done.
> · He was busy _____ his room yesterday.
> · She expects _____ the manager at the airport at six.

❶ to get − to clean − to greet
❷ getting − cleaning − to greet
❸ getting − to clean − greeting
❹ to get − cleaning − greeting
❺ getting − cleaning − greeting

오답노트

[20-21] 다음 빈칸에 들어갈 알맞은 말을 고르시오.

20.

> A: Thank you for _____ me clean the car.
> B: It's my pleasure.

❶ helping ❷ helps ❸ to help
❹ helped ❺ help

21.

> I'm accustomed _____ Italian food because I've been there many times.

❶ to eat ❷ eating ❸ to eating
❹ at eating ❺ on eating

오답노트

22. 다음 문장과 의미가 같은 것은?

> I regret that I fell in love with her.

❶ I can't have fallen in love with her.
❷ I must have fallen in love with her.
❸ I should have fallen in love with her.
❹ I ought to have fallen in love with her.
❺ I shouldn't have fallen in love with her.

오답노트

23. 다음 밑줄 친 부분 중 어법상 어색한 것은?

> My mother is very afraid ❶ of earthquakes. She can feel the smallest tremor that nobody else seems ❷ to notice. We can't ❸ help laugh at her when she panics. But she says she ❹ can't forget the awful earthquake ❺ which struck when she was a child.

오답노트

A. 다음 문장에서 잘못된 부분을 바르게 고쳐 쓰시오.

1. The company is looking forward to work with you again.

→ _____

2. On hear the announcement, all the reporters started to transmit the news.

→ _____

3. Be polite to parents is a must.

→ _____

4. My sister left without finish her dinner.

→ _____

B. 〈보기〉와 같이 주어진 문장을 고칠 때 「전치사 + 동명사」로 빈칸을 완성하시오.

보기	Kelly interrupted me. She apologized for that. → Kelly apologized *for interrupting* me.

1. I like to watch horror movies. I'm interested in that.

→ I'm interested _____ horror movies.

2. We helped an old woman. She thanked us for that.

→ An old woman thanked us _____ her.

3. Lucy wanted to take a taxi to work. She insisted on that.

→ Lucy insisted _____ a taxi.

4. I'm not a good art student. I try to draw paintings, but I'm not good at it.

→ I'm not good _____ paintings.

C. 다음 두 문장이 같은 의미가 되도록 〈보기〉와 같이 동명사를 활용하여 빈칸을 채우시오.

> **보기**
> My teacher is proud that I volunteered as a nurse.
> → My teacher is proud of *my[me] volunteering* as a nurse.

1. I'm sure that he will graduate this time.

→ I'm sure of _____ this time.

2. We are very proud that Yu-na Kim is Korean.

=We are very proud of _____ Korean.

3. She remembers that she would watch the concert together on weekends.

=She remembers _____ the concert together on weekends.

4. I'm afraid that they might be late again.

=I'm afraid of _____ late again.

D. 다음 우리말과 같은 뜻이 되도록 괄호 안의 말을 이용하여 빈칸을 채우시오.

1. 나는 도서관에서 몇 권의 책을 빌려야 하는 걸 기억한다. (borrow)

→ I _____ some books from the library.

2. Jessica와 우연히 마주쳤을 때, 나는 그녀에게 말을 걸려고 멈췄다. (talk)

→ When I ran into Jessica, I _____ to her.

3. 해변에서 그녀를 만났던 일을 잊을 수가 없다. (meet)

→ I can't _____ her at the beach.

4. 나는 그 박물관을 방문했던 것을 잊지 못한다. (visit)

→ I never _____ the museum.

실전 서술형 평가문제

 출제의도 의미에 따른 부정사와 동명사 활용
평가내용 부정사와 동명사를 구별하여 영작하기

A. 〈보기〉와 같이 괄호 안의 동사를 이용하여 동명사가 들어간 문장으로 영작하시오.

[서술형 유형 : 10점 / 난이도 : 중하]

> **보 기**
> Matt said, "Let's go to the beach!" (suggest)
> → *Matt suggested going to the beach.*

1. I try not to use the car when I can walk somewhere. (avoid)

→ _____

2. Mark doesn't go to soccer practice any more because he has broken his leg. (stop)

→ _____

3. Jason won't have a problem working this weekend. (not mind)

→ _____

4. I can't wait to see you again. (look forward)

→ _____

5. Did you take the rubbish out before you left the house? (remember)

→ _____

출제의도 동사에 따른 부정사와 동명사 활용
평가내용 부정사와 동명사를 구별하여 영작하기

B. 주어진 동사를 이용하여 다음 사진에 맞는 문장을 동명사 또는 부정사로 서술하시오. (주어는 I로 쓸 것)

[서술형 유형 : 10점 / 난이도 : 중상]

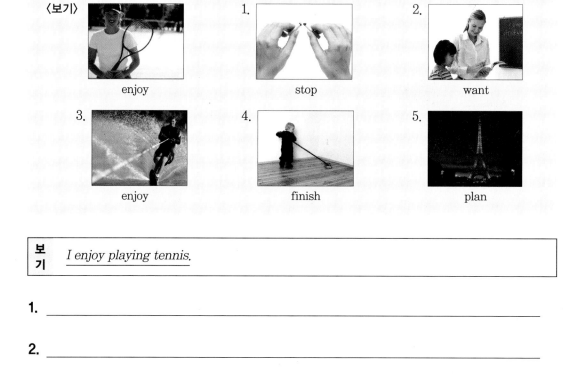

| 〈보기〉 enjoy | 1. stop | 2. want |
| 3. enjoy | 4. finish | 5. plan |

| 보기 | *I enjoy playing tennis.* |

1. _____

2. _____

3. _____

4. _____

5. _____

실전 서술형 평가문제

출제의도 동명사와 to부정사에 따라 의미가 변하는 동사
평가내용 의미에 따른 동명사와 부정사 구별하여 영작하기

C. 다음 정보를 읽고 괄호 안의 동사를 이용하여 빈칸을 완성하시오.　　　　[서술형 유형 : 12점 / 난이도 : 중상]

Mon.	Jessica knocked on the door, but there was no answer.
Tue.	Jessica met the famous actress.
Wed.	Jessica didn't set the alarm, so she was late for work.
Fri.	Jessica is going out to see movies with some friends.
Sat.	Jessica is playing tennis on Saturday afternoon.
Sun.	Jessica is having dinner with Tom.

＊Today is Thursday.

1. Jessica _____ on Monday, but there was no answer. (try)

2. Jessica will never _____ on Tuesday. (forget)

3. Jessica _____ on Wednesday. (forget)

4. Jessica won't _____ on Friday. (forget)

5. Jessica _____ on Saturday afternoon. (remember)

6. Jessica won't _____ on Sunday. (forget)

서술형 평가문제	채 점 기 준	배 점	나의 점수
A		2점×5문항=10점	
B	표현이 올바르고 문법, 철자가 모두 정확한 경우	2점×5문항=10점	
C		2점×6문항=12점	
공통	문법, 철자가 1개씩 틀린 경우	각 문항당 1점씩 감점	
	내용과 전혀 일치하지 않거나 답을 기재하지 못한 경우	0점	

Chapter 6

분사 (Participles)

Unit 01 분사

1-1 분사의 종류와 역할

An old woman is **reading** a book.
연세가 있는 여성분이 책을 읽고 있다.
The woman **sitting** on the chair is my grandmother.
소파에 앉아있는 여자가 내 할머니다.

01 분사를 형용사라고 설명하는 책들이 많은데, 이는 틀린 설명이다. 형용사는 명사의 상태를 설명할 뿐 동작을 표현해 주지 못한다. 반면 **분사는 바로 명사의 행위나 동작을 표현해 줄 수 있다.** 우리말에 '앉다 여자', '공부하다 소녀'를 '앉아 있는 여자', '공부하는 소녀'처럼 '~하는, ~하고 있는'이란 말의 어미를 바꾸듯이, 영어에서도 sit을 sitting으로, study를 studying으로 바꿔 **명사 앞이나 뒤에서 명사의 동작을 설명해 준다.** 이것이 바로 **분사**이다.

02 분사가 명사를 단독으로 꾸밀 경우 명사 바로 앞에 쓴다. **현재분사(-ing)는 명사가 주체적으로 행동**을 할 때 쓰는데 '~하는, 하고 있는'의 뜻이다. **과거분사는 명사가 행동을 받거나 당하는 경우**에 쓰며 '~된, ~되어진'의 뜻이다.

The **sleeping** baby is very cute. 잠을 자고 있는 아기는 매우 귀엽다.

(→ The baby is sleeping) ▶ 진행형으로 쓰인 현재분사 sleeping이 명사 baby의 동작 표현

I visited the **destroyed** city soon after the war. 나는 전쟁이 끝난 후에 파괴된 도시를 방문했다.

(→ The city is destroyed) ▶ 수동태로 쓰인 과거분사 destroyed가 명사 city의 동작 표현

03 분사가 수식 어구를 동반하여 길어지는 경우 **반드시 명사 뒤에서 명사의 동작을 표현**한다. 마찬가지로 현재분사는 '~하는, 하고 있는'의 뜻이고, 과거분사는 '~해진, ~된, ~되어진'의 뜻이다.

People **living** in the city do not know rural pleasure. 도시에 사는 사람들은 시골의 즐거움을 모른다.
(→ People are living in the city) ▶ 진행형으로 바꾼 현재분사 living도 명사의 동작 표현

Look at the leaves **fallen** on the ground. 땅에 떨어진 낙엽들을 봐.
(→ The leaves have fallen on the ground) ▶ 현재완료로 쓰인 과거분사 fallen도 완료의 의미로 명사의 동작 표현

※ 흔히 분사 후치수식일 때 「관계대명사+be」가 생략되었다고 하고 이를 시험에 출제하기도 하는데, 이는 현대영어에서 거의 쓰지 않는 문법이다. People (who are) living in the city ~에서 People are living ~이나 People living in the city나 모두 전달하는 시제와 정보가 같기 때문에 굳이 'who are'를 쓸 필요가 없어 간결하게 표현하게 되었다.

서술형 기초다지기

Challenge 1 다음 괄호 안의 표현 중 어법상 알맞은 것을 고르세요.

01. The (rising / risen) flood waters soon covered the street.

02. Her (smiling / smiled) face made everyone happy.

03. The woman (sitting / sat) over there is a famous singer.

04. Everyone admires the pictures (painting / painted) by him.

05. This coffee cup (making / made) in England is expensive.

06. The garden was covered with (falling / fallen) leaves.

07. The students (talking / talked) loudly in the back seats have no etiquette.

Challenge 2 다음 문장을 분사를 활용하여 다시 쓰세요.

보기	The cars are very nice. They are made in Korea.
	→ *The cars made in Korea are very nice.*

01. Do you know the girl? She is sitting next to Susan.

→ _____

02. The man is sleeping under the tree. He is my father.

→ _____

03. The girl was injured in the accident. She was taken to the hospital.

→ _____

04. The murderer died in jail. He was arrested by the police officer last week.

→ _____

보어 자리에서 명사의 동작을 설명하는 분사

Julia was watering the flowers in the garden.
Julia는 정원에서 꽃에 물을 주고 있었다.
I saw her watering the flowers in the garden.
나는 정원에서 그녀가 꽃에 물을 주고 있는 것을 봤다.

01 분사는 주격 보어 자리에서 주어의 동작을 표현할 수 있다. **주어가 동작을 하는 경우에는 현재분사**(~하고 있는, ~한 채로)를 쓰고, **동작을 당하는 경우에는 과거분사**(~진, ~된 채로)를 쓴다.

The dog kept **barking** all night. 그 개가 밤새 짖고 있었다. ▶ the dog가 보어 barking의 주체
=The dog was **barking** all night.

The children came **running** toward me. 아이들이 내게로 뛰면서 왔다. ▶ the children이 보어 running의 주체
=The children were **running** toward me.

The restaurant remained **closed** for two weeks. 그 레스토랑은 2주 동안 계속 닫혀 있었다.
=The restaurant was **closed** for two weeks.

02 주로 지각동사나 사역동사가 쓰인 5형식 문장에서 **목적어가 동작을 하는 경우에는 현재분사**를 쓰고, **목적어가 동작을 당하는 경우에는 과거분사**를 쓴다.

She kept me **waiting** for a long time. 그녀는 나를 오랫동안 기다리게 했다.
I heard my name **called**. 나는 내 이름이 불리는 것을 들었다.
We heard the doorbell **ringing**. 우리는 초인종이 울리는 소리를 들었다.
I saw a thief **running** down the street. 나는 도둑이 거리를 달려오는 것을 보았다.
I saw a thief **beaten** by some children. 나는 도둑이 어떤 아이들에게 맞는 것을 보았다.
Don't leave the baby **crying**. 아이를 울게 내버려 두지 마라.
I had the roof **repaired** yesterday. 나는 어제 지붕을 고쳤다.
The teacher made the classroom **cleaned** by us. 선생님은 우리에게 교실을 청소하게 했다.

서술형 기초다지기

Challenge 1

다음 괄호 안의 동사를 알맞은 분사형으로 고치고 주격 보어, 목적격 보어, 명사 수식 중 어디에 해당하는지 쓰세요.

보기	I saw her *watering* the flowers in the garden. (water)	→ 목적격 보어

01. She felt her heart _____ wildly. (beat) → _____

02. He came into the room _____ loudly. (cry) → _____

03. Do you know the woman _____ at the bus stop? (stand) → _____

04. We kept _____ for three hours in the train. (stand) → _____

05. I saw the students _____ their classroom after school. (clean) → _____

06. A: What's wrong with you? You look pale.

    B: I saw a boy _____ down by a car. (knock) → _____

07. English is an language _____ all over the world. (speak) → _____

Challenge 2

다음 괄호 안의 단어를 이용하여 문장을 완성하세요.

01. 나는 큰 개 한 마리가 문 앞에 누워 있는 것을 보았다. (in front of, lie, the door)

    → I saw a big dog _____.

02. 나는 그들에게 내 차를 수리하게 할 거다. (repair, them, by)

    → I'll have my car _____.

03. 그녀는 저 주차장에서 차를 도난당했다. (had, steal, her car)

    → She _____ in that parking lot.

04. 나는 교실에서 내 이름이 불리는 것을 들었다. (in the classroom, call)

    → I heard my name _____.

1-3 감정을 나타내는 분사 / 현재분사와 동명사의 구별

I'm not **satisfied** with my job.
나는 내 일에 만족하지 못한다.
My job is **boring**.
내 일은 지루하다.

01 감정 관련 동사가 명사를 수식하거나 설명할 때, 그 명사가 다른 이의 **감정을 일으키는 주체인 경우**에는 **현재분사**를 쓰고 **감정을 느끼거나 받는 대상인 경우**에는 과거분사를 쓴다.

exciting	– excited	surprising	– surprised
흥분시키는	흥분된	깜짝 놀랄만한	깜짝 놀란
amazing	– amazed	confusing	– confused
놀라운(주로 칭찬)	놀란, 감탄한	혼란스럽게 하는	혼동된, 혼란스러운
interesting	– interested	satisfying	– satisfied
흥미로운, 재미있는	관심이/흥미가 있는	만족스럽게 하는	만족스러운
embarrassing	– embarrassed	disgusting	– disgusted
난처하게 하는	난처한	구역질 나는	정떨어진, 넌더리 난

Kelly is **bored** because her job is **boring**. Kelly는 그녀의 일이 지루했기 때문에 따분했다.
We were **disappointed** in the movie. 우리는 그 영화에 실망했다.
The movie was **disappointing**. 그 영화는 실망스러웠다.

※ 현재분사와 과거분사는 주어가 어떤 감정을 일으키는 주체인지 아니면 그 감정을 느끼는 대상이 되는 것인지에 따라 결정되는 것이지, 주어가 사람이냐 사물이냐에 따라 결정되는 것은 아니다.

02 현재분사와 동명사는 둘 다 V-ing형태이기 때문에 명사를 앞에서 꾸며 줄 경우 구별하기 힘들 수 있지만 **현재분사의 수식을 받는 명사는 생물체이면서 언제나 행동 가능한 동작의 주체**가 된다.

현재분사	동명사
명사의 '동작, 행동'을 표현(~하고 있는, ~하게 하는)	명사의 '용도나 목적'을 표현(~하기 위한 것)
a **dancing** girl 춤추고 있는	**dancing** shoes 무용화
(= a girl who is dancing)	(= shoes for dancing)
	(≠ shoes which is dancing)
a **sleeping** puppy 잠자는	a **sleeping** bag 침낭
(= a puppy which is sleeping)	(= a bag for sleeping)
	(≠ a bag which is sleeping)

서술형 기초다지기

Challenge 1 다음 괄호 안의 분사 중 알맞은 것을 고르세요.

01. Su-jin thinks English is very (interesting / interested).

02. Su-jin is very (interesting / interested) in English.

03. Everybody was (surprising / surprised) that he passed the exam.

04. It was quite (surprising / surprised) that he passed the exam.

05. The news was (shocking / shocked).

06. We were (shocking / shocked) when we heard the news.

Challenge 2 〈보기〉와 같이 분사를 이용하여 빈칸을 완성하세요.

보기	The movie disappointed us.	→ The movie was *disappointing*.
		→ We were *disappointed* in the movie.

01. The concert excited all the audience.

   → The concert was _____ to all the audience.

   → All the audience was _____ about the concert.

02. The strange noise frightened the children.

   → The strange noise was _____.

   → The children were _____ by the strange noise.

Challenge 3 다음 밑줄 친 부분이 분사이면 **분**, 동명사이면 **동**으로 쓰세요.

01. Kevin is waiting for you in the <u>waiting</u> room.　　→ _____

02. Susan's plan is <u>making</u> chocolate cake for her boyfriend.　→ _____

03. The man <u>smoking</u> a cigarette over there is a famous actor.　→ _____

04. We sat on the beach and watched the <u>setting</u> sun.　→ _____

2-1 분사구문 만들기

Being sick, she was absent from school.
= **Because** she **was** sick, she was absent from school.
아팠기 때문에 그녀는 학교에 결석했다.

---

01 분사구문은 「접속사＋주어＋동사」로 되어 있는 부사절을 분사가 이끄는 부사구로 간략하게 만든 구문이다. 부정은 분사 앞에 not, never를 쓴다.

When she saw me, she got so embarrassed. 그녀는 나를 보자 매우 난처해했다.

→ **she** saw me, she got so embarrassed. ▶ 접속사 생략

→ **saw** me, she got so embarrassed. ▶ 주어가 같으면 생략

→ **Seeing** me, she got so embarrassed. ▶ saw → seeing으로, 주절은 그대로 씀

02 분사구문은 문맥에 따라 시간, 원인, 이유, 조건, 양보, 동시(연속) 동작의 의미를 나타낸다.

① 시간을 나타내는 접속사(when, after, while, before)

When he got to the bus stop, he found the bus had left.

→ **Getting** to the bus stop, he found the bus had left. 버스 정류장에 도착한 그는 버스가 떠난 것을 알았다.

② 원인, 이유를 나타내는 접속사(because, as, since)

Because she didn't arrive on time, she couldn't take the exam.

→ **Not arriving** on time, she couldn't take the exam.
정시에 도착하지 못했기 때문에, 그녀는 시험을 보지 못했다.

③ 조건을 나타내는 접속사(if)

If you turn to the left, you will find the bookstore.

→ **Turning** to the left, you will find the bookstore. 왼쪽으로 돌면 서점을 찾을 것이다.

④ 양보를 나타내는 접속사(though, although)

Though he lives next door, he doesn't even say hello to us.

→ **Living** next door, he doesn't even say hello to us.
옆집에 살고 있는데도 그는 우리한테 인사조차 하지 않는다.

⑤ 동시 동작 (as), 연속 동작 (and): '~하면서, ~하고 나서'

As she looked at me, she stood by the window.

→ **Looking** at me, she stood by the window. 나를 쳐다보면서 그녀는 창문에 옆에 서 있다.

She sat on the chair, **and** then she read a magazine.

→ She sat on the chair, **reading** a magazine. 그녀는 의자에 앉고 나서 잡지를 읽었다.

서술형 기초다지기

Challenge 1   다음 밑줄 친 부사절을 분사구문으로 바꿔 쓰세요.

> 보기
> *If you turn around*, you will see a service station.
> → *Turning around*, you will see a service station.

01. <u>While I walked in the park</u>, I happened to meet my old friend.

→ _____, I happened to meet my old friend.

02. <u>Although I admit what he says</u>, I still think that he is in the wrong.

→ _____, I still think that he is in the wrong.

03. <u>If you turn to the right at the corner</u>, you will see the lake.

→ _____, you will see the lake.

04. I ate hamburgers for lunch <u>while I was driving to my office</u>.

→ I ate hamburgers for lunch, _____.

Challenge 2   다음 밑줄 친 분사구문을 부사절로 바꿔 쓰세요.

> 보기
> Eating too much, he had a stomachache.
> → *Because(=As) he ate too much*, he had a stomachache.

01. <u>Turning to the left</u>, you will find the post office on the right.

→ _____, you will find the post office on the right.

02. <u>Being poor</u>, she could not afford to buy the car.

→ _____, she could not afford to buy the car.

03. <u>Admitting what you say</u>, I don't like the way you say it.

→ _____, I don't like the way you say it.

04. <u>Picking up the phone</u>, she dialed his number.

→ _____, she dialed his number.

2-2 with＋명사＋분사 / 분사구문의 시제

She stood there with her eyes **closed.**
그녀는 눈을 감은 채로 거기에 서 있었다.

Having graduated from college, she became
a teacher. 대학을 졸업한 후에 그녀는 선생님이 되었다.

01 「with＋명사＋분사」는 '어떤 동작이 벌어지는 상태를 가지고(with) 있다'라는 뜻이다. 이때, 현재분사와 과거 분사를 결정하는 것은 바로 '명사'의 행동 여부에 달려 있다. '~을 ~한 채로'의 뜻으로, **명사가 행위를 하는 주체이면 현재분사를 쓰고 행동을 받는 대상이면 과거분사를 쓴다.**

My mom sat on the sofa **with** her legs **crossed.** 엄마는 다리를 꼰 채로 소파에 앉아 있었다.

She must be crazy to drive **with** her eyes **closed.** 눈을 감은 채로 운전을 하다니 그녀는 미친 것이 틀림없다.

Lisa smiled **with** tears **running** down her cheeks. Lisa는 두 뺨에 눈물을 흘리는 채로 웃고 있었다.

02 분사구문의 시제는 대개 주절의 동사와 같은 시제를 나타낸다. 하지만 주절보다 앞서 행해진 행위를 표현하 고자 할 때는 「having＋p.p.」 형태로 더 이전의 과거임을 표시한다.

Coming with her boyfriend, she **didn't tell** anybody. ▶ coming과 didn't tell은 같은 시제(과거)

→ Although she **came** with her boyfriend, she **didn't tell** anybody.
남자친구와 함께 왔는데도 그녀는 아무에게도 말하지 않았다.

Having finished my homework, I **watched** TV. ▶ having finished가 watched보다 더 과거

→ After I **had finished** my homework, I **watched** TV. 숙제를 끝마치고 TV를 시청했다.

Not having seen my uncle for a long time, I **didn't recognize** him.
삼촌을 오랫동안 보지 못한 나는 그를 알아보지 못했다. ▶ having seen이 didn't recognize보다 더 과거

Having eaten his breakfast, he **went** out to the beach. 아침을 먹고 나서 그는 해변으로 나갔다.

▶ having eaten이 went보다 더 과거

서술형 기초다지기

Challenge 1 다음을 〈보기〉와 같이 「with+명사+분사」를 이용한 문장으로 고쳐 쓰세요.

> **보기** Kelly was sitting on the chair and she was crossing her legs.
> → Kelly was sitting on the chair *with her legs crossed*.

01. I was watching TV and tears were flowing.

    → I was watching TV _____ .

02. Susan worked all afternoon and the door was locked.

    → Susan worked all afternoon _____ .

03. It was a very busy day and the cell phone was ringing all the time.

    → It was a very busy day _____ .

Challenge 2 다음 밑줄 친 부분을 분사구문으로 바꾸세요.

01. After we had finished the project, we had a nice party.

    → _____ , we had a nice party.

02. Since I had a slight cold, I went to bed early.

    → _____ , I went to bed early.

03. As he lived in Spain when he was in high school, he speaks Spanish fluently.

    → _____ when he was in high school, he speaks Spanish fluently.

04. When she heard the news, she turned pale.

    → _____ , she turned pale.

05. As I had met him before, I recognized him at once.

    → _____ , I recognized him at once.

2-3 being과 having been의 생략 / 의미상 주어

Surprised at his behavior, she could not say a word. 그의 행동에 놀란 그녀는 한 마디도 하지 않았다.

The weather **being** fine, I decided to go shopping. 날씨가 좋아서 나는 쇼핑하러 가기로 했다.

---

01 수동태에서 be동사를 Being이나 Having been으로 고칠 때 이 둘을 생략하여 **과거분사로 시작하는 분사구문**을 만들 수 있다.

As this book is written in easy English, it is good for young students.
X   X   ↓

→ (Being) **Written** in easy English, this book is good for young students.
쉬운 영어로 쓰인 이 책은 어린 학생들에게 좋다.
▶ As ~ 부사절의 is(현재)와 주절의 is(현재)의 시제가 같으므로 V-ing형인 Being으로 고치거나 생략

As he was raised in Canada, he speaks English fluently.
X X ↓

→ (Having been) **Raised** in Canada, he speaks English fluently.
캐나다에서 자란 그는 영어를 유창하게 한다.
▶ As ~ 부사절의 was(과거)가 주절의 speaks(현재) 보다 시제가 앞서므로 Having+p.p의 형태로 고치거나 생략

02 주어가 같을 때는 생략하지만, **주어가 서로 다를 경우 각각의 주어를 써주는 것을 독립분사구문**이라고 한다. 분사 바로 앞에 주어를 쓴다.

When the class was over, the students left quickly. ▶ when ~ 부사절의 주어(the class)와 주절의 주어(the
X   ↓   ↓   students)가 서로 다름

The class **being** over, the students left quickly. 수업이 끝났을 때, 학생들은 재빨리 떠나 버렸다.

03 주어가 서로 다르다 하더라도 일반인일 경우에는 주어를 생략하고 하나의 숙어처럼 사용하는데 이를 비인칭 독립분사구문이라고 한다.

strictly speaking 엄밀히 말하면	judging from ~ ~로 판단하건대	frankly speaking 솔직히 말하면
generally speaking 일반적으로 말해	talking/speaking of ~ ~에 대해 말하자면	considering (that) ~ ~을 감안하면, 고려하면
admitting that ~ ~은 인정하지만	granted that ~ ~이 사실이라 해도	roughly speaking 대체로/대강 말하면

Generally speaking, women live longer than men. 일반적으로 말해서 여자가 남자보다 더 오래 산다.

서술형 기초다지기

Challenge 1 다음 문장과 뜻이 같도록 빈칸에 알맞은 말을 쓰세요.

01. As I was excited about the news, I shouted with joy.

→ _____ _____ about the news, I shouted with joy.

→ _____ about the news, I shouted with joy.

02. As he was educated in England, he has a British English accent.

→ _____ _____ _____ in England, he has a British English accent.

→ _____ in England, he has a British English accent.

Challenge 2 다음 밑줄 친 부사절을 분사구문으로 고쳐 쓰세요.

보기	When the sun had set, we started for home. → *The sun having set*, we started for home.

01. As it was fine, they went hiking.

→ _____, they went hiking.

02. As the train was crowded because of the summer vacation, we had to keep standing all the way to Osaka.

→ _____ because of the summer vacation, we had to keep standing all the way to Osaka.

Challenge 3 다음 괄호 안의 표현 중에서 알맞은 것을 고르세요.

01. (Writing / Written) in simple English, this book is good for beginners.

02. (Locating / Located) on the side of a mountain, my house commands a fine view of the Seto Inland Sea.

03. (Graduating / Graduated) from college, she could make her dream come true.

01 출제 100% - 행동의 주체인 명사를 찾아라!

 출제자의 눈 명사 앞뒤에서 명사의 동작을 설명하는 분사의 형태와 「with+명사+분사」 구문에서 분사의 형태를 결정짓는 것은 명사이다. 행위의 주체인 명사를 찾아 행동 가능한 명사일 때는 현재분사를, 행위를 당하는 대상일 경우 과거분사를 쓴다. 이 둘을 고르는 문제가 집중적으로 출제된다.

Ex 1.

A black cat _____ your path is a sign of bad luck to come.
(a) crossed   (b) crossing   (c) crosses   (d) to cross

Ex 2.

He worked with his face _____.
(a) painting   (b) paint   (c) to paint   (d) painted

02 출제 100% - 감정을 주느냐 받느냐 그것이 문제로다!

 출제자의 눈 사람이 충격, 놀람, 감동 등을 받는 경우 과거분사를 쓰고 남에게 감정을 주는 주체가 되는 경우에는 현재분사를 쓴다. 예를 들어, 영화를 보고 그 영화에 의해 사람이 감동을 받을 때 moved를 쓸 것인지 moving을 쓸 것인지 자주 물어본다. 또한 사람이 남에게 감정을 주는 주체가 되기도 하는데 이때는 반드시 현재분사를 써야 한다. 비중 있게 출제되지는 않지만 not의 위치를 묻는 문제도 종종 출제된다. 무엇이 아니라고 부정하는 표현인 not의 위치는 당연히 동작보다 먼저 나와야 뜻을 이해하는 데 혼동이 없다. 따라서 분사구문 바로 앞에 'not'을 쓴다.

Ex 3.

Bob and I went to a movie and it was really _____.
(a) amazed   (b) amazing   (c) to amaze   (d) has amazed

Ex 4.

빈칸에 들어갈 알맞은 말을 쓰시오.
As I didn't know what to do, I asked for his advice.
= _____ knowing what to do, I asked for his advice.

03 출제 100% - 절을 분사구문으로 바꾸는 주관식 문제는 무조건 나온다.

 출제자의 눈 부사절을 분사구문으로 또는 분사구문을 다시 알맞은 접속사와 함께 부사절로 고쳐 쓸 줄 아는지를 묻는 문제가 많이 출제된다. 문장 맨 앞에 현재분사와 과거분사를 구별해서 쓸 줄 아는지를 묻는데 이는 분사구문에 있는 주어의 행동 유무에 따라 행동이 가능하면 현재분사를, 불가능하면 과거분사를 써야 한다.

Ex 5.

_____ from the gallery, the painting by Rubens still hasn't been found.

(a) Stealing   (b) To steal   (c) Stolen   (d) Stealth

Ex 6.

다음 문장을 분사구문으로 바꾸어 다시 쓰시오.

As there was nobody around, she hurried home.

= _____

04 출제 100% - 5형식 문장에서 목적어가 현재분사와 과거분사를 결정한다.

 출제자의 눈 분사가 목적격 보어로 사용될 때, 목적어의 행동 유무에 따라 현재분사와 과거분사가 결정된다. 목적어가 행동의 주체인 경우 현재분사를, 행동의 대상(사물)이 되는 경우 과거분사를 쓴다. 분사구문을 부사절로 바꿀 때 알맞은 접속사를 묻는 문제나, 동명사와 현재분사를 구별하는 문제를 출제하기도 한다. 또한 전체 문맥을 파악하여 주절의 시제보다 더 과거인 경우 완료 분사구문(having+p.p.)을 써야 하는데, 이 문제는 출제빈도는 낮지만 가끔 난이도 있는 문제로 출제될 수 있다.

Ex 7.

I had my picture _____ in the photo studio.

(a) taking   (b) takes   (c) having taken   (d) taken

Ex 8.

빈칸에 들어갈 알맞은 접속사를 고르시오.

Wearing a warm coat, I still felt cold.

= _____ I was wearing a warm coat, I still felt cold.

(a) As   (b) After   (c) Though   (d) When

1. 다음 중 어법상 어색한 부분을 바르게 고치시오.

> The man ❶ sat ❷ by the window,
> ❸ listen to ❹ music ❺ for an hour.

_____ → _____

2. 다음 밑줄 친 부분의 쓰임이 나머지 넷과 다른 것은?

❶ I got to sleep late waiting for my dad to get home.
❷ Smiling brightly, he welcomed her.
❸ Karen was in the kitchen, making coffee.
❹ Jason answered the phone, watching TV.
❺ She is busy cooking in the kitchen.

3. 다음 빈칸에 들어갈 말로 알맞은 것은?

> Opening the door, I found my mom cooking.
> = _____ I opened the door, I found my mom cooking.

❶ If　　　　❷ While　　　　❸ Though
❹ Since　　　❺ When

4. 다음 괄호 안의 말을 알맞은 형태로 고치시오.

> She was reading a newspaper with her legs _____. (cross)

5. 다음 빈칸에 알맞은 것은?

> 그 택시를 운전하고 있는 사람이 나의 삼촌이다.
> → The man _____ is my uncle.

❶ drive the taxi　　　❷ driving the taxi
❸ driven the taxi　　　❹ the taxi driving
❺ the taxi driven

6. 다음 밑줄 친 부분을 바꿔 쓸 때 알맞은 것은?

> After she bowed deeply to the king, she put the brick in front of him.

❶ Bowed deeply to the king
❷ Bowing deeply to the king
❸ Have bowed deeply to the king
❹ Being bowed deeply to the king
❺ She bowed deeply to the king

7. 다음 빈칸에 들어갈 알맞은 말을 고르시오.

> Before leaving the KTX, make sure that you haven't left anything behind.
> → Before _____ the KTX, make sure that you haven't left anything behind.

❶ we leave　　　　❷ you leave
❸ it leaves　　　　❹ you are leaving
❺ they leave

8. 다음 빈칸에 들어갈 말이 알맞게 짝지어진 것은?

> · He left Seoul in the morning, _____ Paris at night.
> · My younger sister insisted on having her new dress _____ by her favorite designer.

❶ reaching − making　　❷ reached − make
❸ reaching − made　　　❹ reached − made
❺ reached − making

9. 분사구문을 이용하여 다음 문장을 다시 쓰시오.

> As she didn't sleep for two days, she is very tired now.
> → _____
> _____

오답 노트 만들기

★틀린 문제 : _____   ★다시 공부한 날 : _____

(1) 문제를 왜? 틀렸는지 곰곰이 생각하고 그 이유를 적어본다.

(2) 핵심 개념을 적는다.

(3) 자신이 몰랐던 단어와 숙어 표현이 있으면 정리한다.

(4) 해설집에서 필요한 부분을 골라 풀이 해법을 정리한다.

★틀린 문제 : _____   ★다시 공부한 날 : _____

(1) 문제를 왜? 틀렸는지 곰곰이 생각하고 그 이유를 적어본다.

(2) 핵심 개념을 적는다.

(3) 자신이 몰랐던 단어와 숙어 표현이 있으면 정리한다.

(4) 해설집에서 필요한 부분을 골라 풀이 해법을 정리한다.

★틀린 문제 : _____   ★다시 공부한 날 : _____

(1) 문제를 왜? 틀렸는지 곰곰이 생각하고 그 이유를 적어본다.

(2) 핵심 개념을 적는다.

(3) 자신이 몰랐던 단어와 숙어 표현이 있으면 정리한다.

(4) 해설집에서 필요한 부분을 골라 풀이 해법을 정리한다.

★틀린 문제 : _____   ★다시 공부한 날 : _____

(1) 문제를 왜? 틀렸는지 곰곰이 생각하고 그 이유를 적어본다.

(2) 핵심 개념을 적는다.

(3) 자신이 몰랐던 단어와 숙어 표현이 있으면 정리한다.

(4) 해설집에서 필요한 부분을 골라 풀이 해법을 정리한다.

1. **다음 우리말에 해당하는 알맞은 말을 고르시오.**

> A: 일반적으로 말해서, it's rainy in July in Korea.
> B: I think you're right.

❶ Frankly speaking   ❷ Strictly speaking
❸ Generally speaking   ❹ Roughly speaking
❺ Judging from

오답노트

2. **다음 빈칸에 들어갈 알맞은 단어를 쓰시오.**

> My mom bought me a watch which was made in Italy.
> =My mom bought me a watch _____ in Italy.

오답노트

3. **다음 빈칸에 들어갈 알맞은 말은?**

> After she had finished her homework, she went out for dinner.
> = _____ her homework, she went out for dinner.

❶ Finished   ❷ Finishing
❸ Being finished   ❹ Having finished
❺ After finished

오답노트

[4-5] 두 문장의 뜻이 같도록 빈칸을 완성하시오.

4. If you turn to the right, you can find the bookstore.
= _____ to the right, you can find the bookstore.

5. As I don't have any money, I can't buy that house.
= _____ _____ any money, I can't buy that house.

오답노트

[6-7] 다음 중 어법상 어색한 것을 고르시오.

6. ❶ Don't step on the broken glass.
❷ I saw the giraffee eating leaves.
❸ She heard the man talking with her husband.
❹ The girl drinking water is my sister.
❺ The puppy slept in the house is very cute.

7. ❶ Who is that girl playing soccer over there?
❷ I'll be pleased if she comes.
❸ I was disappointing in the movie. I had expected it to be better.
❹ Everybody was surprised that he passed the exam.
❺ The goods made by the company are famous for their quality.

오답노트

[8-9] 다음 밑줄 친 부분이 시간이나 이유의 부사절이 되도록 빈칸에 알맞은 말을 쓰시오.

8. Arriving at the restaurant, we found it closed.

   → _____ _____ _____ at the restaurant, we found it closed.

9. Not having any money, I couldn't buy that present.

   → _____ _____ _____ _____ any money, I couldn't buy that present.

오답노트

10. 다음 밑줄 친 (a)와 (b)를 순서대로 바르게 고친 것은?

> (a) Eat his breakfast, he went out to the beach. It was very pleasant to walk along the seashore early in the morning. He stood still, (b) watch fishing boats sailing out of sight.

❶ Eaten – watching
❷ Having eaten – watching
❸ Having eaten – having watched
❹ Eaten – watched
❺ Eating – having watched

오답노트

11. 다음 중 밑줄 친 부분의 표현이 잘못된 것은?

❶ These noodles were made into instant ramen in 1958 by a man called Momofuku Ando.
❷ I can't read books written in Chinese.
❸ Girls often have names taking from small and beautiful things.
❹ More saliva, in turn, helps them feel less bored with eating the same food again and again.
❺ Look at the man singing in the rain.

오답노트

12. 다음 문장의 밑줄 친 부분과 쓰임이 다른 것은?

> Admitting what you are capable of is important.

❶ Admitting what you say, I can't believe it.
❷ Admitting what you are doing is the first step.
❸ The best way to solve this problem is using a computer.
❹ Working as a reporter was a wonderful experience.
❺ When we finish drinking coffee, we'll go home.

오답노트

13. 빈칸에 들어갈 말이 바르게 짝지어진 것은?

> · The concert was _____.
> · I was _____ when I watched the concert.

❶ excite − excited   ❷ exciting − excite
❸ exciting − excited   ❹ excited − exciting
❺ to excite − exciting

오답노트

14. 밑줄 친 부분을 문맥에 맞게 한 단어로 고쳐 쓰시오.

> Our plane leaves at noon, and arrives in Okinawa at 1:30.

→ _____

오답노트

[15-17] 다음 중 알맞은 접속사를 골라 분사구문을 부사절로 바꿔 쓰시오.

> if   because   though   when

15. Being poor, he didn't go to college.

→ _____,
he didn't go to college.

16. Taking this bus, you will get to the museum.

→ _____,
you will get to the museum.

17. Walking along the street, I met an old friend of mine.

→ _____,
I met an old friend of mine.

오답노트

18. 다음 중 밑줄 친 부분의 쓰임이 <u>다른</u> 하나는?

❶ Don't wake the <u>sleeping</u> alligator.
❷ My mom is <u>talking</u> on the phone.
❸ They have already finished <u>eating</u>.
❹ I watched the players <u>warming</u> up.
❺ She sat in the chair all day <u>thinking</u> of past events.

오답노트

[19-20] 괄호 안의 단어를 알맞은 분사형으로 고쳐 쓰시오.

19.

> The soccer team's score was _____ (disappoint). We were _____ (disappoint) with their score.

20.

> The ending of the movie is _____ (shock). I was _____ (shock) by the ending of the movie.

오답노트

21. 다음 두 문장을 한 문장으로 만들 때 빈칸에 알맞을 말을 쓰시오.

· I can't read the book.
· It was written in Japanese.

→ I _____ _____ _____

_____ _____ in Japanese.

오답노트

[22-24] 다음 빈칸에 알맞은 말을 쓰시오.

22. 솔직히 말해서 그의 강의는 지루했다.

→ _____, his lecture was boring.

23. 일반적으로 말해서 한국 사람들은 춤추고 노래하는 것을 좋아한다.

→ _____, Koreans love dancing and singing.

24. 외모로 판단하건대 그는 도둑처럼 보인다.

→ _____ his appearance, he looks like a thief.

오답노트

25. 다음 두 문장의 의미가 같지 <u>않은</u> 것은?

❶ Snoopy is the dog which is barking at the man.
 =Snoopy is the dog barking at the man.
❷ The girl who is dancing on the stage is Sunny.
 =The girl dancing on the stage is Sunny.
❸ I have a friend who is suffering from diabetes.

=I have a friend suffering from diabetes.
❹ The woman who is sitting next to Mina is a ghost.
 =The woman sitting next to Mina is a ghost.
❺ The life guard cured the old lady who was dying from heart disease.
 =The life guard cured the old lady dead from heart disease.

오답노트

26. 다음 밑줄 친 부분과 의미가 같은 것은?

A spaceship hit the earth, <u>killing a lot of people.</u>

❶ but it killed   ❷ if it kills
❸ thought it was killing ❹ and it killed
❺ while it is killing

오답노트

27. 다음 밑줄 친 부분을 가장 알맞게 고친 것은?

After I finished the work, I went to the laundry to <u>dry-clean my suits.</u>

❶ to be dry-cleaned my suits
❷ to have my suits to dry-cleaned
❸ to have dry-clean my suits
❹ to have my suits dry-cleaned
❺ to have my suits dry-cleaning

오답노트

A. 〈보기〉와 같이 분사를 이용하여 한 문장으로 고치시오.

보 기	This is a house. + It was built one hundred years ago. → This is a house *built one hundred years ago.*

1. The book is my father's. It is written in English.

→ The book _____.

2. I'm going to take the train. It leaves in the early morning.

→ I'm going to take the train _____.

3. Look at those leaves. They have fallen under the tree.

→ Look at those leaves _____.

B. 다음 문장을 부사절로 바꿀 때 빈칸에 알맞은 말을 써 넣으시오.

1. While bathing in the river, he was drowned.

→ _____ in the river, he was drowned.

2. Though knowing the difficulty, they undertook the work.

→ _____ the difficulty, they undertook the work.

3. If hungry, you may eat this hamburger.

→ _____, you may eat this hamburger.

4. Although born in New York, Kevin was brought up in Seoul.

→ _____ in New York, he was brought up in Seoul.

C. 다음 두 문장의 뜻이 같도록 빈칸을 완성하시오.

1. Having no money, I could not buy the book.

= _____, I couldn't buy the book.

2. If you turn to the right, you will find the station.

= _____, you will find the station.

3. I received a letter which was written in French.

= I received a letter _____.

4. The girls who are dancing in the hall look very pretty.

= The girls _____ look very pretty.

D. 다음 우리말에 맞게 괄호 안의 말을 이용하여 빈칸을 완성하시오.

1. 일반적으로 말하면 우리는 신선한 공기가 필요하다.

→ _____ _____, we need fresh air. (generally)

2. 밤이 오자, 우리는 집을 향해 떠났다.

→ _____ _____ _____, we left for home. (come, the night)

3. 나는 그녀를 3년 동안 만나지 못했으므로 그녀의 주소를 알지 못한다. (meet)

→ _____ _____ _____ her for three years, I don't know her address.

4. 그의 억양으로 판단하건대, 그는 호주 출신일지도 모른다. (judge)

→ _____ _____ his accent, he may be from Australia.

5. 그녀는 팔짱을 낀 채 그 흥미로운 그림을 보고 있었다. (fold, her, arms)

→ She looked at the interesting painting _____ _____ _____ _____.

실전 서술형 평가문제

출제의도 분사구문 만들기
평가내용 분사구문을 이용한 상황 묘사

A. 다음 사진과 일치하도록 분사구문을 이용하여 문장을 완성하시오.　　　　　[서술형 유형 : 6점 / 난이도 : 중하]

보기

(the news / hear)

Hearing the news, she got surprised.

1.

(very tired / feel)

_____, he threw himself on the bed.

2.

(to music / listen)

_____, I did my homework.

3.

(breakfast / not / eat)

_____, I was very hungry.

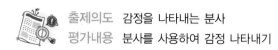

출제의도 감정을 나타내는 분사

평가내용 분사를 사용하여 감정 나타내기

B. 괄호 안의 말을 이용하여 현재분사와 과거분사 문장으로 완성하시오. [서술형 유형 : 10점 / 난이도 : 하]

> **보기**
> The strange noise frightened the children. (frighten)
> → The strange noise *was frightening*.
> → The children *were frightened* by the strange noise.

1. The movie wasn't as good as we had expected. (disappoint)

→ The movie was _____ .

→ We were _____ in the film.

2. Brian's impolite behavior embarrassed his mother. (embarrass)

→ Brian's impolite behavior was _____ .

→ Brian's impolite behavior made his mother _____ .

3. It's been raining all day. I hate this weather. (depress)

→ This weather is _____ .

→ This weather makes me _____ .

4. The children went to the zoo yesterday. They had a great time. (fascinate)

→ The children were _____ by the animals in the zoo.

→ The animals were _____ the children.

5. Kevin is going to Singapore next week. He has never been there before. (excite)

→ It will be an _____ experience for him.

→ Going to new places is always _____ .

→ He is really _____ about going to new places.

출제의도 with + 명사 + 분사

평가내용 현재분사와 과거분사를 구별하여 주어진 상황 묘사하기

C. 〈보기〉와 같이 주어진 문장과 의미가 같도록 영작하시오.

[서술형 유형 : 8점 / 난이도 : 중]

보 기	My brother kept sleeping while the alarm clock was ringing. → *My brother kept sleeping with the alarm clock ringing.*

1.

Kelly always listens to music and she closes her eyes.

→ _____

_____

2.

Susan sobbed loudly as tears were running down her cheeks.

→ _____

_____

3.

Nancy stood by the window, and her arms were folded.

→ _____

_____

4.

Tom was watching TV while his wife was eating popcorn.

→ _____

_____

서술형 평가문제	채 점 기 준	배 점	나의 점수
A	표현이 올바르고 문법, 철자가 모두 정확한 경우	2점 × 3문항 = 6점	
B		2점 × 5문항 = 10점	
C		2점 × 4문항 = 8점	
공통	문법, 철자가 1개씩 틀린 경우	각 문항당 1점씩 감점	
	내용과 전혀 일치하지 않거나 답을 기재하지 못한 경우	0점	

Chapter 7

명사와 관사
(Nouns and Articles)

1-1 셀 수 있는 명사 (Countable Nouns)

Steve works on **a farm**. He has **a horse** and **a pig**.
He takes care of the **cows**, **chickens** and **sheep**.
Steve는 농장에서 일을 한다. 그는 말과 돼지 한 마리씩을 가지고 있다.
그는 소, 닭, 그리고 양들을 돌본다.

01 **보통명사**: **'하나, 둘, 셋'과 같이 낱개로 셀 수 있다.** a나 an을 붙여 단수형을 만들고 -s나 -es를 붙여 복수형을 만든다. 또한, many, a few와 같은 셀 수 있는 수량 형용사(한정사)와 함께 쓸 수 있다.

① 보통명사의 형태

a camera   **an** animal   window**s**   box**es**   dish**es**

countr**ies**   boy**s**   leave**s**   live**s**   book**s**

A girl is surfing the Internet. 한 소녀가 인터넷 검색을 하고 있다.

A few students passed the graduation exam. 몇 명의 학생들이 졸업 시험을 통과했다.

It wasn't your fault. It was **an accident**. 그것은 네 잘못이 아니야. 그것은 사고였어.

② 단수와 복수의 형태가 같은 명사

sheep – **sheep**(복수)   fish – **fish**(복수)   deer – **deer**(복수)

③ 짝을 이루어 복수로 쓰는 보통명사

shoe**s**   sneaker**s**   pant**s**   glove**s**   glass**es**   chopstick**s**

02 **집합명사**: family, class, audience, team, crowd 등은 같은 종류의 개체가 모여 전체를 형성한 것으로, 이때, 전체를 강조하면 단수 취급하고, 그룹의 각 개인을 강조하면 복수형을 쓴다.
단, 기관이나 단체의 명칭이 복수 형태인 경우 단수 취급한다. ex) The United Nations is ~

① 집합명사의 종류

club, committee, council, crew, government, jury, staff, army

My family is living in this house. 내 가족은 이 집에서 살고 있다.

Two families are living in this house. 두 가족이 이 집에서 살고 있다. ▶ 집합명사는 복수형으로도 쓸 수 있음

② 항상 복수 취급하는 집합명사

the police   people   cattle   the nobility   the clergy   poultry

The police are investigating the murder case. 경찰이 그 살인 사건을 수사하고 있다. ▶ 경찰 전체

Cattle are grazing in the field. 소들이 들판에서 풀을 뜯고 있다.

People over 18 have a right to vote in this country. 이 나라에는 18세 이상인 사람들이 투표권을 가지고 있다.

서술형 기초다지기

정답 p. 24

Challenge 1 다음 밑줄 친 부분 중 틀린 것은 바르게 고치고, 맞는 것은 C라고 쓰세요.

| 보기 | Many *boy* are playing soccer with his friends. | → | *boys* |

01. Those girls <u>is</u> my favorite friends.　　　　　　　　→ _____

02. Kevin goes everywhere by bike. He doesn't have <u>car</u>.　→ _____

03. It wasn't your fault. It was <u>accident</u>.　　　　　　　→ _____

04. Five <u>man</u> watched the football game.　　　　　　　→ _____

05. One of her <u>daughters</u> came from New York on Thanksgiving.　→ _____

06. The child should go to bed. His pajamas <u>are</u> on the bed.　→ _____

07. There are 50 <u>class</u> in our school.　　　　　　　　→ _____

Challenge 2 다음 괄호 안에 들어갈 알맞은 말을 고르세요.

01. All our family (gets / get) up early.

02. The clergy (was / were) present at the meeting.

03. The team (has / have) twenty members. I've talked to all of them.

04. The crowd at the baseball game (was / were) huge.

05. The commission (is / are) calling for a global ban on whaling.

06. The Government (exists / exist) for the sum of things.

1-2 셀 수 없는 명사(Uncountable Nouns)

Fresh air is good for your health.
신선한 공기는 건강에 좋다.
Fresh air has a lot of oxygen.
신선한 공기는 많은 산소를 함유하고 있다.

01 **고유명사**: 특정한 대상(사람, 장소, 사물 등)의 이름은 고유하기 때문에 **관사를 붙이지 않고, 단/복수의 개념이 없다.** 항상 첫 글자는 대문자로 쓴다.

Australia, London, Korea, Sunday, January, William Shakespeare, Paris

I'll meet **Joshua** at **Incheon** Airport. 나는 인천공항에서 Joshua를 만날 것이다.
Bob and **Cindy** met last **December** in **Egypt**. Bob과 Cindy는 지난 12월에 이집트에서 만났다.

02 **물질명사**: 음식, 액체, 재료, 입자처럼 구체적인 사물이지만 **분리되어 있지 않아 셀 수 없는 명사**이다. much, (a) little, some, any, no처럼 양을 표현하는 형용사와 함께 쓸 수 있다. 액체(water, tea, coffee, beer, milk, soup, shampoo), 고체(glass, ice, steel, wood, silver, meat, cheese, bread), 기체(air, steam, smoke), 미세한 가루(salt, sand, dirt, flour, dust, corn)가 여기에 해당한다.

Water consists of **oxygen** and **hydrogen**. 물은 산소와 수소로 이루어져 있다.
The **bread** she bought was delicious. 그녀가 사다 준 빵은 맛있었다.
Rice is Korea's main food. 쌀은 한국의 주식이다.
We have much **snow** in this season of the year. 연중 이맘때 눈이 많이 온다.

03 **추상명사**: 눈으로 볼 수도 없고 셀 수도 없기 때문에 **a(n)를 붙일 수 없고 복수형도 없으며 단수 취급**한다. 주로 특별한 형체가 없는 관념적인 단어들이다.

education, knowledge, advice, information, homework, energy, weather, truth, love

Have you done your **homework**? 숙제 다 했니?
Happiness consists in **contentment**. 행복은 만족에 있다.

04 집단 전체(whole group)를 하나로 묶어서 나타내는 명사도 셀 수 없다. 단, 부분은 셀 수 있다.

furniture	⊃ tables, sofas, desks, drawers, chairs, bookshelves
fruit	⊃ apples, grapes, oranges, melons, mangos
mail	⊃ letters, bills(요금 청구서), postcards(엽서), telegrams(전보)
money	⊃ dollars, pennies(=1 cent), cents, nickels(=5 cents), dimes(=10 cents)
clothing	⊃ pants(바지), shirts, jackets, shorts(하의 속옷)
jewelry	⊃ rings, necklaces(목걸이), earrings, bracelets(팔찌)

서술형 기초다지기

정답 p. 24

Challenge 1　다음 밑줄 친 명사가 셀 수 있는 명사면 CN을, 셀 수 없는 명사면 UN으로 쓰세요.

01. His <u>roommate</u> is from Brazil.　　　　　　　→ _____

02. If I had enough <u>money</u>, I would buy a car.　　→ _____

03. This <u>data</u> is very important to me.　　　　　→ _____

04. I'm going to buy some <u>bread</u>.　　　　　　　→ _____

05. They offered me the job because I had a lot of <u>experience</u>.　→ _____

Challenge 2　다음 빈칸에 들어갈 알맞은 말을 아래 박스에서 찾아 쓰세요. (필요시 형태 바꾸기)

picture	friend	coffee	meat	question	advice	day	honesty

보기	There are seven *days* in a week.

01. I had my digital camera, but I didn't take many _____.

02. A vegetarian is a person who doesn't eat _____.

03. Last night I went out with some _____ of mine.

04. Karen has some _____ to ask you.

05. Can you give us some _____?

06. She drinks three cups of _____ every day.

07. A lot of people believed that _____ is the best policy.

1-3 셀 수 있는 명사와 셀 수 없는 명사

I bought **a paper** to read.
나는 읽을 신문을 샀다.

I bought some **paper** to write on.
나는 쓸 종이 몇 장을 샀다.

01 물질명사나 추상명사는 셀 수 없는 명사이므로 a(n)를 붙이지 않고, 복수형으로 만들지도 않는 것이 원칙이다. 그러나 물질로 만든 제품이나 그 물질로 된 개체, 구체적인 종류를 나타낼 경우에는 보통명사로 취급하여 부정관사를 붙이거나 복수형을 쓸 수 있다.

셀 수 있는 명사	셀 수 없는 명사
There's **a hair** in my bowl. (한 개의 머리카락)	John has dark **hair**. (모발 전체)
I handed **a paper** to the teacher. (신문, 보고서, 문서)	I bought some **paper** to write on. (종이)
There are **two cheeses** in the fridge. (두 종류의 치즈)	There's **cheese** in the fridge. (덩어리)
We'll have **two coffees**. (커피 두 잔)	She loves **coffee**. (커피)
I've read this novel **three times**. (횟수, 기간)	Do you have enough **time**? (시간)
There are **two lights** in our bedroom. (두 개의 등불)	**Light** travels faster than sound. (광선, 빛)
You can stay with us. We have **a spare room**. (집에 있는 방)	You can't sit here. There isn't any **room**. (공간＝space)

02 비슷한 뜻을 가진 단어들이 셀 수 있는 명사와 셀 수 없는 명사로 따로 쓰이기도 한다.

셀 수 있는 명사	셀 수 없는 명사
I'm looking for **a job**.	I'm looking for **work**.
What **a beautiful view**!	What beautiful **scenery**!
We have a lot of bags and **suitcases**.	We have a lot of **luggage**.
It is **a good suggestion**.	It is good **advice**.
There are a lot of **vegetables** on the table.	There's a lot of **fruit** on the table.
It's **a nice day** today.	It's nice **weather** today.

서술형 기초다지기

Challenge 1   다음 괄호 안의 표현 중 알맞은 것을 고르세요.

01. She usually reads (paper / the paper) during breakfast.

02. I can't work here. There's too much (a noise / noise).

03. There is (a hair / hair) in my soup!

04. She's got very long (a hair / hair).

05. Is there (a room / room) in your life for helping others?

06. Miss Monica asked us to write three (paper / papers) on history, sociology, and science.

07. I thought there was somebody in the house because there was (light / a light) on inside.

08. At night (light / a light) comes from the moon and the stars.

09. We had (very good weather / a very good weather) while we were in Chicago.

Challenge 2   다음 문장에서 틀린 부분을 찾아 바르게 고치세요.

보기	I need some informations about trains to Madrid.	→ *information*

01. I didn't have much luggages – just two small bags.   → _____

02. If you want to know the news, you can read paper.   → _____

03. Can you give me some advices about which courses to take?   → _____

04. Your hairs is too long. You should have it cut.   → _____

05. A: Did you have a good vacation?
     B: Yes, we had a wonderful times.   → _____

1-4 셀 수 없는 명사를 세는 방법

Susan drinks **a cup of coffee** with **a loaf of bread**. Susan은 빵 한 덩어리와 함께 커피 한 잔을 마신다.

July ate **three pieces of pizza** for lunch.
July는 점심으로 피자 세 조각을 먹었다.

01 셀 수 없는 명사는 much, (a) little, some, any, no를 이용하여 그 양이 많고 적음을 나타낼 수 있으나, **한 개, 두 개 이렇게 셀 수는 없다.**

액체	oil(기름), shampoo(샴푸)
고체	gold(금), soap(비누), silver(은), plastic(플라스틱), furniture(가구), clothing(의류), butter(버터), paper(종이), wood(나무), meat(고기)
기체	air(공기), gas(가스, 기체), smoke(연기), oxygen(산소), nitrogen(질소)
음식	food(음식), butter(버터), cheese(치즈), bread(빵), fruit(과일), water(물), coffee(커피), tea(차), juice(주스), soup(수프), milk(우유), rice(쌀), salt(소금), pepper(후추), sugar(설탕)

02 셀 수 없는 명사를 세기 위해서는 용기나 단위를 사용하며, '물 두 잔'처럼 복수형으로 쓰고자 할 때는 물질명사는 그대로 두고 이 **용기나 단위명사를 복수형으로 나타낸다.**

잔	a cup	tea, coffee
	a glass of	water, milk, wine, beer
조각	a slice/piece of	bread, pizza, toast, meat, cheese
(종이) 장	a piece/sheet of	paper
덩어리	a loaf of	bread, meat
병	a bottle of	milk, juice, wine, ink, shampoo
단지	a jar of	jam
종이 팩	a carton of	milk
(비누) 덩어리	a bar/cake of	soap
추상적인 개념	a piece of	advice, news, information
무게	a pound of	meat, beef, pork, gold
통, 관	a tube of	toothpaste

서술형 기초다지기

Challenge 1 아래의 단어를 활용하여 다음 그림 속 명사의 수량을 나타내 보세요.

cup	beer	carton	sheet	loaf	paper
bread	coffee	water	glass	bottle	milk

01.
_____

02.
_____

03.
_____

04.
_____

05.
_____

06.
_____

Challenge 2 다음 빈칸에 들어갈 알맞은 말을 아래 주어진 단어를 이용하여 써 넣으세요.

bottle	pound	cup	glass	piece

01. Can you buy me _____? (커피 한 잔)

02. I'm going to buy _____ to make dinner for the family. (고기 두 조각)

03. Some Americans carry _____ with them. (물 한 병)

04. She bought _____ for the party. (돼지고기 3파운드)

05. Nutritionists recommend drinking _____ a day for health. (여덟 잔의 물)

1-5 주의해야 할 명사의 수

She bought a pair of jeans.
그녀는 청바지 한 벌을 샀다.

Statistics is a very difficult subject.
통계학은 매우 어려운 과목이다.

01 형태와 의미가 모두 복수형인 명사가 있다. 이들 명사는 항상 복수 취급한다.

clothes	glasses	jeans	pants	shoes	socks
gloves	shorts	arms	contents	scissors	customs
weapons	belongings	goods	remains		

Jeans are my favorite clothes. 청바지는 내가 가장 좋아하는 옷이다.
They use **chopsticks** to eat rice. 그들은 밥을 먹기 위해 젓가락을 사용한다.

※ 항상 복수로 쓰이는 명사인 glasses(안경) pants(바지), jeans(청바지) 등은 똑같은 두 개의 부분이 모여 하나를 이루는 단위명사 pair를 써서 「a pair of+명사」로 개수를 표시한다.
I need **a** new **pair of jeans**. 나는 새 청바지가 한 벌 필요하다.

02 형태는 복수형이지만 **단수 취급하는 명사**도 있는데 이들 명사는 단수 동사를 써야 한다.

physics(물리학)	economics(경제학)	politics(정치학)	mathematics(수학)
linguistics(언어학)	statistics(통계학)	the Philippines(필리핀)	news(뉴스)
analysis(분석)	billiards(당구)	the United States(미국)	

Mathematics <u>is</u> one of the most interesting subjects. 수학은 가장 재미있는 과목 중 하나이다.

03 「수사+명사」가 다른 명사를 수식하는 형용사 역할을 할 때, 수사 뒤의 명사는 반드시 단수 형태로 쓴다. 절대 복수형으로 쓰지 않는다.

They have a five-**year**-old boy. 그들에게는 5살 난 사내아이가 있다. ▶ a five-years-old boy(×)
Here is a ten-**dollar** bill. 여기 10달러 지폐가 있다. ▶ a ten-dollars bill(×)

04 교환이나 상호 관계를 나타내는 경우에는 복수 명사를 쓴다.

She easily <u>makes **friends** with</u> the old. 그녀는 노인들과 쉽게 친해진다. ▶ make friends with: ~와 친해지다
You have to <u>change **buses**</u> on Main Street. 당신은 메인 스트리트에서 버스를 갈아타야 한다.
▶ change buses: 버스를 갈아타다

서술형 기초다지기

정답 p. 24

Challenge 1 다음 괄호 안의 표현 중 알맞은 것을 고르세요.

01. My (belongings / belonging) are still in the car.

02. The (clothes / clothe) are very dirty.

03. The United States (are / is) one of the largest countries in the world.

04. Be careful! These scissors (is / are) very sharp.

05. The news we heard (was / were) very depressing.

06. (Arm / Arms) are weapons, especially bombs and guns.

07. I shook (hand / hands) with the movie star yesterday.

08. She wants to make (friends / friend) with Brian.

09. Physics (was / were) my favorite subject when I was a student.

Challenge 2 우리말과 뜻이 같도록 괄호 안의 말을 이용하여 빈칸을 채우세요.

01. 나는 어제 운동화 두 컬레를 샀다. (pair / sneaker)

   → I bought _____ _____ _____ _____ yesterday.

02. 그는 오늘 안경 하나를 샀다. (pair / glass)

   → He bought _____ _____ _____ _____ today.

03. 그녀는 어제 청바지 세 벌을 샀다. (pair / jean)

   → She bought _____ _____ _____ _____ yesterday.

04. 나는 새 청바지가 한 벌 필요하다. (pair / pant)

   → I need _____ _____ _____ _____ _____.

1-6 명사의 격

My father's car is made in Italy.
아빠의 차는 이탈리아에서 만들어졌다.

This store sells women's clothes.
이 가게는 여성복을 판매한다.

01 명사가 주어로 쓰이면 주격, 목적어로 쓰이면 목적격이라고 한다. 주격과 목적격은 모양이 같다. 명사의 소유격은 '~의'라는 소유 관계를 나타내며 사람과 동물 같은 **생물의 소유격은 '(s)를 붙여** 만든다.

① 단수 명사 뒤에는 's를 붙인다.

My uncle's name is Jim.
내 삼촌의 이름은 Jim이야.

I know the student's name.
나는 그 학생의 이름을 안다.

② -s로 끝나는 복수 명사는 어퍼스트로피(')만 붙인다. 단, 사람의 이름은 -s로 끝나도 's를 붙인다.

I answered the students' questions. 나는 학생들의 질문에 답해 주었다.

Are you going to James's house? James의 집에 갈거니?

③ -s로 끝나지 않는 불규칙 복수형인 경우 's를 붙여 소유격을 만든다.

Which floor is the men's wear on? 남성복은 몇 층에 있나요?

④ 명사의 반복을 피하기 위해서, 또는 서로 알고 있거나 대상이 명백할 때 소유격 뒤의 명사는 생략한다.

Whose dog is this? 이 개는 누구의 것이니? – It's Sandra's.(=Sandra's dog) 그것은 Sandra의 개야.

02 **무생물 명사는 of를 이용**하여 소유격을 나타낸다. 단, 시간, 거리, 장소, 금액을 나타내는 명사는 무생물이지만 's로 소유격을 나타낸다.

the legs **of** the desk 책상의 다리

the cover **of** the book 책의 표지

The answer **of** the question 질문의 답

five pounds' weight 5 파운드의 무게

today's newspaper 오늘의 신문

ten minutes' walk 걸어서 10분

03 a(n), any, this/these, that/those, some, no, which, what 등이 수식하는 명사는 소유격과 나란히 쓸 수 없기 때문에 「of+소유대명사」 또는 「명사의 소유격」 형태의 이중 소유격을 쓴다.

a my friend(×)   →   **a** friend **of mine**(○) 내 친구 중 한 명

this Hemingway's book(×)   →   **this** book **of** Hemingway's(○) 헤밍웨이의 이 책

Which house **of** your neighbor's is the biggest? 네 이웃집 중 어느 집이 가장 크니?

서술형 기초다지기

정답 p. 24

Challenge 1 〈보기〉와 같이 명사의 소유격을 이용하여 빈칸을 완성하세요.

> **보기** I have one friend. My _friend's_ name is Bob.

01. I have two friends. My _____ names are Bob and Paul.

02. I have one child. My _____ name is Anna.

03. I have two children. My _____ names are Anna and Kevin.

04. I know a man. This _____ name is Peter.

05. I know two men. These _____ names are Peter and Joe Lee.

Challenge 2 다음 괄호 안의 표현 중 알맞은 것을 고르세요.

01. Don't forget (meeting of tomorrow / tomorrow's meeting) at 4 o'clock.

02. Give me two (worth of dollars' / dollars' worth) of sugar.

03. I bought six (weight of pounds' / pounds' weight) of beef at that store.

04. We have got (two weeks' holiday / two week's holiday) this summer.

Challenge 3 다음 괄호 안의 단어를 소유격 형태로 바꾸어 빈칸을 완성하세요.

01. _____ is so thin that it may tear apart. (the book, the cover)

02. One of _____ broke while we were moving it. (the desk, the legs)

03. _____ can speak English. (mine / some friends)

04. _____ is the company's latest model. (my brother's, this iPhone)

05. You need at least _____ a day. (sleep, seven hours')

Unit 02 관사

2-1 부정관사 a와 an의 쓰임

There is **an** apple, and there is **some** water.
한 개의 사과와 약간의 물이 있다.

01 '하나, 한 명'이라는 개념으로 셀 수 있어 **단수 명사 앞에 쓰는 a(n)를 부정관사**라고 한다. 대부분의 명사 앞에 a를 쓰지만 첫 소리가 **모음으로 발음되는 명사 앞에는 an**을 쓴다.

a car	**a** doctor	**a** European	**a** university
an umbrella	**an** idea	**an** honest answer	**an** English teacher
an old woman	**a** useful tool	**an** hour	**an** MP3 player

▶ 명사나 형용사의 철자가 자음이냐 모음이냐에 상관없이 자음으로 소리 나면 a, 모음으로 소리 나면 an을 붙인다.

02 **some과 any**는 둘 다 '몇몇의, 약간의'라는 뜻으로 **명사의 수와 양을 정확히 모를 때 사용**한다. some은 긍정문과 의문문(부탁, 권유)에 쓰고 any는 부정문과 의문문에 쓴다.

There is **some** coffee, and there's **some** juice. 약간의 커피와 주스가 있다. ▶ 긍정문: some

Is there **any** milk in the fridge? 냉장고에 우유가 좀 있니? ▶ 의문문: any

Would you like **some** coffee? 커피 좀 드시겠어요? ▶ 의문문(권유): some

03 전달하고자 하는 의미에 따라 구체적인 사물로 쓸 수도 있고, 추상적인 개념으로 쓸 수도 있다. 이때 명사에 a(n)가 붙고 안 붙는 것은 전달하고자 하는 의미에 달려 있다.

There is **a** church over there. 저기에 교회가 하나 있다. ▶ 교회 – 구체적인 건물의 개념

I always go to church on Sundays. 나는 일요일마다 예배를 보러 간다. ▶ '예배를 보러 가다'는 추상적 개념

04 부정관사의 여러 가지 의미

① 하나의(one)	She didn't say **a** word. 그녀는 한마디도 하지 않았다.
② 종족 전체	**A** child needs love. 아이는 사랑을 필요로 한다.
③ 어떤(a certain)	**A** young lady came to see you. 어떤 젊은 여자가 너를 보러 왔다.
④ 같은, 동일한(the same)	Kevin and Bob are of **an** age. Kevin과 Bob은 동갑이다.
⑤ ~당, ~ 마다(per)	We have five English classes **a** week. 우리는 일주일에 영어 수업이 5시간이다.
⑥ 어느 정도, 약간(some)	She thought for **a** while. 그녀는 한동안 생각했다.

서술형 기초다지기

Challenge 1 다음 문장의 빈칸에 a(n) 또는 some을 써 넣으세요.

01. She has _____ computer, but I don't have one.

02. I bought _____ furniture for my apartment.

03. I had _____ unique experience.

04. She will arrive in _____ hour.

05. I often have _____ fruit for dessert.

06. Could you give me _____ information about Korean history?

07. We had _____ easy test yesterday.

Challenge 2 다음 문장의 밑줄 친 a(n)와 같은 의미로 쓰인 것을 찾아 번호를 쓰세요.

① She drinks coffee three times <u>a</u> day.	② You can't do many things at <u>a</u> time.
③ <u>A</u> strange woman came to see you.	④ Albert and I are of <u>an</u> age.
⑤ <u>A</u> puppy is the most popular pet.	⑥ Would you wait here for <u>a</u> while?

01. She takes violin lessons once <u>a</u> week. → _____

02. <u>A</u> Ms. Jones called you while you were out. → _____

03. Birds of <u>a</u> feather flock together. → _____

04. It may take <u>an</u> hour to download this film. → _____

05. She saw a cockroach at <u>a</u> distance. → _____

06. <u>A</u> cheetah can run faster than <u>a</u> tiger. → _____

2-2 정관사 the의 쓰임

We bought a used car. But the car soon broke down.
우리는 중고차 한 대를 샀다. 근데 그 차는 금방 고장이 났다.

01 **앞서 언급된 명사가 다시 반복**될 때, 또는 **상대방이 무엇을 가리키는지 알고 있는** 경우에 쓴다.

I have **a** friend, and **the** friend is a movie star. 나는 친구가 한 명 있다, 그런데 그 친구는 영화배우이다.
　　　　　　　　　　　　　　　　　　　　　　　　▶ 앞서 나온 명사를 다시 언급

Do you mind opening **the** window? 창문을 좀 열어도 될까요? ▶ 서로 알고 있는 것

02 단지 하나밖에 없는 **유일한 것**을 지시하는 경우에는 the를 쓴다.

the sun, the sky, the sea, the world, the south, the North Pole, the universe, the right

The sky is full of clouds today. 오늘 하늘은 구름이 잔뜩 끼었다.

She's traveled all over **the** world. 그녀는 전 세계를 여행했다.

03 **악기 이름 앞**에 정관사 the를 쓴다.

Joy will play **the** violin on the stage. Joy가 무대 위에서 바이올린을 연주할 것이다.

04 **서수(first, second...), 최상급, only, same, very('매우'가 아니라 '바로'의 의미일 경우) 앞**에 정관사 the를 쓴다.

New York is **the** largest city in the world. 뉴욕은 세계에서 가장 큰 도시이다.

The same thing happened to me yesterday. 똑같은 일이 어제 내게 일어났다.

You are **the** only person for the job. 당신은 그 일에 적합한 유일한 사람이다.

Who was **the** first man to walk on the moon? 달에 착륙한 최초의 사람이 누구였니?

05 뒤에서 명사를 수식하는 구나 절이 있어서 **명사가 분명히 정해지는** 경우에 쓴다.

The wine from this region tastes good. 이 지역에서 생산된 포도주는 맛이 좋다.

06 「**the＋형용사/분사**」가 '~한 사람들'이라는 의미로 쓰인 경우나 **신체 일부**를 가리킬 때 쓴다.

The young should respect **the** old. 젊은이들은 노인들을 공경해야 한다. ▶ the young/old＝young/old people

The teacher struck me on **the** head. 선생님이 내 머리를 때렸다. ▶ on my head(×)

She kissed him on **the** cheek. 그녀는 그의 뺨에 키스를 했다. ▶ on his cheek(×)

서술형 기초다지기

정답 p. 25

Challenge 1 다음 빈칸에 a, an, some 또는 the 중에서 알맞은 것을 넣으세요.

> 보기
> I drank *some* coffee and some orange juice.
> *The* coffee was hot. *The* orange juice was cold.

01. I had _____ soup and _____ sandwich for lunch. _____ soup was too salty, but _____ sandwich was pretty good.

02. Yesterday I bought _____ clothes. I bought _____ suit, _____ shirt, and _____ tie. _____ suit is gray and comes with a vest. _____ shirt is pale blue, and _____ tie has black and gray stripes.

03. Yesterday while I was walking to work, I saw _____ birds in _____ tree. I also saw _____ dog under _____ tree. _____ birds didn't pay any attention to _____ dog, but _____ dog was watching _____ birds intently.

Challenge 2 다음 문장에서 관사가 잘못 쓰인 것을 골라 바르게 고치세요.

> 보기
> This is an oldest tower in Korea.   ___an___ → ___the___

01. The teacher patted her on a shoulder.   _____ → _____

02. Our apartment building has the basement. Sunny keeps her bike there at night.
                                                   _____ → _____

03. My friend is an owner of that restaurant.   _____ → _____

04. She is an only friend that I have.   _____ → _____

05. A same thing happened to me two months ago.   _____ → _____

2-3 관사를 쓰지 않는 경우

Kelly's having **lunch** at the cafeteria.
Kelly는 구내식당에서 점심을 먹고 있다.

The students go to **school** by bus.
학생들은 버스를 타고 학교에 다닌다.

01 **식사**를 나타내는 명사 앞이나 **운동 경기**를 나타내는 명사 앞에는 관사를 쓰지 않는다.

She didn't have **breakfast** this morning. 그녀는 오늘 아침에 아침을 먹지 않았다.

They went out for **dinner**. 그들은 저녁 식사 하러 나갔다.

We play **tennis** every Sunday. 우리는 매주 일요일에 테니스를 친다.

※ 식사 이름인 breakfast, lunch, dinner 앞에는 관사를 쓰지 않지만, 이들 단어 앞에 형용사가 오면 관사 a(n)를 쓴다.

We had **a** very **nice dinner**. 우리는 정말 맛있는 저녁을 먹었다.

02 **과목 이름** 앞이나 **교통, 통신수단을 나타내는 by** 다음에는 관사를 쓰지 않는다.

My favorite subject is **history**. 내가 가장 좋아하는 과목은 역사이다.

I'll send the letter **by e-mail** today. 오늘 이메일로 그 편지를 보낼게.

You can get to City Hall **by bus** or **by subway**. 버스나 지하철로 시청에 갈 수 있다.

03 **'공부하다, 잠을 자다, 예배를 보러 가다'**와 같이 건물이나 시설 등이 본래의 목적으로 쓰일 때는 관사를 쓰지 않는다.

We don't have to go to **school** on Saturday.
우리는 토요일은 학교에 갈 필요가 없다. ▶ '공부하러 학교에 가다'라는 의미이므로 무관사

Mom went to **the school** to meet my teacher.
엄마는 선생님을 만나러 학교에 가셨다. ▶ 공부가 목적이 아니므로 관사 사용

Kevin goes to **church** every Sunday.
Kevin은 매주 일요일마다 예배 보러 교회에 간다. ▶ '예배 보러 교회에 가다'라는 의미이므로 무관사

He went to **the church** to repair the roof.
그는 지붕을 수리하러 교회에 갔다. ▶ 예배가 아닌 교회라는 건물을 수리하러 가는 것이므로 관사 사용

04 **가족, 관직, 신분, 호칭**에는 관사를 쓰지 않는다. **listen to music**과 **watch TV**는 관용적으로 관사 없이 쓴다.

Who was **President** of the U.S. ten years ago? 10년 전에 누가 미국의 대통령이었니?

Doctor, I have a slight headache. 의사 선생님, 가벼운 두통이 있어요.

Father is in, but **mother** is out. 아빠는 계시지만 엄마는 나가셨어.

She often **watches TV** at night. 그녀는 종종 밤에 TV를 본다.

서술형 기초다지기

Challenge 1 다음 문장의 빈칸에 a(n), the 중 알맞은 것을 쓰고, 필요 없는 곳에는 X표 하세요.

> **보기** Why isn't your daughter in _x_ school today? Is she sick?

01. There's _____ church near my house.

02. Susan went to _____ school to meet her daughter's teacher.

03. Cindy takes care of patients in the hospital. She is _____ nurse.

04. We watched the news on _____ television.

05. I had a hamburger and fruit for _____ lunch.

06. In Korea, a lot of high school students try to go to _____ college.

07. _____ Officer, could you tell me where the nearest bank is?

08. It takes about thirty minutes to go there by _____ bus.

Challenge 2 다음 문장에서 어법상 어색한 부분을 찾아서 바르게 고치세요.

01. I will send the document by the e-mail. → _____

02. They had the lunch at the cafeteria. → _____

03. I was invited to her birthday party and had the wonderful dinner. → _____

04. When I finish school, I want to go to the college. → _____

05. My favorite subject in school was a physics. → _____

06. Do you think a rich should pay more taxes to help the poor? → _____

"출제자가 노리는 급소" 이것이 시험에 출제되는 영문법이다!

---

01 출제 100 % - 명사의 단수와 복수를 조심하라!

 출제자의 눈 기본적으로 셀 수 있는 명사와 셀 수 없는 명사는 구별해야 한다. 특히 형태는 복수형이지만 단수 취급하는 명사(physics, economics, politics 등) 또는 형태는 단수이지만 복수 취급하는 명사(the police, people, cattle 등)는 주어로 쓰일 때 동사가 단수인지 복수인지 묻는 문제가 출제될 수 있다. 언제나 짝을 이루어서 복수로 쓰이는 명사(pants, sneakers, glasses 등)도 주의하자. 특히, a ten-dollar bill처럼 하이픈(-)으로 연결된 형태는 복수형(ten-dollars)으로 쓰지 않도록 해야 한다.

Ex 1.

The news _____ shocking to the public.

(a) were   (b) are   (c) was   (d) have been

Ex 2.

They have _____ boy.

(a) a five-years-old   (b) a five-year-old

---

02 출제 100 % - 셀 수 없는 명사를 셀 수 있는 것처럼 속인다.

 출제자의 눈 개별 단위로는 셀 수 있지만 집단 전체를 하나로 묶을 때는 셀 수 없는 명사에 -s를 붙여 함정에 빠뜨린다. furniture, fruit, mail, money, clothing 등의 물질명사는 기본적으로 셀 수 없는 명사이다. 셀 수 없는 물질명사는 제아무리 그 양이 많아도 단수 취급하므로 주어로 쓰일 때는 동사도 단수 동사를 써야 한다.

Ex 3.

I can't work here. There _____ too much noise.

(a) are   (b) is   (c) were   (d) will be

Ex 4.

어법상 어색한 부분을 고쳐 쓰시오.

Where are you going to put all your furnitures?

_____ → _____

03 출제 100% - 셀 수 없는 명사의 세는 방법을 묻는다.

 출제자의 눈 셀 수 없는 물질명사 같은 경우 정확한 양을 모를 때는 some, any, a little과 같은 표현으로 수식할 수 있지만 '커피 한 잔, 커피 두 잔'처럼 수를 셀 경우에는 용기나 단위를 이용한다. 이때, 물질명사에는 절대로 -(e)s를 붙이지 않고 그 단위명사에 -(e)s를 붙여서 복수형을 만든다. 이를 집중적으로 물어보거나 물질명사에 알맞은 단위(a cup of, a piece of 등)를 구별해서 쓸 줄 아는지도 물어본다. 또한, 명사의 소유격도 어법상 틀린 것을 고르는 문제로 출제될 수 있다.

Ex 5.

I used two _____ to make a sandwich.

(a) piece of bread   (b) pieces of breads   (c) pieces of bread

Ex 6.

The bus stop is within _____ of my house.

(a) walk of ten minutes   (b) ten minutes' walk

04 출제 100% - 관사의 용법에 익숙해져라.

 출제자의 눈 관사 a(n)의 기본적인 의미를 묻는 문제가 출제되거나 정관사 the를 언제 쓰고, 언제 생략하는지 묻는 문제가 주로 출제된다.

Ex 7.

밑줄 친 a(n)과 의미가 같은 것은?

Mario and I are of <u>an</u> age.

(a) We stayed there for <u>a</u> while.

(b) They are all of <u>a</u> mind.

Ex 8.

다음 중 빈칸에 the/The를 쓸 수 <u>없는</u> 곳은?

(a) Tom sat down on _____ chair nearest the door.

(b) We looked up at all the stars in _____ sky.

(c) What did you have for _____ breakfast?

(d) Every semester parents are invited to _____ school to meet the teachers.

1. 다음 문장 중 표현이 자연스러운 것은?

❶ I eat much rices every day.

❷ It wasn't your fault. It was bad a luck.

❸ I am a fifteen-year-old middle school student.

❹ Many students had questions after the lecture. I answered the student questions.

❺ Please give me two sheets of papers.

2. 다음 두 문장의 뜻이 같도록 빈칸에 알맞은 단어를 쓰시오.

> They liked to help the poor.
> =They liked to help _____ _____.

3. 다음 빈칸에 The/the가 들어갈 수 없는 것은?

❶ She can play _____ piano well.

❷ I saw a dog and a cat. _____ dog was running after the cat.

❸ Where's _____ bathroom? It's on the first floor.

❹ We usually play _____ soccer during lunch time.

❺ Mt. Everest is _____ highest mountain in the world.

4. 다음 빈칸에 공통으로 들어갈 알맞은 말은?

> · I ate eight _____ of pizza.
> · I ate three _____ of cake yesterday.
> · Do you have two _____ of paper?

❶ glasses ❷ loaves ❸ slices

❹ sheets ❺ pieces

5. 다음 밑줄 친 부분 중 어색한 것을 모두 고르시오.

> After shopping they were very tired and hungry. They sat down at the snack bar. Mary bought ❶ three breads and ❷ two glass of milks. Karen drank ❸ a cup of coffee. She also had ❹ a doughnut. They ❺ had a good time.

6. 다음 밑줄 친 단어 중 어법상 틀린 것을 고르시오.

❶ A lot of furniture are for sale now.

❷ The audience in the stadium were deeply moved at the concert.

❸ There is room for everybody to sit down. There are plenty of chairs.

❹ We have no furniture – not even a bed or a table.

❺ We had very good weather while we were in Toronto.

7. 다음 중 밑줄 친 부분이 어색한 것을 고르시오.

❶ Bring me a glass of water.

❷ I need a loaf of paper.

❸ The farmer carried a bag of potatoes.

❹ The child has a piece of cheese.

❺ We had a cup of tea.

8. 다음 밑줄 친 부분의 의미가 주어진 문장과 같은 것은?

> Those shoes are all of a size.

❶ I am paid 8 dollars an hour.

❷ Birds of a feather flock together.

❸ You are right in a sense.

❹ They'll be able to finish it in a day.

❺ A Mr. Kim came to see you.

오답 노트 만들기

★틀린 문제 : _____   ★다시 공부한 날 : _____

(1) 문제를 왜? 틀렸는지 곰곰이 생각하고 그 이유를 적어본다.

(2) 핵심 개념을 적는다.

(3) 자신이 몰랐던 단어와 숙어 표현이 있으면 정리한다.

(4) 해설집에서 필요한 부분을 골라 풀이 해법을 정리한다.

★틀린 문제 : _____   ★다시 공부한 날 : _____

(1) 문제를 왜? 틀렸는지 곰곰이 생각하고 그 이유를 적어본다.

(2) 핵심 개념을 적는다.

(3) 자신이 몰랐던 단어와 숙어 표현이 있으면 정리한다.

(4) 해설집에서 필요한 부분을 골라 풀이 해법을 정리한다.

★틀린 문제 : _____   ★다시 공부한 날 : _____

(1) 문제를 왜? 틀렸는지 곰곰이 생각하고 그 이유를 적어본다.

(2) 핵심 개념을 적는다.

(3) 자신이 몰랐던 단어와 숙어 표현이 있으면 정리한다.

(4) 해설집에서 필요한 부분을 골라 풀이 해법을 정리한다.

★틀린 문제 : _____   ★다시 공부한 날 : _____

(1) 문제를 왜? 틀렸는지 곰곰이 생각하고 그 이유를 적어본다.

(2) 핵심 개념을 적는다.

(3) 자신이 몰랐던 단어와 숙어 표현이 있으면 정리한다.

(4) 해설집에서 필요한 부분을 골라 풀이 해법을 정리한다.

1. 다음 중 빈칸에 들어갈 부정관사(a/an)의 형태가 나머지 넷과 다른 하나는?

❶ There is _____ new student in our class.

❷ Ann is wearing _____ ring on her fourth finger.

❸ I called Kevin by the wrong name. It was _____ honest mistake.

❹ I had _____ banana for dessert.

❺ Will you have _____ glass of orange juice?

오답노트

2. 다음 빈칸에 들어갈 말이 알맞게 짝지어진 것은?

> 지소연은 기념식에서 대통령과 악수를 했다.
> =So-yeon Ji shook _____ with the president at the ceremony.
> 나는 Steve와 친구가 되기를 원한다.
> =I want to make _____ with Steve.

❶ hand – friend ❷ hands – friend

❸ hand – friends ❹ hands – hands

❺ hands – friends

오답노트

[3-7] 다음 밑줄 친 관사의 의미와 같은 것을 찾아 쓰시오.

> (A) the same   (B) some   (C) per
> (D) certain   (E) one

3. I took a trip to Japan once <u>a</u> year. → _____

4. Rome wasn't built in <u>a</u> day. → _____

5. What you say is true in <u>a</u> sense. → _____

6. Tom and Bob are two of <u>a</u> kind. → _____

7. She stayed there for <u>a</u> while. → _____

오답노트

8. 다음 중 밑줄 친 부분의 쓰임이 어색한 것은?

❶ Someone gave him <u>a piece of</u> blue glass.

❷ The farmer carried <u>a bag of</u> potatoes.

❸ I want <u>three glass of</u> water.

❹ We had <u>two cups of</u> tea.

❺ I need <u>a few sheets of</u> paper.

오답노트

[9-13] 다음 빈칸에 a와 an 중 알맞은 것을 쓰고, 필요 없는 경우에는 ×표를 하시오.

9. I brush my teeth twice _____ day.

10. We were very unfortunate. We had _____ bad luck.

11. I want to go to _____ good university.

12. I had _____ interesting experience today.

13. I didn't have _____ time for breakfast.

오답노트

14. 다음 빈칸에 들어갈 말이 알맞게 짝지어진 것은?

> · After work, I watch _____ TV and take it easy.
> · What time did you go to _____ bed last night?

❶ x − the   ❷ the − a   ❸ the − the
❹ x − x   ❺ the − x

오답노트

[15-16] 다음 중 어법상 틀린 문장을 고르시오.

15. ❶ Coffee is an important product of Columbia.
❷ She seized me by a collar.
❸ Those who want to enter a university must study English.
❹ People elected him President of the Republic of Korea.
❺ You may keep the book for a week.

16. ❶ In Alaska in the winter, there is a lot of snow on the ground.
❷ Sunshine is a source of vitamin D.
❸ Prof. Brian has a lot of knowledge about that subject.
❹ Women's shoes are on sale in that store.
❺ I came across my a friend from middle school at the park.

오답노트

17. 다음 빈칸에 알맞은 말을 쓰시오.

> A : What are you doing now?
> B : I'm sending letters by e-mail to some friends _____ _____ in Africa. (내 친구들 중 몇 명)

오답노트

18. 다음 중 빈칸에 The/the가 필요 없는 곳은?

❶ She keeps a puppy. _____ puppy is very cute.
❷ _____ topic of the debate was very controversial.
❸ Neil Amstrong is _____ first man that walked first on the moon.
❹ I was _____ only person in class today.
❺ Do you often listen to _____ classical music?

오답노트

19. 어법상 어색한 부분을 찾아 바르게 고쳐 쓰시오.

> Q : Do you have many rains in this country?
> A : No, we don't.

_____ → _____

오답노트

20. 우리말과 같은 의미가 되도록 다음 빈칸에 알맞은 말을 쓰시오.

> Korean people usually bow when they meet and so do Japanese people. When they meet someone on business, do they (악수를 하다) first?

→ _____

오답노트

[21-22] 다음 대화를 읽고 물음에 답하시오.

> A: Do you know Stephen Hawking?
> B: Yes, I do. He is now the greatest physicist in the world, isn't he?
> A: Yes. It's certain that even (장애를 가진 사람들) can succeed.
> B: Of course. Ⓐ They are just the same as other people.

21. 밑줄 친 우리말에 어울리는 적절한 표현은?

❶ the handicapped   ❷ handicapped
❸ handicap   ❹ the sick
❺ sick people

22. 밑줄 친 Ⓐ가 가리키는 것을 찾아 쓰시오.

→ _____

오답노트

[23-27] 다음 빈칸에 들어갈 알맞은 말을 골라 쓰시오.

sheet	loaf	cup	piece	tube

23. I drank a _____ of coffee.

24. There are 200 _____ of lined paper in my notebook.

25. I need to buy a new _____ of toothpaste.

26. I bought one _____ of bread at the store.

27. Let me give you a _____ of advice.

오답노트

28. 다음 중 어법상 틀린 문장을 고르시오.

❶ The homeless needs more help from the government.
❷ The young have the future in their hands.
❸ Life is all right if you have a job, but things are not so easy for the unemployed.
❹ Next week's meeting has been canceled.
❺ Write your name at the top of the page.

오답노트

A. 다음 문장에서 <u>틀린</u> 부분을 바르게 고쳐 쓰시오.

1. Yesterday I met a your friend in the park.

_____ → _____

2. Does she have much moneys?

_____ → _____

3. She drinks two cup of teas every day.

_____ → _____

4. There is a schoolbag by the desk's legs.

_____ → _____

B. 다음 문장에서 <u>틀린</u> 부분을 바르게 고쳐 쓰시오.

1. There is T-shirt in the closet. T-shirt is my brother's.

_____ → _____, _____ → _____

2. She'll go to church to see the poet's grave before long.

_____ → _____

3. Let me know the result by an e-mail.

_____ → _____

C. 다음 빈칸에 관사가 필요할 경우 알맞은 관사를 쓰고, 필요 없는 곳에는 X표를 하시오.

1. Will you pass me _____ sugar, please? – Here you are.

2. The teacher patted me gently on _____ shoulder.

3. The members unanimously elected him _____ president of FIFA.

4. Seoul is _____ largest city in Korea.

실전 서술형 평가문제

출제의도 보통명사와 물질명사

평가내용 some과 any를 이용하여 명사 표현하기

A. 다음 그림을 보고 some과 any를 이용하여 〈보기〉와 같이 의문문과 대답문을 영작하시오. (단, there be를 이용할 것)

[서술형 유형 : 10점 / 난이도 : 중]

보기	Q: *Is there any orange juice on the table?* (orange juice)
	A: *Yes, there is some orange juice.*

1. Q: _____ (bread)

A: _____

2. Q: _____ (rice)

A: _____

3. Q: _____ (apple)

A: _____

4. Q: _____ (butter)

A: _____

5. Q: _____ (paper)

A: _____

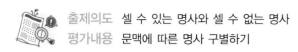

출제의도 셀 수 있는 명사와 셀 수 없는 명사
평가내용 문맥에 따른 명사 구별하기

B. 〈보기〉와 같이 주어진 단어를 문맥에 따라 셀 수 있는 명사와 셀 수 없는 명사로 구별해서 쓰시오.

[서술형 유형 : 18점 / 난이도 : 중]

보기	chicken Kevin, would you like some *chicken* for dinner tonight? My grandfather raises *chickens* in his garden.

time

1. It took a lot of _____ to write those articles.

2. She really likes that movie. She watched it four _____.

paper

3. Students in Prof. Young's literature class have to write a lot of _____.

4. The Korea Herald is a daily English-language _____.

5. I have some _____ to write a letter.

light

6. I thought there was somebody in the house because there were two _____ on inside.

7. If _____ accidentally goes in a darkroom, it can ruin photographic negatives.

hair

8. Lisa has straight _____, and Sally has curly _____.

9. Bob has a black puppy. When I stood up from Bob's sofa, my white slacks were covered with short black _____.

실전 서술형 평가문제

 출제의도 셀 수 없는 명사를 세는 단위의 쓰임과 활용

평가내용 일상생활에서 셀 수 없는 명사 활용하기

C. 다음 그림과 일치하도록 질문에 대한 답을 영작하시오. [서술형 유형 : 8점 / 난이도 : 중상]

보 기	Q: How much milk do you drink in the morning? → *I drink a glass of milk (in the morning).*

1.

Q: How much milk does she have?

→ _____

2.

Q: How many slices of pizza are there in this picture?

→ _____

3.

Q: How much paper does Kelly need?

→ _____

4.

Q: How much meat did you buy yesterday?

→ _____

서술형 평가문제	채 점 기 준	배 점	나의 점수
A	표현이 올바르고 문법, 철자가 모두 정확한 경우	2점×5문항＝10점	
B		2점×9문항＝18점	
C		2점×4문항＝8점	
공통	문법, 철자가 1개씩 틀린 경우	각 문항당 1점씩 감점	
	내용과 전혀 일치하지 않거나 답을 기재하지 못한 경우	0점	

Chapter 8

대명사 (Pronouns)

Unit 01 대명사

1-1 it의 용법 (1)

Nancy is lazy, but she will not admit **it**.
Nancy는 게으르지만, 그녀는 그것을 인정하지 않을 것이다.

It is fun **to play** tennis with Mary.
Mary와 테니스 치는 것은 재미있다.

01 영어는 같은 말의 반복을 싫어해서 대명사를 자주 쓴다. **it은 앞에 나온 특정한 명사**(the+명사)나 구, 절 또는 문장을 대신하기도 한다.

I had an MP3 player, but I left **it** on the train. 나는 MP3가 있었지만 그것을 기차에 놓고 내렸다.
　　　　　　　　　　　　　　　　　　(→ an MP3 player)

I wanted to change my job, but I found **it** difficult. 나는 직업을 바꾸길 원했지만 그것이 어렵다는 것을 알았다.
　　　　　　　　　　　　　　　　　　(→ to change my job)

02 주어나 목적어 자리에 (대)명사가 아닌 부정사, 동명사, 명사절이 올 경우에는, **길어진 주어나 목적어 자리에 it(가주어나 가목적어)을 쓰고 모두 뒤로 보내는 것이 일반적**이다.

For you to start at once is necessary.
=**It** is necessary for you to start at once. 네가 즉시 출발하는 것이 필요하다. ▶ 가주어, 진주어

That she should get angry is natural.
=**It** is natural that she should get angry. 그녀가 화를 내는 것은 당연하다. ▶ 가주어, 진주어

Reading such a book is no use.
=**It** is no use reading such a book. 그러한 책은 읽어도 소용이 없다. ▶ 가주어, 진주어

I found to read his handwriting impossible.
=I found **it** impossible to read his handwriting. 나는 그의 필체를 읽는 것이 불가능하다는 걸 알았다.
　　　　　　　　　　　　　　　　　　　　　　　▶ 가목적어, 진목적어

We found persuading him useless.
=We found **it** useless persuading him. 우리는 그를 설득하는 것이 소용없다는 것을 알았다. ▶ 가목적어, 진목적어

I think that Korea will be unified in 30 years possible.
=I think **it** possible that Korea will be unified in 30 years.
나는 30년 안에 한국이 통일되는 것을 가능하다고 생각한다. ▶ 가목적어, 진목적어

서술형 기초다지기

Challenge 1 밑줄 친 대명사 it이 가리키는 단어/구/절/문장을 찾아 쓰세요.

| 보기 | I had a nice umbrella, but I left it on the subway. | → *a nice umbrella* |

01. She has a car. It is a new car.   → _____

02. I tried to solve the problem, but it was impossible.   → _____

03. I bought some cheese. It was very good.   → _____

04. I'd like to go on a trip to Europe, but I can't afford it.   → _____

05. He advised me to persuade her, but it was useless.   → _____

06. They were all shouting: it was terrible.   → _____

Challenge 2 다음 문장을 가주어와 가목적어를 이용하여 다시 쓰세요.

01. To understand the problem is impossible.

→ _____

02. Behaving like that is foolish.

→ _____

03. That travel broadens our mind is certain.

→ _____

04. I think to make use of solar energy better.

→ _____

05. I believe his taking care of orphans good.

→ _____

1-2 it의 용법 (2) / 지시대명사

It was John **that** told me the story.
내게 그 이야기를 해준 사람은 바로 John이었다.

Her appearance **was that** of a warrior.
그녀의 모습은 전사의 모습이었다.

01 강조하고자 하는 부분을 **It is/was**와 **that** 사이에 넣어 강조할 수 있다. 단, 동사는 불가능하다.

It was James **that[who]** met Tom in the park yesterday. 어제 공원에서 Tom을 만난 것은 James였다.

It was in 1950 **that** the Korean War broke out. 한국전쟁이 발발한 것은 1950년이었다.

02 지시대명사 this, that, these, those

① 시간이나 공간상 **가까우면 this**나 **these(복수형)**를 쓰고, **멀면 that**이나 **those(복수형)**를 쓴다.

Which dictionary is better, **this** one or **that** one? 이것과 저것 중 어느 사전이 더 좋니?

Bob has been staying at the Continental Hotel all **this** week.
Bob은 이번 주 내내 컨티넨탈 호텔에 머물고 있다.

There were no cell phones in **those** days. 그 당시에는 휴대전화가 없었다.

② 앞에 나온 명사의 **반복을 피하기 위해 단수 명사는 that, 복수 명사는 those**를 쓴다.

The population of Japan is larger than **that** of Korea. 일본의 인구는 한국의 인구보다 많다.
▶ that = the population

The ears of a rabbit are longer than **those** of a fox. 토끼의 귀는 여우의 귀보다 길다. ▶ those = the ears

③ 앞에 나온 내용을 가리킬 때는 **this나 that**을 쓴다. 뒤에 나오는 말을 가리킬 때는 **this**를 쓴다.

I tried to persuade her, but **that** was impossible. 그녀를 설득하려고 했으나, 그것은 불가능했다.

I just can't reduce the size of my waist and **this** really bothers me.
도무지 나는 내 허리 사이즈를 줄일 수가 없고 이것이 정말 나를 짜증나게 한다.

Remember **this** : God is always watching you. 이것을 기억해 두어라. 신이 언제나 보고 있다는 것을.

④ **this**는 '**후자**'(the latter), **that**은 '**전자**'(the former)를 가리킨다.

Health is above wealth; **this** cannot give so much happiness as **that**.
건강은 부보다 중요하다. 왜냐하면 후자(부)는 전자(건강)만큼 많은 행복을 줄 수 없기 때문이다.

⑤ 특정한 사람들을 가리킬 때 쓰는 '**those who**'는 '**~하는 사람들**'의 뜻이다.

Heaven helps **those who** help themselves. 하늘은 스스로 돕는 자를 돕는다.

Those who do not try will never learn. 노력하지 않는 사람들은 절대 배우지 못한다.

서술형 기초다지기

Challenge 1 It is/was ~ that 용법을 이용하여 밑줄 친 부분을 각각 강조하는 문장으로 만드세요.

I met Ted at the library this morning.

> **보기** *It was I that met Ted at the library this morning.* (I)

01. _____ (Ted)

02. _____ (at the library)

03. _____ (this morning)

Challenge 2 다음 밑줄 친 지시대명사가 가리키는 내용을 찾아 써 보세요.

01. She didn't answer the letter, and <u>that</u> made him angry.   → _____

02. I will always keep <u>this</u> in mind: "Do your best."   → _____

03. Let's go to the movies. – Oh, <u>that</u>'s a good idea.   → _____

04. Work and play are both necessary to health; <u>this</u> gives us rest and that gives us energy.

→ _____

Challenge 3 다음 빈칸에 that과 those 중 알맞은 것을 써 넣으세요.

01. His skills are like _____ of an expert.

02. Your opinion is quite different from _____ of the authorities.

03. One company's products can be distinguished from _____ of another company.

04. I think London's restaurants are better than _____ of New York.

1-3 재귀대명사

He likes talking about **himself**.
그는 자기 이야기하는 것을 좋아한다.

Tom's looking at **himself** in the mirror.
Tom은 거울 속의 자신을 들여다보고 있다.

01 재귀대명사의 형태는 **단수 대명사에 -self**를 붙이고 **복수 대명사에 -selves**를 붙인다.

I – myself	you – yourself	he – himself	she – herself
it – itself	we – ourselves	you – yourselves	they – themselves

02 재귀대명사는 '~자신(들)'이란 의미로, **주어의 동작이 자기 자신에게 향하는 경우**를 말한다. 재귀대명사는 동사와 전치사의 목적어로 쓰인다.

It's not our fault. You can't blame **us**. 그것은 우리의 잘못이 아니다. 너는 우리를 비난해서는 안 된다.

It's our own fault. We should blame **ourselves**. 그것은 우리의 잘못이다. 우리는 우리 자신에게 책임을 돌려야 한다.

03 강조의 의미로 쓰인 재귀대명사는 **문장의 뒤나 강조하고자 하는 (대)명사 뒤**에 쓴다. 강조하기 위해 사용된 것이므로 생략해도 문장에 영향을 끼치지 않는다. 당연히 생략할 때는 강조의 의미도 없어진다.

She **herself** sent e-mail to me. 그녀가 직접 나에게 이메일을 보냈다.

You have to tell her about it **yourself**. 네가 직접 그녀에게 그것에 관해 얘기해야 한다.

04 「전치사+재귀대명사」 형태의 관용 표현들이 있다.

That machine turns off **of itself**. 저 기계는 저절로 꺼진다. ▶ of oneself 저절로

Between ourselves, I don't like her. 우리끼리 얘긴데, 나는 그녀를 좋아하지 않는다. ▶ between oneselves 우리끼리 얘긴데

Help yourself to the dishes. 음식을 마음껏 드세요. ▶ help oneself to ~을 마음껏 먹다

I want to make it **for myself**. 나는 혼자 힘으로 그것을 해내고 싶다. ▶ for oneself 혼자 힘으로

05 **재귀대명사** vs. **each other**

Bob and Sunny stood in front of the mirror and looked at **themselves**.
Bob과 Sunny가 거울 앞에 서서 자신들을 쳐다보았다.

Bob looked at Sunny; Sunny looked at Bob. They looked at **each other**.
Bob은 Sunny를 보았다. Sunny는 Bob을 보았다. 그들은 서로를 쳐다보았다.

서술형 기초다지기

Challenge 1   다음 인칭에 알맞은 재귀대명사를 쓰세요.

01. I   → _____   **02.** you(단수) → _____

03. you(복수)   → _____   **04.** he   → _____

05. she   → _____   **06.** it   → _____

07. we   → _____   **08.** they   → _____

Challenge 2   빈칸에 알맞은 재귀대명사를 쓰고 생략할 수 있는 재귀대명사에는 ∨ 표시를 하세요.

01. Steve cut _____ while he was shaving this morning.   → _____

02. Let's paint the house _____. It will be much cheaper.   → _____

03. I _____ wrote the entire report.   → _____

04. Susan had a great vacation. She enjoyed _____ very much.   → _____

05. John and Laura are trying to make breakfast by _____.   → _____

06. The movie _____ wasn't very good, but I liked the OST.   → _____

Challenge 3   다음 빈칸에 재귀대명사 또는 each other를 구별해서 쓰세요.

01. Roger and Lucy don't like _____.

02. If people work too hard, they can make _____ sick.

03. How long have you and Jason known _____?

04. Some people are very selfish. They think only of _____.

05. I need you and you need me. We need _____.

Chapter 8 — 대명사 · 221

Unit 02 부정대명사

2-1 one / ones

Do you like the red tie?
빨간색 타이가 맘에 드세요?

– No, I like this **one**.
아니오, 전 이게 마음에 듭니다.

01 one은 앞에 나온 명사와 **종류는 같지만 대상이 다른 경우**에 명사의 반복을 피하기 위해 쓴다. 복수 명사일 경우 ones를 쓴다.

A: Does anyone have a dictionary? 누가 사전을 갖고 있니?

B: Yes, I have **one**. 네, 제가 가지고 있어요.

I sold my old car and bought a new **one**. 나는 오래된 차를 팔고 새 차를 샀다.

I don't have a pencil. Can you lend me **one**? 나는 연필이 없다. 하나 빌려줄 수 있니?

My trousers are too small. I need to buy some new **ones**. 내 바지는 너무 작다. 새 바지를 사야 한다.

02 앞에서 언급한 **바로 그것(똑같은 대상, 동일인)을 나타낼 때 it이나 they**를 쓴다.

She bought an iPhone and gave **it** to me. 그녀는 아이폰을 샀고, 그것을 나에게 주었다.

There is a dictionary on the table. **It** belongs to me. 탁자 위에 사전이 있다. 그것은 내 것이다.

The students aren't in the classroom. **They**'re outside. 그 학생들은 교실에 있지 않다. 그들은 밖에 있다.

03 일반적인 사람들을 가리키는 부정대명사는 one/you/we를 쓴다. one이 더 격식을 갖춘 표현이라 일상 영어에서는 you와 we를 많이 쓴다.

One should obey the traffic regulations. 누구나 교통법규를 지켜야 한다.

We should save the environment. 우리는 환경을 보호해야 한다.

04 일반인을 가리키는 one의 소유격은 one's, 목적격은 one이다. 미국식 영어에서는 다른 인칭대명사와 달리 one이 일단 한번 나오고 나면 그 이후에는 one, one's 대신에 각각 he, his를 쓰는 경우가 많다. '모든 이가, 누구나, 사람은' 등으로 해석한다.

One must learn from **one's(=his)** mistakes. 누구나 실수로부터 배워야 한다.

One should do **one's(=his)** best in everything. 사람은 모든 일에 최선을 다해야 한다.

서술형 기초다지기

Challenge 1   다음 괄호 안의 표현 중 알맞은 것을 고르세요.

01. I like the blue shirt more than the black (one / it).

02. Do you have the letter that I sent you? Yes, I have (one / it).

03. One should listen to (ones / one's) parents.

04. There are a white puppy and a brown puppy. Which (one / ones) do you like?

05. I have several American friends and two Japanese (ones / one).

06. Do you have an MP3 player? – Yes, I have (one / it).

Challenge 2   다음 빈칸에 one 또는 ones를 써 넣으세요.

01. Which is your pencil? – The black _____.

02. Can I borrow your dictionary? – Sorry, I haven't got _____.

03. I like your shoes. – Oh, thanks. They are the _____ I bought yesterday.

04. Which pants fit you better? – The blue _____.

Challenge 3   다음 빈칸에 one, ones, it 또는 them을 넣어 완성하세요.

01. I'm sorry, but I broke this vase. I dropped _____.

02. She bought a cake and ate all of _____.

03. My laptop broke down, so I bought a new _____ this week.

04. Where are my sunglasses? Do you see _____?

05. The dictionaries on this desk are all German _____.

06. Where's the nearest bus stop? – _____ is in front of the bank.

Chapter 8 – 대명사 · 223

2-2 -thing, -body, -one

This is strange. There's **something** wrong.
The window is open.
There wasn't **anybody** in the house.
이상한 일이다. 뭔가 잘못되었다.
창문이 열려 있다.
집 안에는 아무도 없었다.

01 something은 긍정문에서, anything은 부정문이나 의문문에서 **잘 알지 못하는 물건을 가리키는 부정대명사**로 쓰인다. something은 권유나 요구를 나타낼 때 의문문에서도 쓰인다.

I'm thirsty. I want **something** to drink. 나는 목이 마르다. 난 마실 것을 원한다.

Do you know **anything** about this accident? 당신은 이 사고에 대해 아는 것이 있나요?

She didn't eat **anything** for dinner. 그녀는 저녁으로 아무것도 먹지 않았다.

Would you like to have **something** to drink? 마실 것 좀 드릴까요?

02 somebody/someone과 somewhere는 각각 **사람과 장소**를 가리키고 부정문과 의문문에서는 anybody/anyone과 anywhere를 쓴다.

I saw **somebody/someone** in the shop. 나는 누군가 가게 안에 있는 것을 봤다.

She lives **somewhere** near the airport. 그녀는 공항 근처 어딘가에 산다.

Is there **anybody/anyone** in the shop? 가게에 누구 있니?

I'm not going **anywhere**. 나는 아무데도 안 갈 겁니다.

I didn't go **anywhere** yesterday. 나는 어제 아무데도 가지 않았다.

Anybody can come. 누구라도 올 수 있다. ▶ anybody가 '어떠한 ~라도'의 뜻일 때는 긍정문에서 쓸 수 있다.

※ 미국식 영어에서는 -one보다 -body를 더 많이 쓴다.

03 nothing은 사물, no one(=nobody)는 사람, nowhere는 장소 전체를 부정하는 부정대명사이다. '무엇도/누구도 ~가 아니다'의 뜻이다. 긍정문과 의문문에 쓰이며 부정문에서 nothing은 'not+anything'으로 no one(=nobody)은 'not+anybody/anyone'으로 바꿔 쓸 수 있다.

There is **nobody** in the house. 집에는 아무도 없다.

=There isn't **anyone** in the house.

She bought **nothing** yesterday. 그녀는 어제 아무것도 사지 않았다.

=She didn't buy **anything** yesterday.

Where are you going? - **Nowhere**. I'm staying here. 어디 가니? - 아무데도 안가. 여기 머물러 있을 거야.

서술형 기초다지기

Challenge 1 다음 괄호 안의 표현 중 알맞은 것을 고르세요.

01. I lost my MP3 player yesterday. I left it (somewhere / anywhere).

02. She didn't receive (something / anything) from her boyfriend on her birthday.

03. We saw (anyone / someone) in the dark room.

04. Did you tell her (anything / nobody) about me?

05. There's (nothing / anything) wrong with the air conditioner.

06. (No one / Nothing) likes Jessica. She's very selfish.

Challenge 2 알맞은 부정대명사를 사용하여 문장을 완성하세요.

01. She doesn't know _____ about it.

02. Would you like _____ to eat?

03. I have _____ to do this afternoon. Let's go _____. I have my mother's car, so we can go _____ we like.

04. There's _____ at the door. Can you go and see who it is?

05. There isn't _____ in the office.

Challenge 3 nobody는 「not+anybody」로, nothing은 「not+anything」으로 고쳐 쓰세요.

보기	I bought nothing yesterday. → *I didn't buy anything yesterday.*

01. The bus was completely empty. There was nobody on it.

→ _____

02. The teacher said nothing about the result of the exam.

→ _____

2-3 all, every, each, both

All the people in the photo are men.
사진 속에 있는 모든 사람들은 남자들이다.

Every student is in the library.
= All the students are in the library.
모든 학생들이 도서관에 있다.

01 All: '모든, ~모두'의 뜻으로 all 뒤에는 셀 수 있는 명사와 셀 수 없는 명사 모두 올 수 있다. **all 다음에 오는 명사의 수에 동사의 수를 일치**시킨다. 대명사를 쓸 경우 「all of + 대명사」로 쓴다.

All students are wearing jackets. 모든 학생들이 자켓을 입고 있다.
All the information is correct. 모든 정보가 틀림없다.
All of it is correct. 그것 모두가 정확하다.

02 Every: '모든'의 뜻으로 개별적인 것들의 전체를 가리키지만 **단수 취급하여 명사도 단수, 동사도 단수를 쓴다.** 하지만 의미는 복수여서 「All the + 복수 명사」와 같다.

Every runner was fast. = **All the runners** were fast. 모든 주자가 빨랐다. ▶ not each runner

03 Each: '각자, 각기, 각각의'란 뜻으로 전체를 구성하는 개별적인 것들을 가리킨다. Each 뒤에 of가 올 경우 명사 앞에 관사나 소유격 등의 수식어가 붙고 **동사는 반드시 단수 취급**한다.

In a soccer game, **each** team has 11 players. 축구 경기에서는 각 팀에 11명의 선수가 있다. ▶ not every team
Each of the students has his own room. 학생들 각자 자기 방이 있다.

04 Both: '둘 다, 양쪽'의 뜻으로 **복수 명사가 오고 동사도 복수 동사**를 쓴다. 명사 앞에 관사나 소유격 등의 수식어가 있을 때 both 뒤에 'of'를 쓴다.

Both restaurants are very good. 레스토랑 둘 다 매우 좋다.
Both (of) these restaurants are very good. 이 레스토랑 둘 다 매우 좋다.
Both (of) his sons leave for London next Saturday. 그의 아들 둘 다 다음주 토요일에 런던으로 떠난다.

※ of는 생략 가능하다. 단, 대명사가 올 경우에는 반드시 of가 필요하다.
Both of you are acting like children. 너희 둘 다 어린애들 같구나.

서술형 기초다지기

정답 p. 27

Challenge 1   다음 괄호 안의 표현 중 알맞은 것을 고르세요.

01. Every girl (have / has) a bicycle.

02. Each (students / student) has his or her computer.

03. Both my parents (is / are) from Michigan.

04. Each book (was / were) a different color.

05. All the flowers in this garden (is / are) beautiful.

Challenge 2   다음 문장에서 every는 all로, all은 every로 고쳐 다시 쓰세요.

보기	All the rooms have a balcony.	→ *Every room has a balcony.*

01. All the waiters speak excellent English.   → _____

02. Every worker starts at 8 a.m.   → _____

03. Every child wants some pizza.   → _____

04. All the boys always play soccer after school.   → _____

another, other, the other, the others

A: This tea is really nice.
이 차는 정말 맛이 좋군요.

B: Would you have **another** cup of green tea?
녹차 한잔 더 하실래요?

01 another는 '또 하나'의 의미로 **단수 명사를 수식하는 형용사나 대명사**로 쓰인다. 단수의 의미이므로 복수 명사와 함께 쓰지 않는다.

These biscuits are really nice. Can I have **another**? 이 비스킷은 정말 맛있다. 하나 더 먹어도 되니?

Can I ask you **another** question? 질문을 하나 더 해도 될까요?

※ A is one thing, and B is another (thing). A와 B는 별개의 것이다.

To know is **one thing**, and to practice is **another**. 아는 것과 실행하는 것은 별개이다.

02 other는 **복수 명사를 수식하는 형용사나 대명사**로 쓰이는데 대명사는 복수형(others)으로만 쓰인다.

There are many different types of pollution. One of the most common types of pollution is air pollution.
여러 가지 많은 오염 형태가 있다. 가장 흔한 종류의 오염은 대기오염이다.

Other types of pollution are water pollution and noise pollution. 다른 오염들에는 수질오염과 소음공해가 있다.

→ **Others are** water pollution and noise pollution.

03 the other는 '(둘 중) 다른 하나'의 의미로 **단수 또는 복수 명사를 수식하는 형용사 또는 대명사**로 쓰인다. the others는 '(나머지) 다른 사람[것]들'의 의미로 복수를 나타내는 대명사로 쓰인다. 정관사 the를 함께 쓰여 정해져 있는 명사를 가리킨다.

There are two bicycles. I am using one bicycle. 자전거가 두 대 있다. 내가 한 대를 쓰고 있다.

My mom is using **the other** bicycle. 엄마가 다른 자전거를 쓰고 있다.

=My mom is using **the other**.

I invited five friends to the party. 나는 5명의 친구들을 파티에 초대했다.

Sunny and Peter came, but **the other friends** didn't. Sunny와 Peter는 왔지만 다른 친구들은 오지 않았다.

=Sunny and Peter came, but **the others** didn't.

	형용사 + 명사	대명사	단/복수
이미 언급한 이외의 것 하나[한 명]	another boy	another	단수
이미 언급한 이외의 여러 개[명]	other boys	others	복수
주어진 숫자 내에서 남아 있는 것 하나[한 명]	the other boy	the other	단수
주어진 숫자 내에서 남아 있는 나머지 전부	the other boys	the others	복수

서술형 기초다지기

Challenge 1 다음 빈칸에 another와 the other 중 알맞은 것을 골라 쓰세요.

01. There are two apples on the table. Bob's going to eat one of them. Sunny is going to eat _____ apple.

02. The child has a lot of toys, but he wants _____ one.

03. Many cities in the U.S. have warm weather. One city is Miami. _____ one is San Diego.

04. To learn is one thing, and to teach is _____.

05. It is one thing to acquire knowledge; it is quite _____ to apply it.

06. Do you know the capital of this state? Do you know _____ 49 state capitals?

Challenge 2 다음 빈칸에 other(s)와 the others 중 알맞은 것을 골라 쓰세요.

01. Johnson is a common last name in the U.S. _____ common last names are Smith, Wilson, and Jones.

02. The bank is going to close now. Plese come back some _____ time.

03. Some people like classical music, but _____ like rock music.

04. There are four seasons in Korea. Spring and summer are two. _____ are fall and winter.

05. There are four roses in the vase; one is red and _____ are white.

06. Some people went by bus, and _____ by train.

2-5 자주 쓰이는 부정대명사

There are three women here. **One** is from Japan, **another** is from China and **the other** is from Korea.
여기에 세 명의 여자가 있다. 한 명은 일본 출신이고, 다른 한 명은 중국 출신, 그리고 나머지 한 명은 한국 출신이다.

01 두 개의 명사를 순서 없이 가리킬 때 **(둘 중의) 하나는 one**을 쓰고, **나머지 다른 하나는 the other**를 쓴다.

There are two countries I want to visit. **One** is France, and **the other** is Italy.
내가 방문하고 싶은 두 나라가 있다. 한 곳은 프랑스이고 다른 한 곳은 이탈리아이다.

02 세 개의 명사를 순서 없이 가리킬 때 **첫 번째는 one, 두 번째는 another, 마지막 정해진 세 번째는 the other 또는 the third**를 쓴다.

I have three brothers; **one** is in Seoul, **another** is in Incheon, and **the other**(=the third) is in Busan.
나는 세 명의 형이 있다. 한 명은 서울에, 또 한 명은 인천에, 다른 한 명은 부산에 있다.

03 불특정 다수를 표현하여 **몇몇은 some, 다른 사람[것]들은 others**를 쓴다. others는 「other+복수 명사」로 표현할 수 있다.

Some people believe that the development of technology leads to happiness, and **others**(=other people) don't. 어떤 사람들은 기술의 발전이 행복을 가져온다고 생각하고, 다른 사람들은 그렇게 생각하지 않는다.

04 정해져 있는 수에서 몇몇을 가리킬 때 some, 나머지는 the others를 쓴다. the others는 정관사 the와 함께 쓰여 정해져 있는 명사들을 가리킨다.

Some of them said "yes", but **the others** said "no".
그들 중 몇몇은 "yes"라고 말했지만 나머지 사람들은 "no"라고 말했다.

05 each other는 둘 사이, one another는 셋 이상일 경우에 '서로서로'를 뜻한다. 하지만 일상 영어에서는 둘 다 구분 없이 쓰는데 each other가 더 자주 쓰인다.

Those two boys are always laughing at **each other**. 저 두 소년들은 항상 서로를 보고 웃는다.
All the students helped **one another** prepare for the test. 모든 학생들이 서로 도와가며 시험 준비를 한다.

서술형 기초다지기

Challenge 1 다음 빈칸에 another, others, the other, the others 중 알맞은 것을 골라 쓰세요.

01. I have two gifts. One is for you, Bob. _____ is for you, Jason.

02. Some animals live in land and _____ live in water.

03. There are many kinds of animals in the world. The cheetah is one kind. Some _____ are elephants, whales, and tigers.

04. One country in Europe is France. _____ is Italy.

05. There are three European countries where people speak French. One is France, _____ is Belgium, and _____ is Switzerland.

06. I have five dogs. Some are white, but _____ are black.

07. I have two sisters. One lives in Seoul and _____ lives in Daegu.

08. People usually eat three meals a day. Breakfast is one meal, lunch is _____ and dinner is _____.

09. Some of the girls were dressed up, and _____ were not.

10. There are a lot of flowers. Some are white and _____ are yellow.

11. There are four seasons. Summer is one. _____ are fall, winter, and spring.

12. What's your favorite season? Some people like spring the best. _____ think fall is the nicest season.

13. There are four oceans. The Pacific and the Atlantic are two. _____ are the Indian and the Arctic Oceans.

14. Paris is a beautiful city in Europe. Prague is _____ beautiful city in Europe.

01 출제 100% – 대명사 it과 지시대명사를 구별하라!

출제자의 눈 대명사 it이나 복수형인 they는 앞에 나온 특정한 명사를 대신하고, one(s)은 종류는 같지만 대상이 다른 명사를 대신해서 쓴다. 이 둘을 구별하는 문제나 it ~ that 강조용법의 it과 대명사 it을 구별하는 문제가 출제된다. 특히 지시대명사 that과 those는 앞에 나온 단/복수 명사를 대신하는 데 쓰이는데 this와 these를 쓰지 않도록 조심하자.

Ex 1.

A: Does anyone have a dictionary?

B: Yes, I have _____.

(a) it   (b) one   (c) ones   (d) them

Ex 2.

Mr. Schmidt's performance is far superior to _____ of his associates.

(a) these   (b) those   (c) this   (d) that

02 출제 100% – all, every, each, both는 수의 일치를 묻는다.

출제자의 눈 every와 each 뒤에는 반드시 단수 명사를 쓰고 동사도 단수로 일치시킨다. both는 항상 복수 동사를 쓰고, all은 뒤에 나오는 명사에 따라 단/복수의 수를 일치시켜야 한다.

Ex 3.

All the food _____ delicious.

(a) are   (b) is   (c) all   (d) each

Ex 4.

There were four books on the table. Each _____ was a different color.

(a) books   (b) every book   (c) book   (d) has

03 출제 100% - 재귀대명사의 형태와 용법을 알아두자.

출제자의 눈 재귀대명사는 문장에서 목적어로 쓰일 때는 생략할 수 없지만 부사가 되어 강조용법으로 쓰일 때는 생략이 가능하다. 인칭과 단/복수에 따른 재귀대명사의 형태를 묻거나 강조용법과 구별하는 문제가 출제된다. -thing, -body로 끝나는 부정대명사는 긍정문, 부정문, 의문문에 따라 알맞은 대명사를 쓸 줄 아는지를 물어본다.

Ex 5.

Julia had a great vacation. She enjoyed _____ very much.
(a) himself　　　(b) her　　　(c) yourself　　　(d) herself

Ex 6.

A: I'm hungry. I want _____ to eat.
B: What would you like?
(a) anything　　　(b) something　　　(c) nothing　　　(d) somewhere

04 출제 100% - 출제 빈도가 높은 부정대명사를 기억해 두자.

출제자의 눈 부정대명사 one, another, the other, others, the others의 쓰임을 반드시 기억해 두자. 특히 정관사 the가 붙은 부정대명사는 갯수가 정해진 것들을 가리킬 때 쓴다. 불특정한 것을 가리킬 때 단수는 another, 복수는 others 또는 「other+복수 명사」로 나타낸다. 갯수가 정해지지 않은 복수 명사 중에 몇몇을 가리킬 때는 some이고 나머지는 others이며, 정해진 명사일 때는 some과 the others를 쓴다.

Ex 7.

One of the students is from Mexico. _____ student is from Japan.
(a) The other　　　(b) Another　　　(c) Others　　　(d) The others

Ex 8.

Travelers by air go on increasing in number year after year. Some of them utilize airplanes for business, and _____ enjoy flights as recreation.
(a) others　　　(b) another　　　(c) the others　　　(d) one

1. 다음 그림과 일치하도록 재귀대명사를 이용하여 문장을 완성하시오.

A: What is she doing now?

B: She is _____ _____ _____ in the mirror. (look at)

2. 다음 밑줄 친 부분이 어법상 틀린 것을 고르시오.

❶ The car he is driving is not <u>his</u>.

❷ I've lost my pencil. Can you lend me <u>it</u>?

❸ My watch is broken. I need to get another <u>one</u>.

❹ Tell me <u>this</u>. Who is responsible for the mistake?

❺ <u>It</u> was only a few days ago that I talked with Lisa.

3. 다음 빈칸에 알맞은 것을 고르시오.

_____ is Mike that helps me with my English homework.

❶ That ❷ Such ❸ This

❹ It ❺ He

4. 다음 빈칸에 들어갈 말로 알맞은 것은?

Franklin, on the $100 bill, and Hamilton, on the $10 bill, were not American presidents. All _____ bills have pictures of American presidents.

❶ some ❷ other ❸ another

❹ the other ❺ the others

5. 다음 글의 밑줄 친 <u>ones</u>가 가리키는 것은?

You have lost your confidence over the years. You need to learn how to turn negative thoughts into positive <u>ones</u>. The process is simple, but it takes time and practice. No matter how much someone offends you or how bad a situation was, try to avoid letting it have a negative effect on you. Take a deep breath and turn your thoughts to positive <u>ones</u>. Your day will be much better if you do.

❶ yourselves ❷ practice

❸ negative effects ❹ confidence

❺ thoughts

6. 다음 빈칸에 들어갈 말이 바르게 짝지어진 것은?

Many people in the world speak English. _____ people use English as their first language, and _____ use it as their second language.

❶ Some – some ❷ One – the other

❸ Some – others ❹ One – another

❺ Any – none

7. 다음 빈칸에 공통으로 들어갈 말로 알맞은 것은?

· The ears of rabbits are longer than _____ of dogs.

· _____ who break the rules will be punished.

❶ that ❷ these ❸ those

❹ some ❺ themselves

234

오답 노트 만들기

★틀린 문제 : _____　★다시 공부한 날 : _____

(1) 문제를 왜? 틀렸는지 곰곰이 생각하고 그 이유를 적어본다.

(2) 핵심 개념을 적는다.

(3) 자신이 몰랐던 단어와 숙어 표현이 있으면 정리한다.

(4) 해설집에서 필요한 부분을 골라 풀이 해법을 정리한다.

★틀린 문제 : _____　★다시 공부한 날 : _____

(1) 문제를 왜? 틀렸는지 곰곰이 생각하고 그 이유를 적어본다.

(2) 핵심 개념을 적는다.

(3) 자신이 몰랐던 단어와 숙어 표현이 있으면 정리한다.

(4) 해설집에서 필요한 부분을 골라 풀이 해법을 정리한다.

★틀린 문제 : _____　★다시 공부한 날 : _____

(1) 문제를 왜? 틀렸는지 곰곰이 생각하고 그 이유를 적어본다.

(2) 핵심 개념을 적는다.

(3) 자신이 몰랐던 단어와 숙어 표현이 있으면 정리한다.

(4) 해설집에서 필요한 부분을 골라 풀이 해법을 정리한다.

★틀린 문제 : _____　★다시 공부한 날 : _____

(1) 문제를 왜? 틀렸는지 곰곰이 생각하고 그 이유를 적어본다.

(2) 핵심 개념을 적는다.

(3) 자신이 몰랐던 단어와 숙어 표현이 있으면 정리한다.

(4) 해설집에서 필요한 부분을 골라 풀이 해법을 정리한다.

1. 다음 빈칸에 들어갈 말로 알맞은 것은?

> I didn't apologize to her because I had _____ to be sorry for her.

❶ all ❷ anything ❸ something
❹ nothing ❺ anyone

오답노트

2. 다음 빈칸에 들어갈 말이 순서대로 나열된 것은?

> Just use this simple form if you want to transfer funds from _____ of your existing accounts to _____.

❶ one – the others ❷ other – the other
❸ one – another ❹ one – the other
❺ some – the others

오답노트

3. 다음 문장의 밑줄 친 부분과 쓰임이 같은 것은?

> We take it for granted that he is opposed to the plan.

❶ It was in the park that I met her for the first time.
❷ It can help scientists work out problems.
❸ It is always pleasant to have a match.
❹ It is too dark in this room.
❺ I think it natural for you to think so.

오답노트

4. 다음 밑줄 친 부분이 어법상 어색한 것은?

❶ Both of us were very tired.
❷ Every student wears a school uniform.
❸ All animals eat in order to live.
❹ There were four toys on the table. Each of them have a different shape.
❺ All of their oil comes from the Middle East.

오답노트

5. 다음 빈칸에 들어갈 말로 알맞은 것은?

> Some kids get an allowance for doing nothing. _____ kids have to do chores to get an allowance. But not all kids get an allowance.

❶ Another ❷ The other ❸ Others
❹ The others ❺ Other

오답노트

6. 다음 중 밑줄 친 재귀대명사를 생략할 수 있는 것은?

❶ She wrote most of the songs herself.
❷ Peter sometimes blames himself.
❸ Be careful! Don't hurt yourself.
❹ You must be proud of yourself.
❺ They introduced themselves to the whole class.

오답노트

7. 다음 밑줄 친 Ⓐ, Ⓑ가 가리키는 것을 찾아 순서대로 쓰시오.

> Work and play are both necessary to health; Ⓐ <u>this</u> gives us rest, and Ⓑ <u>that</u> gives us energy.

Ⓐ _____ / Ⓑ _____

오답노트

8. 다음 빈칸에 알맞은 것은?

> The cost of living in the city is higher than _____ in the country.

❶ one ❷ it ❸ this
❹ those ❺ that

오답노트

9. 다음 중 밑줄 친 It이 가주어로 쓰인 것은?

❶ <u>It</u> was Mary that broke the vase yesterday.
❷ <u>It</u> is ten miles from here to the station.
❸ What was <u>it</u> that said so?
❹ <u>It</u> doesn't matter which team will win the game.
❺ If <u>it</u> were not for water, nothing could live.

오답노트

10. 다음 빈칸에 들어갈 말로 알맞은 것은?

> Nowadays many different types of English are used by people all over the world. Some of these people use English as their first language, and _____ use it as their second language.

❶ the other ❷ others ❸ the others
❹ one ❺ the one

오답노트

11. 두 문장이 같은 뜻이 되도록 빈칸에 알맞은 말을 쓰시오.

> The question is difficult to answer.
> = _____ _____ difficult to answer the question.

12. 다음 우리말과 같은 뜻이 되도록 빈칸에 알맞은 말을 쓰시오.

> 그녀는 양손에 가방을 들고 있었다. 그래서 내게 문을 열어달라고 부탁했던 것이다.
> =She had bags in _____ hands. That's why she asked me to open the door.

❶ most ❷ almost ❸ all the
❹ both ❺ each

오답노트

[13-17] 다음 빈칸에 들어갈 알맞은 말을 아래에서 골라 쓰시오.

one   the others   another   some   the other

13. To attack the hill is one thing, to defend the hill is _____.

14. Many people gathered here. _____ came from Korea, others from Thailand, and others from China.

15. Bob has two suits. One is blue, and _____ is gray.

16. There are nine students here. Some have cell phones, and _____ don't.

17. This towel is too dirty. Can I have a clean _____?

오답노트

18. 다음 문장을 It was ~ that 강조구문으로 바꿀 때 어법상 틀린 것은?

Park Tae-hwan won the second gold medal at the Guangzhou Asian Games in 2010.

❶ It was Park Tae-hwan that won the second gold medal at the Guangzhou Asian Games in 2010.

❷ It was won that Park Tae-hwan did the second gold medal at the Guangzhou Asian Games in 2010.

❸ It was the second gold medal that Park Tae-hwan won at the Guangzhou Asian Games in 2010.

❹ It was at the Guangzhous Asain Games that Park Tae-hwan won the second gold medal in 2010.

❺ It was in 2010 that Park Tae-hwan won the second gold medal at the Guangzhous Asian Games.

오답노트

19. 다음 밑줄 친 부분의 용법이 다른 하나를 고르시오.

❶ He did his homework <u>himself</u>.
❷ We enjoyed <u>ourselves</u> at the party.
❸ The Turtle ship was invented by General Yi <u>himself</u>.
❹ I made the desk <u>myself</u>.
❺ I <u>myself</u> carried the box.

오답노트

20. 다음 빈칸에 알맞은 말은?

I invited six friends to the party. But only Sunny and Steve came. _____ didn't come.

❶ The others   ❷ Another
❸ One   ❹ Both of them
❺ Either of them

오답노트

21. 다음 중 밑줄 친 부정대명사가 잘못 쓰인 것은?

❶ Is there <u>anything</u> else I can help you with?

❷ <u>Nobody</u> knows what the afterlife will be like.

❸ I put my glasses <u>somewhere</u>, and now I can't find them.

❹ Would you like <u>anything</u> to eat?

❺ <u>No one</u> can live without air and water.

오답노트

22. 다음 빈칸에 들어갈 말이 바르게 짝지어진 것은?

The air is composed of two different kinds of substances, oxygen and nitrogen. The _____ is necessary for the process of burning, while _____ does not allow things to burn.

❶ some − others   ❷ one − the other

❸ one − another   ❹ one − others

❺ some − the others

오답노트

23. 다음 중 밑줄 친 부분을 생략할 수 있는 것은?

❶ I washed <u>myself</u> after school.

❷ He did the work <u>himself</u>.

❸ Please talk about <u>yourself</u>.

❹ She went there by <u>herself</u>.

❺ Did you enjoy <u>yourself</u> at the party?

오답노트

24. 다음 빈칸에 공통으로 들어갈 대명사를 고르시오.

· He bought a watch and give _____ to me.

· _____ is not easy to solve this problem.

❶ it   ❷ one   ❸ that

❹ some   ❺ this

오답노트

[25-27] 다음 우리말과 의미가 같도록 빈칸에 알맞은 말을 하나씩 골라 쓰시오.

| each | all | every |

25. 모든 사회는 그 사회만의 규칙이 있다.

→ _____ society has its own rules.

26. 각각의 사람들은 이루어야 할 다른 목표들이 있다.

→ _____ person has different goals to achieve.

27. 모든 학생들이 학교 축제에 참석했다.

→ _____ the students were present at the school festival.

오답노트

A. 다음 빈칸에 something, someone, anything, anyone 중 하나를 사용하여 문장을 완성하시오.

1. 사무실에 아무도 없었다.

→ There isn't _____ in the office.

2. 나는 그것이 지겹다. 난 뭔가 새로운 것을 원해.

→ I'm tired of it. I want _____ new.

3. 나는 어떤 것도 마시고 싶지 않다. 난 목이 마르지 않다.

→ I don't want _____ to drink. I'm not thirsty.

4. 문에 누군가가 있다. 그 여자를 아니?

→ There's _____ at the door. Do you know the woman?

B. 다음 빈칸에 들어갈 알맞은 대명사를 써 넣으시오.

1. The ears of a rabbit are longer than _____ of a dog.

2. Do _____ speak English in Australia?

3. _____ is hot in the summer.

4. I found _____ true that he passed the examination.

C. 다음 우리말에 맞게 빈칸에 알맞은 말을 넣어 문장을 완성하시오.

1. 나는 두 명의 친구를 만났다. 한 명은 Jason이고 다른 한 명은 Susan이다.

→ I met two friends. _____ is Jason and _____ _____ is Susan.

2. 사람들은 해상 여행을 원한다. 몇몇은 제주도로, 다른 사람들은 독도로 가고 싶어 한다.

→ People want to travel by water. _____ want to go to Jejudo and _____ want to go to Dokdo.

D. 다음 문장에서 목적어를 찾아 표시한 후 가목적어를 이용하여 문장을 다시 쓰시오.

> | 보 기 | Don't regard <u>forgiving everything</u> generous. |
> |---|---|
> | | → *Don't regard it generous forgiving everything.* |

1. We think that she should leave without telling us strange.

→ _____

2. My parents see to wear a miniskirt in cold winter crazy.

→ _____

3. Western people believe to break a mirror unlucky.

→ _____

E. 아래의 표현과 알맞은 재귀대명사를 이용하여 다음 문장을 완성하시오.

> | blame | enjoy | cut | help | teach |
> |---|---|---|---|---|

> | 보 기 | Ouch! I just *cut myself* with a knife. |
> |---|---|

1. When I was young, I _____ to ride a bicycle. Then I taught the other children in the neighborhood.

2. Jessica _____ for the accident, but it wasn't her fault. There was nothing she could have done when the car came toward her.

3. Eat! Eat! There's a lot more pizza in the oven. Please, all of you, _____.

4. They went to a party last night. Let's ask them if they _____.

실전 서술형 평가문제

 출제의도 지시대명사
평가내용 지시대명사를 활용한 문장 이해

A. 우리말과 같은 의미가 되도록 괄호 안의 표현을 이용하여 문장을 완성하시오. (단, 지시대명사 that, those 를 이용할 것)   [서술형 유형 : 8점 / 난이도 : 중]

1. 호주의 인구는 일본의 인구보다 훨씬 적다. (much smaller / the population of Australia / Japan)

→ _____

2. 이 호수의 물은 저 호수의 물보다 맑다. (that lake / cleaner than / the water in this lake)

→ _____

3. 토끼의 귀는 사람의 귀보다 더 길다. (a human / longer than / the ears of a rabbit)

→ _____

4. Jason의 태도는 종종 아이들의 태도보다 훨씬 못하다.

(a child / often much better / Jason's manners)

→ _____

5. 한국의 기후는 이탈리아의 기후와 비슷하다.

(Italy / like / the climate of Korea)

→ _____

출제의도 부정대명사
평가내용 부정대명사의 올바른 활용

B. 다음 그림과 일치하도록 주어진 단어와 부정대명사를 이용하여 문장을 완성하시오. (단, 부정대명사 one, another, the other, the others, other를 이용할 것) [서술형 유형 : 6점 / 난이도 : 중하]

보기	 Sunny / Tiffany	There are two women in this picture. *One is Sunny and the other is Tiffany.*

1.

doctor / teacher

I have two daughters.

_____

2.

red / blue / black

There are four colors in the Korean flag. One of the colors is white.

_____

3.

go outside /
play soccer

Our physical education class was divided into two groups.

Half of the students stayed inside and played basketball.

_____

실전 서술형 평가문제

정답 p. 30

출제의도 It is/was ~ that 강조구문
평가내용 강조구문을 이용하여 질문에 답하기

C. 아래 사진을 보고 It is/was ~ that 강조구문을 이용하여 질문에 답하시오. [서술형 유형 : 6점 / 난이도 : 중]

보 기		Scott : I'm sorry that I broke your glasses yesterday. Peter : You were really drunk. It was very terrible.

1. Q : Who broke the glasses?

　　A : _____

2. Q : What did Scott break yesterday?

　　A : _____

3. Q : When did Scott break the glasses?

　　A : _____

서술형 평가문제	채 점 기 준	배 점	나의 점수
A	표현이 올바르고 문법, 철자가 모두 정확한 경우	2점×4문항=8점	
B		2점×3문항=6점	
C		2점×3문항=6점	
공통	문법, 철자가 1개씩 틀린 경우	각 문항당 1점씩 감점	
	내용과 전혀 일치하지 않거나 답을 기재하지 못한 경우	0점	

Chapter 9

형용사 (Adjectives)

1-1 형용사의 역할

Nancy is a **kind** girl. Nancy는 친절한 소녀이다.
She is **kind** and **pretty**. 그녀는 친절하고 예쁘다.
I think her **kind** and **pretty**. 나는 그녀가 친절하고 예쁘다고 생각한다.

01 **형용사가 명사를 직접 수식하는 용법을 한정용법**이라고 한다. 형용사의 정의가 '명사와 함께 하는 단어'인 만큼 형용사는 명사의 종류와 마찬가지로 고유형용사와 일반형용사로 구분된다.

There's an **Italian** restaurant near my house. 집 근처에 이탈리안 레스토랑이 있다. (고유형용사)

I have a **red** coat. 나는 빨간색 코트가 하나 있다. (일반형용사>묘사형용사)

I have a date **this** evening. 나는 오늘 저녁에 데이트가 있다. (일반형용사>지시형용사)

What floor are you going to? 몇 층 가십니까? (일반형용사>의문형용사)

02 형용사가 보어(주격 보어, 목적격 보어)로 쓰여 **주어와 목적어인 명사의 상태나 성질을 설명하는 역할**을 한다. 이를 형용사의 서술적 용법이라고 한다.

This flower is **beautiful**. 이 꽃은 아름답다. ▶ 주격 보어

We consider him **innocent**. 우리는 그가 무죄라고 생각한다. ▶ 목적격 보어

03 look, feel, smell, taste, sound, get 등의 감각을 나타내는 동사들은 **뒤에 형용사만 쓰며 주어의 상태가 어떤지를 표현**한다. 이러한 연결동사 뒤에 명사를 쓰려면 「like+명사」로 쓴다.

She **looks** happy. 그녀는 행복해 보인다.

She **looks like** a soldier. 그녀는 군인처럼 보인다.

04 대부분의 형용사는 명사 앞과 동사 뒤에 자유롭게 쓰지만 어떤 형용사들은 둘 중 한 가지로만 쓸 수 있다.

① 명사 앞에서만 수식하는 형용사(한정적 용법)

main, only, live, drunken, elder, golden, wooden, former, inner, indoor, outdoor, major

② 연결동사 뒤에서만 수식하는 형용사(서술적 용법)

afraid, asleep, alone, alive, alike, aware, ashamed, content, drunk, fine, glad, pleased

The **drunken** man was lying on the road. 술 취한 사람이 길에 누워 있었다.

You were really **drunk** yesterday. 너 어제 정말 취했었어.

I saw a **live** fish in the fishbowl. 나는 어항에서 살아있는 물고기를 봤다.

The fish is **alive**. 그 물고기는 살아있다.

246

서술형 기초다지기

정답 p. 30

Challenge 1   다음 밑줄 친 형용사의 용법을 한정적 용법과 서술적 용법으로 구별하세요.

01. It's <u>cold</u> weather today.   →_____ 용법

02. The weather is <u>cold</u> today.   →_____ 용법

03. Everyone has <u>ill</u> feeling towards the war.   →_____ 용법

04. When his wife was <u>ill</u>, Jason cared for her night and day.   →_____ 용법

05. The room smelled very <u>terrible</u>.   →_____ 용법

Challenge 2   다음 괄호 안의 형용사 중에서 알맞은 것을 고르세요.

01. These are (live / alive) fish.

02. These fish are (live / alive).

03. A (drunk / drunken) man was wandering in the parking lot.

04. A cute baby is (sleep / asleep) on the bed.

05. The twins look (like / alike).

Challenge 3   괄호 안의 형용사를 다음 문장의 알맞은 위치에 넣어 다시 쓰세요.

01. She is taller than her sister. (elder)

    →_____

02. Tennis is a game. (outdoor)

    →_____

03. I think the drivers are very dangerous. (drunken)

    →_____

04. My concern now is to take care of my parents. (main)

    →_____

1-2 형용사의 다양한 쓰임

There's **something suspicious** about that man.
저 남자에 관해 수상쩍은 것이 있다.

We should donate money for **the poor**.
우리는 가난한 사람들을 위해 돈을 기부해야 한다.

01 같은 형태의 형용사이지만 위치에 따라 그 의미가 달라지는 경우가 있다.

	한정적 용법	서술적 용법
right	오른쪽의, 옳은	옳은
certain	어떤, 특정한	확실한
ill	나쁜	아픈
present	현재의	출석한
late	작고한, 돌아가신(=dead)	늦은

I don't know her **present** address. 나는 그녀의 현재 주소를 모른다.
The king was **present** at the meeting. 국왕이 회의에 참석했다.
She's got a **certain** charm. 그녀는 어떤 매력을 갖고 있다.
It is **certain** that he failed in the exam. 그가 시험에 떨어진 것은 확실하다.
The **late** Mr. Walker was such a nice person. 작고한 워커 씨는 참 좋은 사람이었다.
He was **late** for the meeting. 그는 회의에 늦었다.

02 -thing, -one, -body로 끝나는 부정대명사는 **형용사가 반드시 뒤에서 수식**한다.

She always wants **something** special. 그녀는 항상 특별한 것을 원한다.
I don't know **anyone** selfish like Jane. Jane처럼 이기적인 사람을 모른다.

※ thing, body, one 그 자체가 한 단어로 쓰인 경우에는 형용사가 앞에서 수식한다.

I don't want anyone to see my secret **diary**. 나는 누구도 내 비밀 일기장을 보는 걸 원치 않는다.
A lot of bad **things** happened to me in my life. 내 인생에서 나쁜 일들이 많이 일어났다.

03 「the＋형용사」는 사회적으로 잘 알려진 **사람들의 집단을 나타내며 복수로 취급**한다.

The rich are not always happy. 부자라고 항상 행복한 것은 아니다. ▶ The rich＝rich people
The unemployed want their job back. 실업자들은 다시 일자리를 갖길 원한다. ▶ the unemployed＝unemployed people

248

서술형 기초다지기

Challenge 1 다음 밑줄 친 단어의 의미를 써 보세요.

| 보기 | It is <u>certain</u> that Jack will read this message. | → | 확실한 |

01. <u>Certain</u> plastic containers produce environmental hormones. → _____

02. His <u>ill</u> manner made us embarrassed. → _____

03. I was feeling <u>ill</u> last night. → _____

04. His <u>late</u> wife was an expert in this field. → _____

05. Kathy was <u>late</u> for school this morning. → _____

06. She got sunburn in the <u>right</u> leg. → _____

07. You are <u>right</u> in a sense. → _____

Challenge 2 다음 빈칸에 괄호 안의 단어들을 바르게 배열하여 쓰세요.

01. I don't have _____ to tell you. (particular, anything)

02. Would you give me _____? (nice, something)

03. I want _____. (hot, drink, to, something)

04. Do you have _____? (anything, drink, cold, to)

05. I saw _____ in the room. (white, nothing)

06. There isn't _____ with Bob's eyes. (wrong, anything)

Challenge 3 다음 문장의 밑줄 친 부분과 같은 의미가 되도록 빈칸을 채우세요.

01. Our city's subway system is equipped with facilities for <u>blind people</u>.

= Our city's subway system is equipped with facilities for _____ _____.

02. Lots of volunteers are trained to help <u>the handicapped</u>.

= Lots of volunteers are trained to help _____ _____.

Unit 02 수량형용사

2-1 many, much, a lot of, lots of

many books   **much** money   **a lot of** cars   **lots of** water

01 many, much, a lot of, lots of 등은 모두 '많은'이라는 뜻인데, **many는 셀 수 있는 명사**에, **much는 셀 수 없는 명사**에, a lot of나 lots of는 셀 수 있는 명사와 셀 수 없는 명사 모두에 쓴다.

Do you have **many** friends at school? 학교에 친구가 많이 있니?

I don't have **much** money. 나는 돈이 많지 않다.

A lot of(=**Lots of**) people immigrated to America. 많은 사람들이 미국으로 이민을 갔다.

※ many와 much는 주로 부정문과 의문문에 쓰고 a lot of(=lots of)는 긍정문에 많이 쓴다. 특히 much는 긍정문에는 잘 쓰지 않는다.

02 'how much'는 셀 수 없는 명사 앞에, 'how many'는 셀 수 있는 명사 앞에 쓴다. 둘 다 어떤 수나 양이 '얼마나 많은지'를 물어보는 표현이다.

How much water do you drink? 얼마나 많은 물을 마시니?

How many books do you have? 얼마나 많은 책을 가지고 있니?

03 'too many', 'too much'는 **지나치게 많은 수나 양**을 나타낼 때 쓰는데 too many는 셀 수 있는 명사 앞에, too much는 셀 수 없는 명사 앞에 쓴다. too는 어떤 문제가 있음을 암시하는 어조와 함께 불평하는 어조도 있다.

Too many people came to dinner. There wasn't enough food for everyone.
너무 많은 사람들이 만찬에 왔다. 모든 사람들을 위한 충분한 음식이 없었다. ▶ 문제가 있음을 암시함

※ **A lot of** people came to dinner. We all had a great time.
많은 사람들이 만찬에 왔다. 우리는 모두 즐거운 시간을 가졌다. ▶ 문제를 암시하지 않음

There is **too much** noise in this restaurant. 이 식당은 너무 시끄럽다.

서술형 기초다지기

정답 p. 30

Challenge 1 다음 밑줄 친 부분을 many 또는 much로 바꾸어 문장을 다시 써 보세요.

01. Was there <u>a lot of</u> yellow dust in Seoul yesterday?

→ _____

02. Did you prepare <u>lots of</u> food for Thanksgiving?

→ _____

03. This year I didn't invite <u>a lot of</u> people. I just invited my immediate family.

→ _____

Challenge 2 주어진 대답을 참고하여 빈칸에 How many(much) ~? 의문문을 만들어 보세요.

| 보기 |  | 당신은 설탕이 얼마나 많이 필요한가요?
Q: *How much sugar do you need?* .
A: I need two pounds of sugar. |

01.

그는 얼마나 많은 닭을 기르나요?

Q: _____

A: He raises ten chickens.

02.

그녀는 얼마나 많은 피자를 원하나요?

Q: _____

A: She wants six pieces of pizza.

Challenge 3 다음 빈칸에 too many, too much, a lot of 중 알맞은 것을 써 넣으세요.

01. I love garlic. This recipe calls for _____ garlic, so it's going to be delicious.

02. I can't eat this soup. It has _____ salt.

03. I think I ate _____ pieces of pumpkin pie. Now I feel sick.

04. Before the Europeans arrived, there were _____ Indians in America.

2-2 some, any, no, none

There are **some** cars in the parking lot. 주차장에 몇 대의 차가 있다.
There aren't **any** bicycles in the parking lot.
=There are **no** bicycles in the parking lot.
주차장에 자전거가 한 대도 없다.

01 some과 any는 '몇몇의, 약간의, 조금의'라는 뜻으로 **어떤 것에 대해 정확한 개수나 양을 모를 때** 사용한다. some과 any는 셀 수 있는 명사나 셀 수 없는 명사 앞에 모두 쓸 수 있다.

some	any
1. 주로 긍정문에 쓴다. We bought **some** books about Korean history. 우리는 한국 역사에 관한 몇 권의 책을 샀다. 2. 부탁하거나 권유할 때 의문문에 쓴다. Would you like **some** green tea? 녹차 좀 드시겠어요? 3. 긍정의 대답을 기대하거나 그렇게 대답할 것을 알고 있을 때 의문문에 쓴다. Do you have **some** money? 돈 좀 가지고 있지? 4. some of+복수/단수 명사+복수/단수 동사 **Some of** the students speak English. 학생들 중 몇몇은 영어로 말한다. **Some of** his information is correct. 그의 정보 중 일부는 정확하다.	1. 주로 부정문과 의문문에 쓴다. There aren't **any** classes on Saturday. 토요일에는 어떤 수업도 없다. Do you have **any** money? 돈이 좀 있니? ▶ 돈이 있는지 없는지 궁금하여 물어보는 상황 2. 긍정문에 쓰일 때는 '어떤 ~라도'의 뜻이 된다. Choose **any** flowers you like. 좋아하는 꽃을 어느 것이든 고르시오. 3. 조건을 나타내는 if절 안에서 주로 any를 쓴다. If you have **any** pencils, please lend me one. 연필 가진 게 있으면 하나만 빌려주세요.

02 no와 none (of)도 셀 수 있는 명사와 셀 수 없는 명사에 모두 사용한다. 둘 다 '전혀 없다'는 뜻으로, **no**는 **형용사**처럼 쓰이고 **none**은 **대명사**처럼 쓰인다.

I have **no** brothers and sisters. 내겐 형제자매가 없습니다.
None of my friends call me any more. 더 이상 어떤 친구도 나한테 전화하지 않는다.

03 부정문에 쓰인 not ~ any 또는 not a는 no로 바꾸어 쓸 수 있다. '조금도 없는, 아무것도 없는'의 의미이다.

There aren't **any** cars in the parking lot. 주차장에 차가 한 대도 없다.
=There are **no** cars in the parking lot.

It's a nice house, but there isn't a garage(=there's **no** garage). 아주 좋은 집이지만 차고가 없다.

서술형 기초다지기

정답 p. 30

Challenge 1   다음 빈칸에 some, any, no, none 중 알맞은 것을 써 넣으세요.

01. I bought _____ cheese, but I didn't buy _____ bread.

02. I haven't seen _____ good movies recently.

03. There aren't _____ gas station near here.

04. I'm going out tonight with _____ friends of mine.

05. Can I have _____ sugar in my coffee, please?

06. The teacher can't help you now because she has _____ time.

07. The teacher can't help you now because she doesn't have _____ time.

08. I understand this lesson completely. I have _____ questions.

09. "How many eggs do we have?" – "_____. Should I go and buy some?"

10. We canceled the party because _____ of the people we invited were able to come.

Challenge 2   다음 문장을 not ~ any는 no로, no는 not ~any로 바꿔 다시 써 보세요.

보기	She doesn't have any pencils to write with. =*She has no pencils to write with.*

01. There's no sugar in your coffee.

    = _____

02. Kevin has no free time.

    = _____

03. My sister is married, but she doesn't have any children.

    = _____

04. I couldn't make an omelette because there weren't any eggs.

    = _____

2-3 (a) few, (a) little

Laura runs **a few** miles every day.
로라는 매일 몇 마일을 달린다.

She drinks a lot of milk and eats **a little** fruit.
그녀는 많은 우유를 마시고, 약간의 과일을 먹는다.

01 a few(=some) vs. few(=not many)

a few와 few 둘 다 셀 수 있는 명사 앞에 쓴다. **a few는 '많지 않은 수이지만 충분한'이라는 긍정의 의미**가 담겨 있고 **few는 '(수가) 거의 없는'의 뜻으로 부정의 의미**가 담겨 있다.

I have **a few** apples. I can make an apple pie. 나는 약간의 사과를 가지고 있다. 애플파이를 만들 수 있다.
There are **few** apples. We must go and buy some. 사과가 거의 없다. 우리는 가서 몇 개 사와야 한다.
Scott has **very few** friends at the company. Scott은 회사에서 친구가 정말 거의 없다.

※ very few는 '(수가) 매우 적음'을 강조하기 위하여 사용된다.

02 a little(=some) vs. little(=not much)

a little과 little은 둘 다 셀 수 없는 명사 앞에 쓴다. **a little은 '많지 않은 양이지만 충분한'이라는 긍정의 의미**가 담겨 있고 **little은 '(양이) 거의 없는'의 뜻으로 부정의 의미**가 담겨 있다.

I have **a little** time. I can finish this work. 나는 약간의 시간이 있다. 이 일을 끝낼 수 있다.
I have **little** time. I must hurry. 나는 시간이 거의 없다. 서둘러야 한다.
There was **very little** time to think. 생각할 시간이 너무 없었다.

※ very little은 '양이 매우 적음'을 강조하기 위하여 사용된다.

03 few와 little은 딱딱하고 형식적이어서 일상 영어에서는 잘 쓰지 않고 not ~ many 또는 not ~ much를 많이 쓴다.

There was **little** food in the refrigerator. 냉장고에 먹을 음식이 거의 없다.
=There **wasn't much** food in the refrigerator. 냉장고에 먹을 음식이 많지 않다.
She eats **few** sweets for her teeth. 그녀는 치아를 위해 단것을 거의 먹지 않는다.
=She **doesn't** eat **many** sweets for her teeth. 그녀는 치아를 위해 단것을 많이 먹지 않는다.

서술형 기초다지기

Challenge 1 다음 빈칸에 a few, few, a little, little 중 알맞은 것을 쓰세요.

01. She drinks _____ glasses of juice every day.

02. It's raining. There are _____ people in the park now.

03. I know _____ Japanese. I can understand Japanese people.

04. I like to listen to _____ music when I drive, especially _____ old Beatles songs.

05. She's a strange woman. I think she has _____ secrets. _____ people understand her.

06. He knows _____ English, so he's going to take _____ English classes.

07. There's _____ food in the refrigerator. Let's make a sandwich.

Challenge 2 다음 빈칸에 very few 또는 very little 중 알맞은 것을 골라 쓰세요.

01. He isn't very popular. He has _____ friends.

02. She has _____ extra money. She can't buy anything.

03. Sunny is very busy these days. She has _____ free time.

04. The weather has been very dry recently. We've had _____ rain.

05. Home computers were very rare 25 years ago. _____ people had a home computer.

06. _____ high schools teach Latin. It's not a very popular language to study anymore.

Challenge 3 다음 문장을 not ~ many 또는 not ~ much로 고쳐 다시 써 보세요.

| 보기 | She's lucky. She has few problems. | = _She's lucky. She doesn't have many problems._ |

01. I have few books in my schoolbag. = _____

02. There is little milk in the bottle. = _____

Unit 03 형용사로 쓰이는 분사

3-1 형용사 역할을 하는 분사

Steve is an easily **frightened** person.
Steve는 쉽게 놀라는 사람이다.
He was **frightened** to see her face.
그는 그녀의 얼굴을 보고 무서워했다.

01 형용사와 마찬가지로 분사도 명사를 앞뒤에서 수식하는 역할을 한다. 단, 형용사는 명사의 동작을 표현해 주지 못하기 때문에 **동사의 현재분사형(-ing)이나 과거분사형(-ed)을 이용**하여 명사의 동작을 표현해 준다.

There was a **flickering** light in the distance. 저 멀리에 깜박이는 불빛이 있었다.

Do you know the man **talking** to Susan? Susan과 얘기하는 저 남자를 아니?

The garden was covered with **fallen** leaves. 정원은 낙엽들로 덮여 있었다.

Do you like symphonies **composed** by Beethoven? 베토벤이 작곡한 교향곡을 좋아하니?

02 분사는 주어와 목적어의 **행위를 표현하기 위해** 연결동사 뒤의 **주격 보어와 목적격 보어 자리에 위치**한다.

The teenagers are **excited**. 10대들은 흥분했다.

Kevin is **bored** because his job is **boring**. Kevin은 자신의 일이 지루했기 때문에 따분해 한다.

The old man sat **surrounded** by his children. 그 노인은 그의 아이들에 둘러싸인 채로 앉아 있다.

I saw him **writing** a letter. 나는 그가 편지 쓰고 있는 것을 보았다.

03 현재분사와 과거분사를 구별하여 써야 한다. 사람(생물체)은 남에게 감정을 주기도 하고(현재분사 사용), 받기도 한다(과거분사 사용). 하지만 사물이나 어떤 대상은 사람에게 감정을 줄 뿐(현재분사 사용), 감정을 받지 못한다.

Look at the woman **frightened** by the snake. 그 뱀에 놀란 여자를 봐라.

Jane thinks history is very **interesting**. Jane은 역사가 매우 재미있다고 생각한다.

Everybody was **surprised** that he passed the exam. 모든 사람들은 그가 그 시험을 통과해서 놀랐다.

The movie was **disappointing**. We expected it to be much better.
그 영화는 실망스러웠다. 우리는 훨씬 재미있을 거라고 기대했었다.

서술형 기초다지기

Challenge 1 다음 빈칸에 알맞은 말을 아래에서 골라 알맞은 형태로 고쳐 쓰세요.

read/a book   break/vase   write/in easy English

01.

Look at the _____ on the floor.

02.

The girl _____ is one of my friends.

03.

This book _____ is very popular.

Challenge 2 아래에 있는 단어를 알맞은 분사 형태로 바꿔 쓰세요.

bore   disappoint   interest   embarrass   shock

> **보기** The movies was *disappointing*. We were *disappointed* in the film.

01. The ending of the movie is _____. We were _____ by the ending of the movie.

02. Scott's impolite behavior embarrassed his teacher. Scott's teacher was very _____.

03. Nancy thinks physics is very _____. She is very _____ in physics.

04. I don't have anything to do in my office. My job is _____. I'm _____.

01 출제 100% - 형용사와 부사를 구별하라!

 출제자의 눈 연결동사(be동사, seem, taste, look, smell…) 뒤에는 반드시 형용사가 보어로 온다. 하지만 부사처럼 해석되기 때문에 부사를 써놓고 틀린 곳을 찾으라는 문제가 자주 출제된다. 수량 형용사 many와 much를 구별해야 하는데, 특히 much는 셀 수 없는 명사 앞에는 쓰고 아무리 양이 많아도 단수 취급하여 동사도 단수형을 써야 한다.

Ex 1.

Kevin told me about his new job. It sounds very _____.

(a) interested　　　(b) happy　　　(c) interesting　　　(d) interest

Ex 2.

빈칸에 들어갈 수 없는 것은?

Did you take _____ pictures when you were on vacation?

(a) many　　　(b) a lot of　　　(c) some　　　(d) much

02 출제 100% - 부정대명사는 형용사가 반드시 뒤에서 수식한다.

 출제자의 눈 우리말에는 '아름다운 그녀'처럼 쓰지만, 영어는 'beautiful she'로 쓰지 못한다. -thing, -body, -one으로 끝나는 부정대명사도 마찬가지로 형용사가 앞에서 수식하지 않고 반드시 뒤에서 수식한다. 또한 「the+형용사」는 복수 명사 취급하므로 반드시 동사도 복수형을 써야 한다는 것도 알아두자.

Ex 3.

괄호 안의 말을 올바른 순서로 쓰시오.

Wilson: Would you like (to, hot, something, drink)? It'll keep you warm.

Jane ： Sure, what can I have?

→ _____

Ex 4.

빈칸에 알맞은 말이 바르게 짝지어진 것은?

Do you think _____ should pay more taxes to help _____?

(a) the rich − the poors　　　(b) the riches − poor people

(c) the rich − poor people　　　(d) rich people − a poor

03 출제 100 % - (a) few와 (a) little은 구별하여 알아두자!

 출제자의 눈 셀 수 있는 명사 앞에는 (a) few, 셀 수 없는 명사 앞에는 (a) little을 써야 한다. 'a'를 긍정이냐 부정이냐에 따라 구별하여 정확하게 쓸 줄 알아야 한다. 한편, 하이픈(-)으로 숫자와 결합하여 명사를 꾸밀 때는 단수형으로 쓰므로 ten-year-old boy를 years로 쓰지 않도록 조심하자. to부정사 앞에 의미상 주어로 「of+목적격」이 오면, 앞에는 kind, nice, stupid, foolish 등 사람의 성격을 나타내는 형용사를 쓴다는 것도 기억하자. 여기에 부사를 쓰면 안 된다.

Ex 5.

빈칸에 들어갈 말이 바르게 짝지어진 것은?

Some scientists think a giant tortoise has _____ enemies, spends _____ energy and so on.

(a) few – little   (b) little – a few   (c) a little – few

Ex 6.

다음 밑줄 친 부분 중 잘못 쓰인 것은?

"I can't (a) <u>live</u> (b) <u>without my cell phone</u>," (c) <u>says</u> (d) <u>sixteen-years-old</u> Min-su.

04 출제 100 % - 사물은 행위나 감정의 주체가 되지 못한다.

 출제자의 눈 분사가 명사를 수식하거나 보어로 쓰일 때 사람(생물체)은 그 행위나 감정의 주체가 되거나 받는 대상이 될 수 있으므로 현재분사와 과거분사를 쓸 수 있다. 하지만 사물의 경우 감정을 받을 수 없으므로 과거분사를 쓰지 못한다는 것을 반드시 알아두어야 한다.

Ex 7.

괄호 안의 단어를 이용하여 빈칸을 완성하시오.

The soccer game was quite _____. We had a great time. (excite)

Ex 8.

괄호 안의 단어를 이용하여 빈칸을 완성하시오.

He's one of the most _____ people I've ever met. (bore)

1. **다음 빈칸에 들어갈 말이 바르게 짝지어진 것은?**

> David has a _____ dog and an _____ cat.

❶ four-year-old   eighteen-month-old
❷ four-years-old   eighteen-months-old
❸ four-year-olds   eighteen-months-olds
❹ four-years-olds   eighteen-months-olds
❺ fours-year-olds   eighteens-months-olds

2. **다음 빈칸에 들어갈 수 없는 것은?**

> It was _____ of you to do such a thing.

❶ foolish   ❷ important   ❸ wise
❹ careless   ❺ clever

3. **다음 우리말을 영어로 옮길 때 빈칸에 들어갈 말로 알맞은 것은?**

> 저에게 뜨거운 마실 것 좀 주세요.
> → Please give me _____.

❶ hot something to drink
❷ something hot to drink
❸ to drink hot something
❹ hot to drink something
❺ something to drink hot

4. **다음 밑줄 친 ⓐ~ⓔ 중에서 어법상 틀린 것을 고르시오.**

> I can't help ⓐ worrying about young people in these days. It ⓑ seems that all ⓒ that they are interested in is ⓓ unimportant something ⓔ such as hair color, fashion, idol stars, etc.

[5-6] **빈칸에 들어갈 알맞은 말을 고르시오.**

5.

> It was a very difficult test, _____ students passed it.

❶ little   ❷ few   ❸ many
❹ much   ❺ a lot of

6.

> Most of the town is modern. There are _____ old buildings.

❶ a few   ❷ not a little   ❸ much
❹ little   ❺ few

7. **다음 중 밑줄 친 부분의 쓰임이 어색한 것은?**

❶ The girl injured in the accident was taken to the hospital.
❷ Kathy always talks about the same thing. She's really boring.
❸ Are you interested in buying a car? I'm trying to sell.
❹ A boy swimming in the river nearly drowned. He called out to a truck that was passing by for help, but could not make himself heard.
❺ You don't have to get annoying just because I'm a few minutes late.

8. **다음 문장에서 어색한 부분을 찾아 바르게 고치시오.**

> When I was a child, I liked to listen to a bedtime story before I fell sleep.

_____ → _____

오답 노트 만들기

★틀린 문제 : _____   ★다시 공부한 날 : _____

(1) 문제를 왜? 틀렸는지 곰곰이 생각하고 그 이유를 적어본다.

(2) 핵심 개념을 적는다.

(3) 자신이 몰랐던 단어와 숙어 표현이 있으면 정리한다.

(4) 해설집에서 필요한 부분을 골라 풀이 해법을 정리한다.

★틀린 문제 : _____   ★다시 공부한 날 : _____

(1) 문제를 왜? 틀렸는지 곰곰이 생각하고 그 이유를 적어본다.

(2) 핵심 개념을 적는다.

(3) 자신이 몰랐던 단어와 숙어 표현이 있으면 정리한다.

(4) 해설집에서 필요한 부분을 골라 풀이 해법을 정리한다.

★틀린 문제 : _____   ★다시 공부한 날 : _____

(1) 문제를 왜? 틀렸는지 곰곰이 생각하고 그 이유를 적어본다.

(2) 핵심 개념을 적는다.

(3) 자신이 몰랐던 단어와 숙어 표현이 있으면 정리한다.

(4) 해설집에서 필요한 부분을 골라 풀이 해법을 정리한다.

★틀린 문제 : _____   ★다시 공부한 날 : _____

(1) 문제를 왜? 틀렸는지 곰곰이 생각하고 그 이유를 적어본다.

(2) 핵심 개념을 적는다.

(3) 자신이 몰랐던 단어와 숙어 표현이 있으면 정리한다.

(4) 해설집에서 필요한 부분을 골라 풀이 해법을 정리한다.

1. 빈칸에 들어갈 말이 알맞게 짝지어진 것은?

> · It is _____ to ride a bicycle along a country road in fine weather.
> · I am a little _____ now because this is my first letter in English.

❶ exciting – exciting   ❷ excited – excited

❸ exciting – excited   ❹ excited – exciting

❺ to excite – to excite

오답노트

2. 다음 우리말을 영어로 잘못 옮긴 것은?

> 영어를 배우기 위해서는 많은 시간이 필요하다.

❶ A lot of time is needed to learn English.

❷ A great deal of time is needed to learn English.

❸ Plenty of time is needed to learn English.

❹ Many time is needed to learn English.

❺ Lots of time is needed to learn English.

오답노트

3. 다음 중 어색한 문장을 고르시오.

❶ Kevin saw a big animal in the lake.

❷ Nancy likes to eat something special.

❸ She likes to buy popular shoes.

❹ Cindy wants an interesting book.

❺ Christina has different something.

오답노트

4. (a)와 (b)에 들어갈 말이 바르게 짝지어진 것은?

> · One person may say the glass is half full. She sees something positive about the quantity of water in the glass: The glass has (a) _____ water.
> · Another person may say the glass is half empty. He sees something negative about the quantity of water in the glass. The glass has very (b) _____ water.

	(a)	(b)
❶	a few	a little
❷	little	a little
❸	few	a few
❹	a little	little
❺	a few	few

오답노트

5. 다음 밑줄 친 부분의 쓰임이 바른 것은?

❶ Do you know the woman <u>talked</u> to Tom?

❷ I received a letter <u>written</u> in English yesterday.

❸ Who were those people <u>waited</u> outside?

❹ Some of the people <u>inviting</u> to the party can't come.

❺ Most of the goods <u>making</u> in this factory are exported.

오답노트

[6-8] 다음 중 틀린 부분을 찾아 바르게 고쳐 쓰시오.

6. Because he spoke too fast, little people understood what he said.

_____ → _____

7. Every time I go to a bookstore, I buy any books. As a result, I have more books than I'll ever be able to read.

_____ → _____

8. The children approached the abandoned house and looked in the breaking windows. What they saw almost scared them to death. There was a very old lady sitting on the living room floor crying.

_____ → _____

오답노트

9. **다음 빈칸에 들어갈 말이 바르게 짝지어진 것은?**

To make some cake, we need _____ sugar, a pound of flour, three eggs, some milk and _____ salt.

❶ some – a little ❷ a few – few
❸ little – little ❹ any – some
❺ some – any

오답노트

10. **다음 빈칸에 들어갈 말로 알맞지 않은 것은?**

To some people, trying to talk over the telephone in a foreign language seems _____.

❶ difficult ❷ hard ❸ confused
❹ difficulty ❺ tough

오답노트

11. **다음 밑줄 친 부분이 틀린 것은?**

❶ He always wants something new.
❷ I'd like to eat something special.
❸ Do you have anything cold to drink?
❹ I have nothing particular to do today.
❺ When she goes shopping, she always buys shoes popular.

오답노트

12. **다음 밑줄 친 부분의 용법이 나머지 넷과 다른 것은?**

❶ The government decided to create more jobs for the unemployed.
❷ The kind girl I met in the park yesterday was an American.
❸ The homeless need more help from the government.
❹ You'd better take care of the injured first.
❺ The government should make more efforts to narrow the gap between the poor and the rich.

오답노트

[13-14] 다음 밑줄 친 부분이 어법상 어색한 것은?

13. ① I have <u>a little</u> food in my refrigerator.
② I eat <u>a few</u> meat every day.
③ My <u>73-year-old</u> grandmother is well.
④ Can you give me <u>some</u> information?
⑤ If there are <u>any</u> words you don't understand, use a dictionary.

14. ① I enjoy my life here. I have <u>a few</u> friends, and we get together pretty often.
② He felt <u>uncomfortable</u> in that party.
③ <u>Left-handed</u> people usually use their left hand more often.
④ To me, computer games are more <u>interested</u> than playing outside.
⑤ I turn the lights off when <u>leaving</u> my office.

오답노트

15. 밑줄 친 부분과 바꿔 쓸 수 있는 것을 고르시오.

> <u>A lot of</u> people came to dinner. There wasn't enough food for everyone.

① Too much   ② Too many
③ Very few   ④ A few
⑤ Several

오답노트

16. 빈칸에 들어갈 알맞은 말을 쓰시오.

> Steve can't wear the cap. The cap isn't large enough and his head is too ____.

오답노트

17. 다음 우리말을 영어로 바르게 옮긴 것은?

> 오늘 밤 TV에 재미있는 거라도 있나요?

① Is there interesting something on TV tonight?
② Is there anything interesting on TV tonight?
③ Is there interesting anything on TV tonight?
④ Is there interesting on TV tonight?
⑤ Is there something interesting on TV tonight?

오답노트

18. 다음 빈칸에 알맞은 단어를 쓰시오.

Life is all right if you have a good job, but things are not so easy for unemployed people.
=Life is all right if you have a good job, but things are not so easy for _____ _____.

오답노트

264

19. 다음 중 빈칸에 (a) few 또는 very few가 들어갈 수 없는 곳은?

❶ _____ young American Indians speak the language of their ancestors.

❷ Before I bought my computer, I talked to _____ people about which computer to buy.

❸ I want to say _____ words about my country. Please listen.

❹ Women are still rare as political leaders. _____ countries have a woman president.

❺ Listen carefully. I'm going to give you _____ advice.

오답노트

[20-21] 아래와 같이 빈칸에 알맞은 분사를 넣으시오.

> The movie disappoints us.
> → The movie is *disappointing*.
> → We are *disappointed*.

20. The strange woman frightened the children.
→ The strange woman was _____.
→ The children were _____.

21. The murderer was arrested. The news shocked the citizens.
→ The news was _____.
→ The citizens were _____.

오답노트

22. 다음 두 문장의 의미가 서로 다른 것은?

❶ There was no bus, so we walked home.
= There wasn't any bus, so we walked home.

❷ My sister is married, but she has no children.
= My sister is married, but she doesn't have any children.

❸ We had to make a quick decision. There was little time to think.
= We had to make a quick decision. There wasn't much time to think.

❹ We've got a little time before the train leaves.
= We've got some time before the train leaves.

❺ She didn't have any pencils to write with.
= She had a few pencils to write with.

오답노트

23. 다음 밑줄 친 단어의 뜻이 잘못된 것은?

❶ A <u>certain</u> woman came to see you while you were out. (어떤)

❷ All the students were <u>present</u> at the event. (참석한)

❸ The <u>late</u> Mr. James was a great scientist. (작고한)

❹ His <u>ill</u> manner made us embarrassed. (나쁜)

❺ You will find the bank <u>right</u> on your left. (오른쪽의)

오답노트

A. 다음 빈칸에 현재분사와 과거분사 중 알맞은 형태를 써 넣으시오.

> Laura is going to Seattle next week. She has never been there before. (excite)

1. It will be an _____ experience for her.

2. Going to new places is always _____.

3. Laura is really _____ about going to Seattle.

> It's been snowing all day. I hate this cold weather. (depress)

4. This cold weather is _____.

5. This cold weather makes me _____.

6. It's silly to get _____ because of the weather.

B. 빈칸에 a few, few, a little, little 중 알맞은 것을 써서 문장을 완성하시오.

1. It's raining. There are _____ people in the street now.

2. There are _____ eggs in the fridge. We should buy some today.

3. I should visit my grandfather more often, but I have _____ time these days.

4. There's _____ chance that she will pass the exam. She rarely studies.

C. 다음 괄호 안의 말을 이용하여 영작하시오. (필요하면 변형할 것)

1. 구급차는 사고현장에 도착했고 부상자들을 인근의 병원으로 옮겼다. (injured)

= Ambulances arrived at the scene of the accident and took _____ to a nearby hospital.

2. 춥죠? 따뜻한 것 좀 마실래요? (hot / something / drink)

= It's cold, isn't it? Would you like _____?

실전 서술형 평가문제

> 출제의도 수량 형용사 이해하기
> 평가내용 some과 any를 이용한 문장 완성하기

A. 〈보기〉와 같이 괄호 안의 단어와 **any**를 이용하여 의문문을 만들고 그 대답까지 영작하시오.

[서술형 유형 : 10점 / 난이도 : 중]

보 기	*Is there any coffee on the table*? (coffee) → Yes, *there is some coffee (on the table)*.

1. _____ (bread)

→ Yes, _____.

2. _____ (pineapples)

→ No, _____.

3. _____ (kiwis)

→ Yes, _____.

4. _____ (cheese)

→ No, _____.

5. _____ (orange juice)

→ Yes, _____.

실전 서술형 평가문제

출제의도 막연한 수와 양을 나타내는 의문문 만들기
평가내용 How many ~ / How much ~를 이용하여 문장 완성하기

B. 괄호 안의 단어를 이용하여 How many ~, How much ~? 의문문을 만들고, 대답은 본문에서 찾아 완성하시오.

[서술형 유형 : 12점 / 난이도 : 중]

Scott is always hungry. He drinks six glasses of milk. He eats five eggs and seven slices of bread with a lot of butter and cheese. Then he drinks some coffee with four doughnuts. He spends a lot of money on breakfast.

보기	Q: *How much milk does he drink?* (milk / drink) → *He drinks six glasses of milk.*

1. Q: _____ (eggs / eat)

→ _____

2. Q: _____ (slices of bread / eat)

→ _____

3. Q: _____

(butter and cheese / put on the bread)

→ _____

4. Q: _____ (doughnut / eat)

→ _____

5. Q: _____ (coffee / drink)

→ _____

6. Q: _____ (money / spend / breakfast)

→ _____

출제의도 주어진 정보로 자신의 생각 표현하기

평가내용 (a) few / (a) little을 이용하여 문장 완성하기

C. 주어진 음식에 대한 자신의 선호도를 a lot of, (a) little, (a) few, not ~ many, not ~ much 중 하나를 이용하여 영어로 표현해 보시오.　　　　　　　　　　　　　　[서술형 유형 : 16점 / 난이도 : 중]

> **보기** apples : I eat a lot of apples. / I don't eat many apples. / I eat a few apples.

1. eggs _____

2. ice cream _____

3. potatoes _____

4. meat _____

5. chocolate _____

6. bananas _____

7. coffee _____

8. fruit _____

출제의도 분사를 이용한 문장 완성하기

평가내용 감정을 나타내는 현재분사와 과거분사를 구별하여 표현하기

D. 다음 문장을 읽고 알맞은 분사를 괄호 안의 우리말에 맞게 영작하시오.　　　[서술형 유형 : 8점 / 난이도 : 중상]

보기	The movie moved us. → *The movie was moving.* (그 영화는 감동적이었다.) → *We were moved.* (우리는 감동을 받았다.)

1. The strange scream frightened the children.

→ _____ (그 이상한 비명소리는 무서웠다.)

→ _____ (그 아이들은 무서워했다.)

2. The serial killer was arrested. The news shocked the citizens.

→ _____ (그 뉴스는 충격적이었다.)

→ _____ (그 시민들은 충격을 받았다.)

3. Politics interests Julia.

→ Julia thinks (that) _____ (Julia는 정치학이 매우 재미있다고 생각한다.)

→ _____ (Julia는 정치학에 매우 관심이 많다.)

4. Her story amazed everyone.

→ _____ (그녀의 이야기는 몹시 놀라웠다.)

→ _____ (모든 사람들은 몹시 놀랐다.)

서술형 평가문제	채 점 기 준	배 점	나의 점수
A	표현이 올바르고 문법, 철자가 모두 정확한 경우	2점 × 5문항 = 10점	
B		2점 × 6문항 = 12점	
C		2점 × 8문항 = 16점	
D		2점 × 4문항 = 8점	
공통	문법, 철자가 1개씩 틀린 경우	각 문항당 1점씩 감점	
	현재분사, 과거분사, some/any/no, 수량 형용사의 사용이 잘못된 경우	0점	
	내용과 전혀 일치하지 않거나 답을 기재하지 못한 경우		

Memo

Memo

한국에서 유일한
중학영문법

알짜 3000제

BOOK 정답 및 해설

am books

중학교 3학년 영문법

3-A

한국에서 유일한

중학영문법

알짜 3000제

정답 및 해설

I am books

Chapter 01 시제 I

1-1 현재시제의 활용   p. 11

Challenge 1

01 speaks
02 doesn't drink
03 flows
04 opens / closes
05 takes
06 boils

Challenge 2

01 The concert begins at eight tonight.
02 The game starts at one tomorrow afternoon.
03 What time does the movie begin tomorrow?

Challenge 3

01 will finish / returns   02 is / will drive

2-1 과거시제의 활용   p. 13

Challenge 1

01 took
02 went
03 wasn't
04 laughed
05 didn't bother
06 didn't enjoy
07 flew

Challenge 2

01 Did Marie and Pierre Curie discover penicillin? / No, they didn't. They discovered radium.
02 Did Marilyn Monroe come from France? / No, she didn't. She came from the United States.
03 Did Romeo love Cleopatra? / No, he didn't. He loved Juliet.

2-2 used to   p. 15

Challenge 1

01 used to be lazy   02 would watch

Challenge 2

01 used to be
02 did you used(d) to live
03 used to watch / didn't use(d) to watch / did you use(d) to watch

Challenge 3

01 to jog   02 to living   03 to be   04 to eating

3-1 현재진행형과 과거진행형   p. 17

Challenge 1

01 eats / is eating   02 sleeps / is sleeping
03 boils / is boiling

Challenge 2

01 arrived / was drinking
02 was driving / rang
03 were walking / started

3-2 미래진행형 / 진행형으로 쓸 수 없는 동사   p. 19

Challenge 1

01 will be reading   02 will / be doing
03 will be working   04 will be watching

Challenge 2

01 am smelling / smell   02 weighs / is weighing
03 prefer   04 is looking / sees

4-1 미래를 나타내는 시제(1)   p. 21

Challenge 1

01 will   02 am going to   03 am going to

Challenge 2

01 No, they aren't. They are going to buy new cell phones.
02 No, she isn't. She is going to ride a horse.

4-2 미래를 나타내는 시제(2)   p. 23

Challenge 1

01 is playing tennis on Saturday
02 is having dinner with Bob

03 is going to the movies tonight
04 are going to the party

Challenge 2

01 He is about to wash his hands.
02 She is about to leave outside.
03 She is about to go to bed.

이것이 시험에 출제되는 영문법이다!   p. 24

Ex1 (c)	Ex2 (d)	Ex3 (c)	Ex4 (b)
Ex5 (d)	Ex6 (b)	Ex7 (c)	Ex8 (d)

| 해설 |

Ex1 반복적인 일상을 나타내고 주어가 복수이므로 현재시제 meet을 쓴다.

Ex2 과학적인 진리도 현재시제를 쓴다.

Ex3 when 부사절이 과거시제이므로 문맥상 과거의 습관을 나타내는 「used to+동사원형」이 올바르다.

Ex4 과거 연도(2001년)가 함께 있으므로 반드시 과거시제를 써야 한다.

Ex5 조건의 부사절 내에서 의미상 미래시제라 하더라도 현재시제로 미래를 대신한다.

Ex6 이미 확실히 정해져 있는 일정은 현재시제로 미래를 나타낼 수 있다.

Ex7 동사가 감정, 지각, 소유를 나타낼 때는 원칙적으로 진행형이 불가능하다. 따라서 look은 진행형을 쓸 수 없고 주어가 You이므로 look을 쓴다. 단, '~을 보다'의 뜻인 look at은 진행형이 가능하다.

Ex8 비가 내리기 전에 이미 앉아 있었으므로 과거진행형(was sitting)을 쓰고 나중에 짧게 일어난 비가 오는 행위는 과거시제(began)를 쓴다.

기출 응용문제   p. 26

1 ①   2 ④   3 ③
4 will rain → rains   5 have felt → felt
6 No, I'm going to call her tonight.   7 ④
8 ①

| 해설 |

1 '막 ~하려고 하다'의 뜻인 be about to를 쓴다. 주로 5분 이내에 이루어질 일을 나타낸다.

2 동사 want는 진행형으로 쓰지 않는다.

3 last night은 과거시제와 함께 쓴다. 또한 과거시제로 답하고 있으니 과거시제로 물어야 한다. 따라서 What did you do last night?이 올바르다. ②번은 Where did you go last night?이 되면 답이 될 수 있다.

4 조건의 부사절 내에서는 현재시제가 미래를 대신한다. 따라서 will rain이 아닌 현재시제 rains를 써야 한다.

5 앞서 이미 진행되고 있던 동작은 과거진행형을 쓰고, 나중에 일어난 일에 대해서는 과거시제를 쓴다. 따라서 have felt를 과거시제인 felt로 써야 한다.

6 이미 하기로 결정했거나 마음먹은 일은 be going to를 쓴다. 따라서 No, I'm going to call her tonight.으로 쓴다.

7 나머지는 모두 현재 진행의 뜻이고, ④는 진행형을 이용하여 미래를 나타내고 있다. 진행형이 미래를 나타낼 때는 this evening과 같은 미래를 나타내는 어구와 함께 쓰인다.

8 과거의 습관을 묻고 있으므로 대답 또한 과거의 습관을 나타내는 「used to+동사원형」을 사용한다.

중간·기말고사 100점 100승   p. 28

1 ⑤	2 ②	3 ⑤	4 ②
5 used to	6 ④	7 ③	8 ③
9 ⑤			
10 No, he wasn't. He was born in (Malaga) Spain.			
11 ③	12 ②	13 Han-Gul	14 ②
15 bought	16 ②	17 ④	18 ①
19 ③	20 ⑤	21 ③	22 ②

| 해설 |

1 미래에 진행되고 있을, 즉 '테니스를 치고 있을 거다'라는 말이므로 알맞은 시제는 ⑤의 미래진행시제이다.

2 last night을 보고 과거시제임을 알 수 있으므로 hurried를 쓴다.

3 '작년에 가족과 함께 아프리카에 갔다'라는 말로 글이 시작되므로 지문의 모든 시제는 특별한 경우를 제외하고 과거시제를 써야 한다. 따라서 ⓔ의 are를 과거 were로 써야 한다.

4 '목이 길다'라는 표현으로 빈칸에 들어갈 동물은 기린(giraffe)이라는 것을 알 수 있다.

5 '예전에는 ~하곤 했었다'란 뜻의 과거의 습관을 나타내는 used to를 쓴다.

6 미래시제가 필요한데 개인의 예정된 계획이나 일정을 나타낼 때에는 be going to 또는 현재진행형으로 미래를 나타낼 수 있다. 따라서 ④가 정답이다. ②, ③은 미래를 나타내지만, 이미 어떤 일을 하기로 마음먹은 일을 나타내는 미래와는 거리가 멀다.

7 지구가 점점 더 더워지는 지속적인 변화나 추세를 나타내므로 현재진행형을 쓴다. 현재진행형은 오랜 기간에 걸쳐 변화하고 있는 동작이나 상태를 나타낼 때도 쓴다.

8 역사적 사실은 과거시제를 쓴다.

9 등위접속사 and 앞이 과거시제(was)이므로 learn 또한 learned로 일치시켜야 한다. 과거의 인물을 서술하는 내용이므로 특별한 경우를 제외하고 모두 과거시제를 쓴다.

10 스페인의 말라가(Malaga)에서 태어났다는 내용이 본문에 언급되어 있다.

11 미래시제와 함께 쓸 수 없는 표현은 last year이다. last year는 과거시제와 함께 사용되는 어구이다.

12 조건의 부사절 내에는 현재시제가 미래를 대신한다. 따라서 주어가 단수이므로 lives를 쓴다.

13 it은 대명사로 앞에 나온 단수 명사를 받는다. 따라서 Han-Gul을 대신하는 대명사인 것을 쉽게 알 수 있다.

14 어떤 동작이 있기 이전에 이미 진행되고 있었던 동작은 과거진행형을 쓰고 나중에 짧게 일어난 동작은 과거시제를 쓴다. 따라서 과거진행형인 ②의 was reading이 올바르다.

15 Last week는 '지난주'라는 과거를 표시하므로 동사 buy는 과거형인 bought로 써야 한다.

16 과거에 습관적으로 행했던 동작은 「used to+동사원형」이나 would로 나타낼 수 있다.

17 시간의 부사절 내에서는 그 의미가 미래라 하더라도 현재시제를 써서 미래를 나타낸다. 따라서 주어가 3인칭 단수 현재인 comes를 써야 한다.

18 조건의 부사절에서 미래를 나타낼 때에는 현재시제를 쓴다. 따라서 주어가 you이므로 close를 쓴다.

19 주절의 동사가 과거(drank)이므로 부사절에서도 과거로 시제를 일치시킨다. 과거의 동작이 순차적으로 일어났음을 나타낸다.

20 be going to를 이용하여 상대방의 예정된 계획을 물어보고 있다. 따라서 대답 또한 be going to를 쓰거나 현재진행형으로 써야 한다.

21 Kevin이 도착한 것보다 숨어 있었던 동작이 먼저 행해지고 있었기 때문에 과거진행시제인 were hiding을 쓰고 나중에 일어난 동작에는 과거시제 arrived로 쓴다.

22 7:30에는 Steve가 TV로 축구경기를 보고 있을 것이다. 따라서 미래진행시제인 will be watching을 써야 한다.

중간·기말고사 평가대비 단답형 주관식　　p. 32

A 1 Nancy was watching TV when the phone rang.
  2 It began to rain while I was walking home.
  3 John took a picture of me while I was not looking.
  4 I was walking along the street when suddenly I heard footsteps behind me.
B 1 am going to wash
  2 am going to walk
  3 am going to eat
  4 are going to buy
C 1 I'll have the same.
  2 I won't accept his invitation.
  3 I won't let you leave now.
  4 Will you help me?
D 1 used to go to the beach every weekend
  2 used to wear blue jeans

  3 used to crawl under her bed / put her hands over her ears

| 해설 |

A 과거에 먼저 이미 진행되고 있었던 동작은 과거진행시제를 쓰고 나중에 일어난 동작은 과거시제를 쓴다.
  1 was watching TV / rang
  2 began / was walking
  3 took a picture / was not looking
  4 was walking / heard
B 1 손이 더럽다는 내용으로 보아 손을 씻는다는 것을 알 수 있다. 따라서 am going to wash를 쓴다. 2 '날씨가 좋아, 버스를 타지 않고 걸어갈 것이다'라는 의미이므로 am going to walk를 쓴다. 3 '배가 고프다'라는 표현으로 am going to eat로 문장을 완성해야 한다는 것을 알 수 있다. 4 '생일 선물을 살 것이다'라는 내용을 추론해 낼 수 있으므로 are going to buy로 문장을 완성한다. 주어가 We이므로 be동사는 are를 쓴다.
C 1 What will you have?의 대답으로 '나도 똑같은 것을 가질 것이다'라는 I will have the same.이 알맞다. 2 He invited you to the party.의 대답으로 '나는 그의 초대를 받아들이지 않을 거야.'라는 I won't accept his invitation.이 알맞다. 3 '하지만, 지금 떠나야 해.'라는 대답에 어울리는 문장은 I won't let you leave now.가 알맞다. 4 '좋아, 기꺼이 그러지.'에 대한 질문으로 Will you help me?가 알맞다.
D 1 '매주 해변에 가곤 했었다'는 I used to go to the beach every weekend로 쓴다. 2 '(과거에) 청바지를 입고 다녔었다'는 used to wear blue jeans로 쓴다. 3 '침대 밑으로 기어들어가 귀를 막곤 했었다'의 표현으로 Sunny used to crawl under her bed and put her hands over her ears로 문장을 완성한다.

실전 서술형 평가문제 A　　p. 34

모범답안

1 I'm going to go to the gym. / I'm going to the gym.
2 I'm going to read a lot of books. / I'm reading a lot of books.
3 I'm going to walk to school. / I'm walking to school.

실전 서술형 평가문제 B
p. 35

모범답안

1 she wasn't / She was waiting for a train. 또는 She was standing at the subway station.
2 she wasn't / She was eating[having] breakfast [dinner, meals].
3 she wasn't / She was washing the car.

실전 서술형 평가문제 C
p. 36

모범답안

1 Jane didn't use(d) to have short hair. / She used to have very long hair.
2 We didn't use(d) to take a school bus. / We used to walk to school.
3 Bob didn't use(d) to play soccer. / He used to play basketball.

실전 서술형 평가문제 D
p. 37

모범답안

1 Who is Kevin meeting at 10:30 / He is meeting Jason and Lisa
2 What is Kevin doing at 12:00 / He is having lunch with Jason, Lisa, and the boss
3 Where is Kevin waiting for Lucy / He is waiting for Lucy in the hotel lobby
4 What is Kevin doing at 22:00 / He is returning to the hotel and preparing for the meeting on Wednesday

실전 서술형 평가문제 E
p. 38

모범답안

1 If the dress is expensive, Linda may not buy it.
2 If you don't take a subway, you will be late for work.
3 If you feel tired, you must go to bed.

Chapter 02 시제 II
p. 39~68

1-1 현재완료 형태와 용법
p. 41

Challenge 1

01 met
02 have known
03 eaten
04 just

Challenge 2

01 has lost his key
02 has broken her leg
03 has washed his car

Challenge 3

01 Has she lost her purse? / she has / she hasn't
02 I have never forgotten her name.
03 Have you / been to Egypt / I have / I haven't

1-2 현재완료 계속적 용법
p. 43

Challenge 1

01 have known / ten years
02 has worked / since
03 have met / was
04 has had / came
05 have known / were
06 has risen / bought

Challenge 2

01 have you known
02 have you studied

Challenge 3

01 Lisa has read two history books since Monday.
02 My sisters haven't played beach volleyball since last summer.
03 Laura has been a photographer for ten years.

1-3 현재완료시제와 과거시제 p. 45

Challenge 1

01 have known   02 read   03 eaten
04 broke   05 lived   06 have lived

Challenge 2

01 have already seen / saw
02 have / have been / was
03 have you visited / have visited / visited / was

Challenge 3

01 Maria graduated from high school in 1999.
02 I didn't read a newspaper yesterday.
03 Have you taken a vacation recently?

1-4 현재완료 진행시제 p. 47

Challenge 1

01 Alice has been talking with her friend for an hour.
02 I've been studying Korean since December.
03 They have been playing soccer for three hours.

Challenge 2

01 How long has he been using his computer? / When did he start using his computer?
02 How long has she been eating lunch? / When did she start eating lunch?

Challenge 3

01 have been planning   02 has been looking

1-5 현재완료와 현재완료 진행시제 p. 49

Challenge 1

01 has been painting / has painted
02 has been writing / has already sent
03 has been driving / has driven

Challenge 2

01 Nancy has been learning Korean for two years.
02 We have had this car since 2006.
03 Amy and Kevin have been married for twenty years.
04 We have been waiting for you since six o'clock this morning.

1-6 과거완료시제 p. 51

Challenge 1

01 had lent   02 had known
03 had lived   04 had

Challenge 2

01 had taken off   02 had not seen
03 had studied

Challenge 3

01 It had changed a lot.
02 The bus fare has gone up.
03 they were playing tennis

1-7 과거완료 진행시제 p. 53

Challenge 1

01 had been living   02 had been sitting
03 hadn't been working   04 had been waiting

Challenge 2

01 caught / had been singing
02 have been waiting
03 had been playing / started
04 had been working / came

Challenge 3

01 Somebody had been smoking in the room.
02 He had been watching TV.

이것이 시험에 출제되는 영문법이다! p. 54

| Ex1 (a) | Ex2 (b) | Ex3 (b) | Ex4 (c) |
| Ex5 (c) | Ex6 (d) | Ex7 (b) | Ex8 (c) |

| 해설 |

Ex1 명백한 과거표시어구 last week가 있으므로 현재완료가 아닌 과거시제 visited를 쓴다.

Ex2 「since+주어+과거시제」는 주절에 현재완료와 함께 쓴다. 따라서 has hated를 쓴다.

Ex3 시간의 길이 the last half hour가 있으므로 전치사 for 를 쓴다.

Ex4 과거와 현재의 시간이 내포되어 있으므로 현재완료 has been을 쓴다.

Ex5 과거시제 moved보다 더 이전 과거에 일어난 일은 과거완료(had never spoken)로 쓴다.

Ex6 과거보다 더 먼저 일어난 일은 과거완료로 쓰고 나중에 일어난 일을 과거시제 entered로 쓴다.

Ex7 현재완료 진행과 함께 쓸 수 있는 것은 since이다. when 은 현재의 의미를 내포한 시제와 함께 쓸 수 없고 과거완료 진행시제와는 함께 쓸 수 있다.

Ex8 과거보다 더 이전에 진행되었던 행위를 강조하고자 할 때 에는 과거완료 대신 과거완료 진행시제를 쓸 수 있다. 따 라서 had been waiting으로 쓴다.

기출 응용문제
p. 56

1 ④		2 ①	
3 have been playing		4 had begun	
5 ③	6 ⑤	7 ④	8 ⑤

| 해설 |

1 현재완료 의문문에 대한 대답도 have/has를 이용한다. 적 절한 대답은 Yes, I have read it twice.이다. ③은 No, ⑤ 는 Yes로 고치면 답이 될 수 있다.

2 현재완료의 여러 용법들 중에서 ②④는 완료, ③은 결과, ⑤ 는 경험을 나타낸다. 주어진 문장은 ①과 동일한 '계속'의 의미를 나타낸다.

3 한 시간 전부터 현재까지 농구를 하고 있는 것은 현재완료 진행형이므로 'have been V-ing'를 쓴다.

4 콘서트 홀에 들어간 시점(과거)보다 콘서트가 먼저 시작되었 으므로 대과거를 쓴다.

5 MP3를 빌린 것이 잃어버린 것보다 더 이전의 과거이므로 과 거완료시제인 had borrowed로 써야 한다.

6 콘서트가 시작하기 전부터 시작할 때까지 기다리고 있었으 므로 과거완료 진행시제를 쓴다.

7 '~이후 지금까지'의 뜻을 나타낼 때는 since를 쓴다. 이때 주절에는 현재완료형을 쓰고 since가 이끄는 종속절에서는 과거형을 쓴다.

8 과거와 현재를 연결하는 현재완료 have learned를 쓴다.

중간 · 기말고사 100점 100승
p. 58

1 ④	2 ⑤	3 ④	4 ③
5 ④	6 have been playing		7 ⑤
8 ④	9 ①	10 ③	
11 was interested → have been interested			
12 ②	13 ⑤		
14 ⓐ got ⓑ had already started		15 ①	
16 ⑤	17 ④		
18 has been held by teachers		19 ③	
20 ③			
21 How long have you been studying Korean?			

| 해설 |

1 현재완료 경험을 나타내는 have ever seen을 쓴다. ever 는 '여태껏, 지금까지'의 의미로 현재완료 경험의 표현에 자 주 쓰인다.

2 반지를 준 것이 반지를 분실한 것보다 더 앞선 시제이므로 과거완료인 had given을 쓴다.

3 since는 '~이래로'의 의미로 현재완료와 함께 계속을 나타 낸다. 따라서 현재완료 또는 현재완료 진행시제(has been working)를 쓴다.

4 역에 도착하기 전에 이미 먼저 기차가 떠났으므로 과거완료 시제인 had already left를 쓴다.

5 '과거부터 지금까지 계속 ~해오고 있는 중이다'라는 의미는 현재완료 진행형 have/has been+V-ing를 써서 나타낸 다.

6 '과거부터 지금까지 계속 ~해오고 있는 중이다'라는 의미인 현재완료 진행형 I have been playing since then.으로 쓴 다.

7 과거의 어떤 시점보다 더 이전에 행해진 일을 나타낼 때는 과거완료시제를 쓴다.

8 과거에 시작하여 현재도 진행 중임을 강조할 때는 현재완료 진행시제를 쓴다. 구체적인 기간 two years가 있으므로 전 치사 for를 쓴다.

9 한 번도 하지 못한 경험에는 never, 구체적인 시간의 길이 앞에는 전치사 for, '지금까지, 여태껏'이란 의미의 부사로 ever를 쓴다.

10 '2년이 지났다'는 완료 표현인 have passed로 쓰고 since 뒤에 「주어+동사」를 쓸 경우 동사는 반드시 과거시제를 쓴 다.

11 '어렸을 때부터 지금까지 옷과 패션에 관심이 있다'는 의미 이므로 was interested를 완료시제 have been interested 로 써야 한다. have interested로 쓰지 않도록 조심한다.

12 시간의 길이 over an hour가 있으므로 전치사 for를 쓰고 시작점을 나타내는 2 o'lock 앞에는 since를 쓴다.

13 주어진 문장은 경험을 나타내는 현재완료 표현으로 ⑤가 같은 용법의 경험이다.

14 두 개의 동작 중 어느 것이 먼저 일어났는지를 시간적으로 구별할 때 과거완료시제를 쓴다. 홀에 도착했을 때 이미 콘 서트가 시작되었으므로 had got은 과거시제인 got으로 쓰 고 그 보다 더 이전에 있었던 일은 과거완료인 had already started로 써야 한다.

15 when은 현재완료시제와 어울리지 않는다. 따라서 ①은 When did you first meet Lucy?로 써야 한다.

16 「How long+현재완료 ~?」는 과거에 시작해서 지금까지 의 어떤 행동이나 상태의 특정한 기간을 물어보므로 쓰임이 같은 것은 계속을 나타내는 ⑤가 알맞다.

17 과거에 시작된 행동이 현재까지 계속되고 있으므로, 현재완 료진행(have been+V-ing)인 ④가 알맞다.

18 현재완료 have+p.p.의 수동태 문장은 has been held by teachers로 쓴다. 주어(The music night)가 3인칭

단수로 바뀌었으므로 have 대신 has를 써야 한다.

19 ① 완료, ②④ 결과, ⑤ 계속을 나타내고, ②는 경험을 나타낸다.

20 they는 복수를 나타내는 대명사이므로 앞에 있는 African people을 대신한다.

21 특정한 기간을 물어보므로 「How long have+주어+p.p. ~?」로 문장을 완성한다.

중간·기말고사 평가대비 단답형 주관식
p. 62

A 1 She has lived in this town for three years.
  2 He has not eaten anything for two days.
  3 They have not visited the city yet.
B 1 We had just eaten lunch.
  2 The movie had already begun.
  3 She had made plans to do something else.
  4 I had never been there before.
C 1 has collected stamps for two years
  2 have worked for the company since 1995
  3 has rained (everywhere) since last night
D 1 She has been travelling for three months.
    She has visited three countries so far.

| 해설 |

A 1 주어가 3인칭 단수이므로 has를 사용한 She has lived in this town for three years.로 문장을 완성한다. 2 주어가 3인칭 단수이므로 has를 사용한 He has not eaten anything for two days.로 쓴다. 부정문은 have+p.p. 사이에 not을 쓴다. 3 yet은 부정문에서는 문장 맨 끝에 쓰고 not을 넣어 have not visited로 완성한다.

B 1 배고프지 않은 상태보다 점심을 먹은 것이 먼저이므로 have를 had로 써서 과거완료시제로 써야 한다. 2 극장에 도착한 것보다 영화가 먼저 상영되었으므로 began을 과거완료시제인 had already begun으로 써야 한다. 3 make의 과거분사형 made를 쓴다. 4 런던에 가보지 못한 것은 지난달에 갔었던 것보다 더 이전의 일이므로 과거완료시제를 이용한 had never been으로 써야 한다.

C 1 2년 동안 우표를 수집하고 현재도 수집하고 있으므로 현재완료를 이용한 has collected stamps for two years로 문장을 완성한다. 2 1995년부터 회사에서 일을 했고 현재도 일하고 있으므로 현재완료시제를 이용한 have worked for the company since 1995로 문장을 완성한다. 3 어젯밤부터 비가 내렸으므로 has rained (everywhere) since last night으로 문장을 완성한다.

D 1 3개월간 여행을 하고 있으므로 현재완료 진행시제인 She has been travelling for three months.로 문장을 완성한다. / so far는 '여태까지, 지금까지'의 의미로 She has visited three countries so far.로 문장을 완성한다.

실전 서술형 평가문제 A
p. 64

모범답안

1 Peter has already tried scuba diving.
2 Peter has not travelled around Australia yet.
3 Peter has not tasted snake yet.
4 Peter has already stayed in the jungle for a week.

실전 서술형 평가문제 B
p. 65

모범답안

1 Steve has travelled abroad many times since he started working.
2 Karen has improved her Spanish since she decided to study more.
3 Sunny has lost ten kilos since she started going to the gym.
4 I haven't seen Jim since he moved to Scotland.
5 Nancy hasn't gone out with her friends since she found a new job.

실전 서술형 평가문제 C
p. 66

모범답안

1 She has been working for a newspaper since 2005.
2 She has been jogging in the park for two hours.
3 He has been talking on the phone since 5 o'clock.

실전 서술형 평가문제 D
p. 67

모범답안

1 By the time the police arrived, the thieves had run away.
2 After Lucy had done the shopping, she had coffee with Susan. 또는 Lucy had coffee with Susan after she had done the shopping.
3 When Sarah had finished her assignment, she gave it to the teacher.
4 Scott had typed up his story before his computer broke down.

모범답안

1 had broken / called the police
2 met my dad / had / come back from vacation / looked very tired
3 there was / had gone

Chapter **03** 조동사
p. 69~98

1-1 can, could
p. 71

Challenge 1

01 Can Kevin write with his left hand? / No, he can't.
02 Can Ron eat with chopsticks? / Yes, he can.
03 Can you go shopping with me this afternoon? / Yes, I can.

Challenge 2

01 couldn't   02 couldn't
03 could   04 couldn't

Challenge 3

01 My friends and I are able to play tennis outdoors.
02 I am not able to go ice skating now, but I was able to go ice skating last winter.
03 When Sunny comes home, she is able to help you with your homework.

1-2 must be, may, might
p. 73

Challenge 1

01 He is a traffic policeman.
02 You may(=can) use my car.
03 She must be tired.
04 She may(=might) become a great musician.

Challenge 2

01 possibility   02 possibility   03 permission

Challenge 3

01 may well   02 may(=might) as well
03 may(=might) be

1-3 정중한 부탁(요청)
p. 75

Challenge 1

01 May I
02 Can I 또는 Could I 또는 May I
03 Could I 또는 May I / Could I 또는 May I

Challenge 2

01 Can[Could, May] I have a picnic at the park with my friends?
02 Can[Could, Will, Would] you teach me how to drive a car?

Challenge 3

01 Would you like to sit down?
02 Would you like something to drink?

1-4 must, have (got) to
p. 77

Challenge 1

01 You mustn't swim in the river.
02 The man mustn't eat the hamburger.
03 He mustn't smoke in the museum.
04 You must be quiet in class.

Challenge 2

01 I had to study for my medical school exams.
02 Next week, John will have to interview five people.

Challenge 3

01 mustn't   02 mustn't   03 don't have to

1-5 should, ought to, had better, would rather

p. 79

Challenge 1

01 should   02 would   03 ought not to
04 rather not   05 better

Challenge 2

01 He shouldn't go to bed late at night. / He should use an alarm clock.
02 He shouldn't work so hard. / He should take a break.

Challenge 3

01 would rather watch TV
02 had better not listen
03 would rather be a freelancer

2-1 과거 추측(조동사+have+p.p.)

p. 81

Challenge 1

01 must not be   02 may have been
03 must have forgotten 04 must not have seen
05 might not have known

Challenge 2

01 can't have known about it
02 may be in her office
03 might have revealed the secret
04 must have forgotten the promise

2-2 과거 추측 must have p.p. / should have p.p.

p. 83

Challenge 1

01 should have listened
02 must have forgotten
03 shouldn't have laughed

Challenge 2

01 must have practiced
02 should have written

Challenge 3

01 She ought not to have gone to the party last night.
02 We ought to have reserved a table.

이것이 시험에 출제되는 영문법이다!

p. 84

| Ex1 (d) | Ex2 (b) | Ex3 (c) | Ex4 (d) |
| Ex5 (d) | Ex6 (b) | Ex7 (d) | |

| 해설 |

Ex1 could not과 바꿔 쓸 수 있는 것은 was not able to이다. 주어가 3인칭 단수이므로 was를 써야 한다.
Ex2 '(과거에) ~해야 했었다'의 의미로 had to를 쓴다.
Ex3 '피아니스트일 리가 없다'의 의미로 can not을 쓴다.
Ex4 '~임에 틀림이 없다'의 의미로 must be를 쓴다.
Ex5 '~하지 않는 게 좋겠다'는 had better 바로 뒤에 not을 쓴다.
Ex6 want to와 같은 뜻은 would like to이다.
Ex7 도로가 젖어 있는 것을 보고 과거에 대한 강한 추측을 할 수 있다. 따라서 must have+p.p.를 써야 한다.

기출 응용문제

p. 86

1 ③	2 had better cut down	3 ④
4 must be	5 cannot(=can't) be	
6 don't have to		7 ⑤
8 would rather / than	9 must have	
10 ③	11 should have been	

| 해설 |

1 주차 금지 표지판이다. 강한 금지를 나타내는 ③의 You must not park here.가 올바르다.
2 had better 뒤에 동사원형을 쓴다. 따라서 had better cut down으로 문장을 완성한다.
3 had better 뒤에 동사원형만 가능하다.
4 '~임에 틀림없다'의 뜻은 must be를 쓴다.
5 '~일 리가 없다'의 뜻은 cannot be 또는 can't be를 쓸 수 있다.
6 '~할 필요가 없다'의 뜻은 don't have to 또는 don't need to를 쓸 수 있다.
7 ① ought to는 인칭에 상관없이 항상 ought to로 써야 한다. ought to의 과거형은 ought to have+p.p.를 사용한다. ② 「need not+동사원형」을 쓴다. need가 조동사 역할을 하므로 needs를 need로 써야 한다. ③ 조동사 뒤에는 항

상 동사원형을 쓰므로 helps를 help로 써야 한다. ④ 항상 「ought to+동사원형」으로 쓰므로 ought go를 ought to go로 써야 한다.

8 어떤 일에 대한 선호도를 나타낼 때 would rather를 쓴다. 「would rather+동사원형 ~ than+동사원형」은 '(than 이하) 하느니 차라리 ~하겠다'의 뜻이다.

9 과거 상황에 대해 논리적으로 강한 추측을 할 경우에는 must have+p.p.로 쓴다.

10 과거 사실에 대한 유감이나 안타까움을 나타내고 있다. 따라서 과거에 '~했어야 했다'를 나타내는 should have+p.p. 또는 ought to have+p.p.를 쓸 수 있다.

11 '거기에 갔어야 했는데 가지 않았다'라는 말이 내포되어 있으므로 should have+p.p.를 이용한 should have been을 쓴다.

중간·기말고사 100점 100승   p. 88

1 ③	2 ought to shave	3 ④
4 ④	5 ③	
6 would rather meet my friends		7 ②
8 ⑤	9 ③	10 ④
11 would	12 ④	13 ⑤ 14 ⑤
15 ③	16 must have 17 should have	
18 ①	19 ⑤	20 ① 21 ④
22 ②	23 should / need	

| 해설 |

1 ③ ought to not을 ought not to로 고쳐야 한다.

2 should와 같은 표현은 ought to이다.

3 '~했을 리가 없다'는 must not have+p.p.를 쓴다.

4 과거 일에 대한 후회나 유감을 나타낼 때 should (not) have+p.p.를 쓴다.

5 '가이드의 말을 들었어야 했다'는 의미로 should have+p.p.를 써야 한다.

6 「would rather+동사원형」으로 쓴다.

7 must have+p.p.는 과거 상황에 대한 논리적인 확신이나 추측을 나타낼 때 쓰는 표현이므로 '과거(remembered)의 일을 현재 확신한다(be sure)'의 뜻이 된다.

8 과거의 능력 '~할 수 없었다'의 의미이므로 couldn't를 써야 한다.

9 미래의 능력을 나타낼 때 will be able to로 쓴다.

10 ④는 cannot be 형태로 강한 부정의 추측(~일 리가 없다)을 나타내고, 나머지는 능력(~할 수 있다)을 나타내는 can의 부정 표현이다.

11 「would like to+동사원형」에서 would는 소망의 의미를 나타내는 조동사이다. '~하는 게 낫겠다'의 의미는 would rather이므로 공통 단어는 would이다.

12 '~해야만 했다'는 had to를 쓴다. must와 have to의 과거 표현이다.

13 '~하지 말았어야 했는데 (사실은 했다)'의 의미는 should not have+p.p.로 쓴다.

14 ⑤는 논리적인 근거를 가지고 말하는 강한 추측, 나머지는 모두 강한 의무를 나타낸다.

15 「had better+동사원형」은 '~하는 편이 낫다'의 의미로, 충고나 가벼운 명령의 표현이다. Why do you obey the safety rules?는 단순히 이유를 묻는 의문문이다.

16 「must have+과거분사」는 과거의 일에 대한 확신으로 '~했음에 틀림없다'라고 해석한다.

17 '먹을 것을 가져왔어야 했는데 가져오지 않았다'의 의미이므로 should have+p.p.를 쓴다.

18 have to는 '~해야 한다'는 '의무'의 뜻을 나타내는 표현이다. 이러한 의미의 부정으로 don't have to(~할 필요가 없다)를 쓰는데 don't need to나 need not을 쓸 수도 있다.

19 '~했을지도 모른다'의 의미인 may[might, could] have+p.p.로 쓴다.

20 ①은 허락을 나타내고 나머지는 모두 추측을 나타낸다.

21 '주차를 하면 안 된다'의 의미가 되어야 하는데 don't have to는 '~할 필요가 없다'의 의미이므로 빈칸에 들어갈 수 없다.

22 had better 뒤에는 반드시 동사원형을 써야 한다. ②의 to calm down을 calm down으로 고쳐야 한다.

23 첫 번째 문장은 '~하지 말아야 한다'의 의미이고 두 번째는 '~했어야 했는데 하지 않았다'의 뜻이므로 빈칸에는 공통적으로 should나 need가 들어가야 한다.

중간·기말고사 평가대비 단답형 주관식   p. 92

A 1 would rather / than 2 should not
  3 must   4 cannot(=can't)

B 1 She might not sit here.
  2 It might snow tomorrow.
  3 I might not travel to India.

C 1 Are you able to speak any foreign languages?
  2 Most students aren't able to understand what the teacher is saying.
  3 When I was a child, I was able to swim in the river.

D 1 ought to   2 need not
  3 would like   4 must(=should) keep

E 1 should not(=ought not to) have seen
  2 may(=might) have met
  3 had better not listen

| 해설 |

A 1 선호를 나타낼 때는 had better가 아닌 would rather를 쓴다. would rather A than B는 'B하느니 차라리 A하겠다'의 뜻이다. 2 '~하지 말았어야 했는데 사실은 했다'의 의미이므로 should not have+p.p.를 쓴다. 3 과거의 상황에 대한 강한 추측의 경우 must have+p.p.를 쓴다. 4 '~일

리가 없다'의 의미로 can't(=cannot) have+p.p.를 쓴다.

B 1 '그녀가 여기에 앉지 않을지도 모른다.'의 뜻이므로 She might(=may) not sit here.로 문장을 완성한다. 2 '내일 눈이 올지도 모른다.'의 뜻이므로 It might(=may) snow tomorrow.로 문장을 완성한다. 3 '인도로 여행을 하지 않을지도 모른다.'의 뜻이므로 I might(=may) not travel to India.로 문장을 완성한다.

C 1 주어가 you이므로 be동사 are를 이용하여 Are you able to speak~?로 문장을 완성한다. 2 주어가 복수 명사이므로 be동사 are를 이용하여 Most students aren't able to understand~로 문장을 완성한다. 3 주어가 I이고 과거(could)이므로 be동사 was를 써서 When I was a child, I was able to swim in the river.로 문장을 완성한다.

D 1 should와 같은 뜻인 「ought to+동사원형」으로 바꾸어 쓸 수 있다. 2 don't have to와 같은 뜻인 「need not+동사원형」으로 바꾸어 쓸 수 있다. 3 want to와 같은 뜻인 would like to로 바꾸어 쓸 수 있다. 4 명령문과 같은 의미로 must나 should 또는 have to로 바꾸어 쓸 수 있다.

E 1 '보지 말았어야 했는데 봤다'는 의미이므로 should not have+p.p. 또는 ought not to have+p.p.로 쓸 수 있다. 2 과거에 대한 가능성이 현저히 낮은 추측이므로 may(=might) have+p.p.로 쓸 수 있다. 3 '~하지 않는 게 좋겠다'의 의미인 「had better not+동사원형」으로 쓸 수 있다.

실전 서술형 평가문제 A　　　p. 94

모범답안

1 You mustn't run in the hallway.
2 You must listen to the teacher.
3 You mustn't talk with your friend.
4 You mustn't sleep in class.

실전 서술형 평가문제 B　　　p. 95

모범답안

1 You mustn't take　　2 You must pay
3 You must return　　4 You must leave
5 You must leave

실전 서술형 평가문제 C　　　p. 96

모범답안

1 She should(=had better) call the police. / She shouldn't have left her handbag open.
2 He should(=had better) study more. / He should(=had better) stop watching so much TV.
3 He should(=had better) put some cream on. / He shouldn't have stayed in the sun so long.

실전 서술형 평가문제 D　　　p. 97

모범답안

1 I would rather(=I'd rather) be a school teacher than a journalist. 또는 I would rather(=I'd rather) be a journalist than a school teacher.
2 I would rather(=I'd rather) live in a big city than in a country. 또는 I would rather(=I'd rather) live in a country than in a big city.
3 I would rather(=I'd rather) have tuna salad than chicken salad. 또는 I would rather(=I'd rather) have chicken salad than tuna salad.
4 I would rather(=I'd rather) study English than Japanese. 또는 I would rather(=I'd rather) study Japanese than English.

실전 서술형 평가문제 E　　　p. 98

모범답안

1 We should have brought umbrellas.
2 We should have studied last night.
3 We should have got(=gotten) up earlier.
4 Can[Could, Will] you help me with my homework?
5 Can[Could, Will, Would] you teach me how to drive a car?
6 Can[Could, May] I help you clean up when the party is over?

Chapter **04** 부정사

1-1 주어와 보어로 쓰이는 to부정사　　　p. 101

Challenge 1

01 To live in a foreign country
02 to reach a decision

Challenge 2

01 It is not good to spend so much time playing computer games.
02 It is very dangerous to camp alone in the woods.

Challenge 3

01 is to see things clearly
02 is to go to Egypt

1-2 목적어로 쓰이는 to부정사　　　p. 103

Challenge 1

01 to go　　　　　　02 to get
03 to visit　　　　　04 to be

Challenge 2

01 what to say　　　02 where to get
03 who to send

Challenge 3

01 to get married　　02 to tell him her name

1-3 목적격 보어로 쓰이는 to부정사　　　p. 105

Challenge 1

01 to tell　　02 clean　　03 rise　　04 burning
05 move　　06 to finish　　07 learn

Challenge 2

01 her husband repair the window
02 let him buy a bicycle
03 the crowd to leave the building

Challenge 3

01 didn't let the students use

2-1 형용사처럼 쓰이는 to부정사　　　p. 107

Challenge 1

01 They're looking for an apartment to live in.
02 Bring me several pieces of paper to write on.
03 She needs a friend to talk with.

Challenge 2

01 are to gain trust / 의도
02 was to be seen / 가능
03 is to speak / 예정
04 were to work / 운명

3-1 목적을 나타내는 to부정사　　　p. 109

Challenge 1

01 to　　　　02 for　　　　03 to　　　　04 for

Challenge 2

01 open the bedroom windows (in order) to let in some fresh air
02 writes a letter to his parents (in order) to ask them for some money
03 have the radio on (in order) to listen to a soccer game

Challenge 3

01 The teacher(=She) spoke very slowly so that we could understand what she said.
02 I'm going to go to the nursing home so that I can take part in volunteer work.

3-2 결과, 원인, 조건, 판단을 나타내는 to부정사　　　p. 111

Challenge 1

01 to hear　　　　02 to fail　　　　03 to believe
04 to come

Challenge 2

01 Are you happy to go to the party?
02 I was excited to eat such delicious food.

03 She grew up to become the greatest leader in history.

Challenge 3

01 grew up to be   02 to fix
03 never to come back

3-3 too ~ to / enough to   p. 113

Challenge 1

01 You are strong enough to carry the box.
02 The smart phone is too expensive to buy.
03 This MP3 player is small enough to fit in my pocket.
04 The water was too cold (for me) to swim in.
05 He has enough money to travel around the world.
06 There is enough room in the car (for us) to get on.

Challenge 2

01 This coffee is so hot that I can't drink it.
02 The wind was so strong that it could break windows.
03 Jane was so young that she couldn't get married.
04 Jessica is so kind that she can help the poor people.
05 My father was so sleepy that he couldn't watch the movie on TV.

4-1 부정사의 시제 / 부정사의 의미상 주어   p. 115

Challenge 1

01 to have been   02 for
03 to have happened   04 of

Challenge 2

01 Susan seems to enjoy writing on her blog.
02 They seem to have worked together in the past.
03 She appeared to have stopped smoking.

Challenge 3

01 for a child to sit still for a long time
02 of her to give up her new job

4-2 대부정사 / 독립부정사   p. 117

Challenge 1

01 would love to   02 didn't ask me to

Challenge 2

01 want to   02 offered to
03 don't have time to

Challenge 3

01 To be frank with you
02 To make matters worse
03 To begin with

이것이 시험에 출제되는 영문법이다!   p. 118

Ex1 don't know what to wear to the party
Ex2 (b)   Ex3 (d)   Ex4 (b)
Ex5 strong enough to kill an alligator
Ex6 of him to have left without saying goodbye
Ex7 seem to feel tired

| 해설 |

Ex1 「의문사+to부정사」는 명사구 역할을 한다. 여기서 '무엇을 입고 가야 할지'라는 뜻이므로 what to wear로 써야 한다.
Ex2 목적어가 동작을 하는 경우 to부정사를 쓴다.
Ex3 「make+목적어+동사원형」을 쓴다. 따라서 목적격 보어에 동사원형 memorize를 써야 한다.
Ex4 지각동사는 목적격 보어에 '동사원형 또는 현재분사'를 쓸 수 있다. 따라서 답은 playing이 된다.
Ex5 「so+형용사/부사+that+주어+can」은 「형용사/부사+enough to부정사」로 바꾸어 쓸 수 있다. 따라서 형용사 strong을 enough 앞에 써서 strong enough to kill an alligator로 문장을 완성한다.
Ex6 impolite은 사람의 성질이나 성격 등을 나타내므로 의미상 주어 앞에는 전치사 of를 써서 of him으로 쓰고 예의 없다(is impolite)고 말하는 시점보다 떠난 것이 더 이전의 일이므로 to have left로 고쳐 써야 한다.
Ex7 「It seems that+주어+동사」는 추측하여 말할 때 사용하며, 「주어+seem to ~」로 바꿀 수 있다.

기출 응용문제   p. 120

1 ④	2 how to use	3 ⑤
4 ⑤	5 ①	6 what to do
7 for me to write	8 ②	

| 해설 |

1 사람의 성질이나 성격을 나타내는 특정한 형용사 몇 개를 제외하고 모두 의미상 주어 앞에 전치사 for를 쓴다.

2 직접화법을 간접화법으로 바꿔 준다. 따라서 「how to부정사」를 이용하여 how to use로 쓴다.

3 ⑤의 to help 앞에 명사가 없는 것만 봐도 용법이 다르다는 것을 알 수 있다. 여기서 to help는 부사적 용법으로 '~위하여'의 뜻이다. 나머지는 모두 형용사 용법이다.

4 말하는 시점과 같으므로 「to+동사원형」을 쓴다.

5 「형용사/부사+enough to부정사」의 어순으로 쓴다.

6 what I should do를 what to do로 고칠 수 있다.

7 「for+의미상 주어+to부정사」의 어순으로 쓴다.

8 아픈 것이 말하는 시점보다 더 과거이므로 「to have+p.p.」로 써야 한다.

중간·기말고사 100점 100승　　　p. 122

1 ⑤　　2 how to ride
3 small enough　　4 seems to fix
5 ①　　6 ③, ⑤　　7 ⑤　　8 ③
9 he is honest　　10 enough to
11 ②　　12 to have kept
13 to have read　　14 to　　15 ⑤
16 ④　　17 ④　　18 ③　　19 ③
20 ④　　21 ④　　22 ③　　23 ③
24 advised him not to go
25 strong enough to rule　　26 ④

| 해설 |

1 과거시제임에 유의한다. 「too ~ to ~」는 '너무 ~해서 ~할 수 없다'는 뜻으로 「so+that+주어+can't」로 바꿔 쓸 수 있다.

2 how I should ride는 '의문사+to부정사」를 이용해 how to ride로 쓸 수 있다.

3 형용사 small이 enough 앞에 위치하여 small enough로 쓸 수 있다.

4 주절과 종속절의 시제가 모두 현재이므로 seems to fix로 쓴다.

5 주어 자리에 It을 쓰고 주어인 to play reggae music을 뒤로 보낸다. It is very hard to play reggae music.으로 쓴 ①번이 의미가 같다.

6 why와 that은 「의문사+to부정사」로 쓰지 않는다.

7 ①~④ 모두 명사 뒤에서 명사를 수식하는 형용사적 용법이다. ⑤의 to say는 명사 gentleman 뒤에 위치하여 형용사 용법처럼 보이지만 앞의 명사를 수식할 수 없다. 이때 to say는 부사적 용법으로 우리말 '~하다니'로 해석된다.

8 ③ selfish는 사람의 성질을 나타내므로 의미상 주어로 of를 쓰고 나머지는 모두 for를 쓴다.

9 의미상 him과 to be는 주어와 동사 관계이다. 따라서 that절

안에 him을 주격 he로 바꾸고 to be를 동사 is로 바꾼다.

10 「so ~ that 주어+can ~」=「enough to ~」 매우 ~해서 ~하다

11 나머지는 모두 '예정'의 의미이고, ②의 be to는 의도 즉 want to의 의미이다. 예정은 주로 시간을 나타내는 표현과 자주 쓰이고 의도는 If와 자주 쓰이며 want to의 의미를 나타낸다.

12 기다리게 한 행위는 말하는 시점보다 더 이전의 일이므로 완료 부정사인 to have kept로 써야 한다.

13 소설을 읽는 행위는 더 이전부터 일어난 일이므로 완료 부정사인 to have read로 쓴다.

14 'It seems that ~' 구문은 「주어+seem+to부정사」 구문으로 바꿀 수 있다. seemed와 were가 모두 과거이므로 완료 부정사가 아닌 to+동사원형으로 써야 한다.

15 enough fast의 어순이 아닌 fast enough가 되어야 한다.

16 「make+목적어+동사원형」을 쓴다. 따라서 to feel에서 to를 생략해야 한다.

17 「told+목적어+to부정사」의 5형식 어순에서 부정문은 to부정사 바로 앞에 not을 쓴 ④가 올바르다.

18 보기의 문장에서 It은 진주어 to meet 이하를 대신하는 가주어로 쓰였다. ①⑤는 때를 나타내는 비인칭 주어, ②는 날씨를 나타내는 비인칭 주어, ④는 대명사이다.

19 so to speak(말하자면, 즉)는 글의 흐름상 자연스럽지 않다.

20 그녀를 싫어하는 이유를 나열하고 있으므로 '우선'이란 의미의 to begin with가 적절하다.

21 저널리스트인 것이 말하는 시점과 같으므로 She seems to be a journalist.로 쓴다.

22 사역동사 let은 목적격 보어에 동사원형을 쓴다. 따라서 to carry를 carry로 써야 한다.

23 ③의 old enough to stay는 so old that he could stay로 고쳐야 한다.

24 5형식 동사 advise는 「동사+목적어+to부정사」로 문장을 만든다. 시제가 과거이고 '가지 말라'는 부정의 의미이므로 not을 넣어 advised him not to go로 문장을 완성한다.

25 「so+형용사+that+주어+can/could」는 「형용사+enough to부정사」로 바꾸어 쓸 수 있다. 따라서 형용사 strong을 enough 앞에 위치시켜 strong enough to rule로 완성한다.

26 이상한 꿈을 꾼 것은 말하는 시점보다 더 과거이므로 완료 부정사(to have had a strange dream)로 써야 한다. seem은 현재시제로 써야 하는 것에 주의한다.

중간·기말고사 평가대비 단답형 주관식　　p. 126

A 1 expected to meet　　2 what to read
　3 never to come back
B 1 of her to lend　　2 for them to solve
C 1 to hear　　2 to speak
　3 to marry

D 1 to know → know　　2 to not → not to
　　3 to play → play / playing
　　4 finish → to finish
E 1 You are so short that you can't ride this
　　　rollercoaster.
　　2 She stayed up late in order to study for
　　　the final exam.
F 1 too hot / cool enough
　　2 tall enough to touch / too short to touch

| 해설 |

A 1 '~할 것을 기대했다'의 의미이므로 과거동사 expected 뒤
　　에 목적어로 부정사 to meet를 쓴다. 2 '무엇을 읽어야 할지'
　　는 what to read로 쓴다. 3 '결코 돌아오지 않았다'는
　　never to come으로 쓴다.
B 1 사람의 성질을 나타내는 형용사 kind가 있으므로 she를
　　의미상 주어 of her로 바꾸어 of her to lend로 문장을 완
　　성한다. 2 전치사 for를 이용하여 they를 의미상 주어 for
　　them으로 바꾸어 for them to solve로 문장을 완성한다.
　　전치사 뒤에는 대명사의 목적격을 써야 한다.
C 1 was shocked와 heard는 서로 같은 시제이므로 to부정
　　사의 형태는 완료형(to have heard)이 아닌 to hear로 쓴다.
　　2 was와 couldn't speak는 서로 같은 시제이므로 「to+동
　　사원형」으로 쓴다. 3 감탄문+to부정사로 쓴다. She was
　　stupid enough to marry such a man.으로 써도 된다.
D 1 let은 목적격 보어로 '동사원형'을 쓴다. 따라서 목적격 보
　　어로 쓰인 to know를 know로 고친다. 2 부정사를 부정할
　　때에는 부정사 바로 앞에 not을 쓴다. 따라서 to not을 not
　　to play로 고친다. 3 지각동사 hear는 목적격 보어로 동사
　　원형이나 현재분사(V-ing)를 쓴다. 따라서 to play를 play
　　나 playing으로 써야 한다. 4 동사 get은 목적격 보어로
　　to부정사를 취한다. 따라서 finish를 to finish로 써야 한다.
E 1 too ~ to는 「so ~ that+주어+can't」로 바꿔 쓸 수 있
　　다. 따라서 You are so short that you can't ride this
　　rollercoaster.로 쓴다. 형용사 short는 so와 that 사이에
　　쓴다. 2 in order를 to study 앞에 써서 in order to
　　study로 문장을 완성한다.
F 1 형용사 hot은 too 뒤에 써서 too hot to drink로 문장을
　　완성한다. / cool은 enough 앞에 써서 cool enough to
　　drink로 문장을 완성한다. 2 tall을 enough 앞에 써서 tall
　　enough to touch로 완성한다. / 형용사 short는 too와 to
　　사이에 넣어 too short to touch로 문장을 완성한다.

실전 서술형 평가문제 A　　　　p. 128

모범답안
1 She's exercising in order to keep in shape.
2 She turned up the volume in order to hear the
　 news better.
3 She must drive all night in order to get there
　 by tomorrow.
4 She must save money in order to buy a new
　 motorcycle.
5 She's going to the library in order to study for
　 the test.

실전 서술형 평가문제 B　　　　p. 129

모범답안
1 her use his cell phone
2 him(=the patient) to exercise every day
3 her to give him a hand
4 him(=her son) to be careful

실전 서술형 평가문제 C　　　　p. 130

모범답안
1 isn't old enough to drive this car
2 is good enough to take part in the math
　 competition
3 is warm enough for us to jump in the water

실전 서술형 평가문제 D　　　　p. 131

모범답안
1 let Kevin[him] borrow her camcorder
2 didn't allow them to watch TV
3 helped Peter[him] (to) find information
4 had Maria[her] drive her sister to soccer practice
5 made Dan[him] show her his licence

실전 서술형 평가문제 E　　　　p. 132

모범답안
1 saw Peter and Julia playing badminton
2 heard Laura playing the drum
3 watched the girls walking along the street

1-1 명사처럼 쓰이는 동명사　　　　p. 135

Challenge 1

01 is doing yoga　　　　02 Taking a walk is
03 Keeping a diary teaches
04 not bringing my camera

Challenge 2

01 Learning new languages is very interesting.
02 Watching TV for too long is bad for your eyes.

Challenge 3

01 having a picnic　　　　02 laughing
03 talking to her　　　　　04 breaking down
05 sitting on the floor

1-2 전치사의 목적어로 쓰이는 동명사 /
　　　go+동명사　　　　　　　　　　p. 137

Challenge 1

01 I'm worried about being late for the concert.
02 Are you interested in going to the zoo with us?
03 She apologized for being so rude to me.
04 Are you afraid of flying in small planes?
05 Bob insisted on paying the restaurant bill.

Challenge 2

01 went swimming　　　　02 go camping
03 went shopping

2-1 목적어로 쓰이는 동명사와 부정사　　p. 139

Challenge 1

01 dating　　　02 to get　　　03 studying
04 not to do　 05 to help　　 06 living
07 to give　　 08 to travel　　09 helping
10 eating

Challenge 2

01 asking　　　　　　　02 to boil / boiling
03 to rise / rising　　　 04 to go
05 drinking　　　　　　 06 to play / playing
07 to eat / eating

2-2 동명사와 to부정사를 모두 목적어로 쓰는 동사
　　　　　　　　　　　　　　　　　p. 141

Challenge 1

01 to turn off　 02 meeting　　03 to keep
04 changing　　05 to lock　　 06 being
07 washing / to be washed　　08 laughing

Challenge 2

01 watching the accident last year
02 to say that you are not on the list
03 to avoid using the bicycle when I can walk
　 somewhere
04 going to yoga class because she has broken
　 her arm

3-1 동명사의 의미상 주어　　　　　p. 143

Challenge 1

01 my[me] being　　　　02 my[me] staying
03 her singing　　　　　04 daughter('s) leaving
05 my[me] smoking　　　06 Lisa('s) lying

Challenge 2

01 her hitting　　　　　02 my riding
03 our[us] coming

3-2 동명사 없이는 못 사는 표현들　　p. 145

Challenge 1

01 prevented me from enjoying
02 is worth reading
03 never see your face without smiling
04 it is no use taking medicine
05 On seeing him

Challenge 2

01 have difficulty remembering
02 worth watching(=seeing)
03 keep(=prevent) / from coming
04 look forward to working

8 과거에 했던 일을 나타내므로 동명사인 lending을 쓴다.

이것이 시험에 출제되는 영문법이다!　　　　p. 146

Ex1 (a)	Ex2 (c)	Ex3 (d)	Ex4 (b)
Ex5 (a)	Ex6 (b)	Ex7 (a)	Ex8 (b)
Ex9 (b)			

| 해설 |

Ex1 주어가 동명사이므로 단수 취급하여 makes를 쓴다.

Ex2 전치사(by) 뒤에는 반드시 명사 또는 동명사를 쓴다.

Ex3 앞으로 해야 할 일을 나타내므로 동사의 목적어로 부정사를 써야 한다.

Ex4 「can't help+V-ing」로 동명사 laughing을 쓴다.

Ex5 동사 remember는 문맥을 통해서 부정사와 동명사를 결정해야 한다. 어떤 행위를 했던 것을 기억했다는 의미이므로 remembered 뒤에 동명사를 목적어로 써야 한다.

Ex6 한번 해봄 직한 일, 또는 경험이나 기억을 가지고 있을 때에는 tried 뒤에 동명사를 목적어로 써야 한다.

Ex7 have no trouble 뒤에는 동명사를 쓴다.

Ex8 look forward to의 to는 전치사이다. 따라서 전치사 뒤에는 반드시 동명사를 쓴다.

Ex9 「be used to+V-ing」는 '~하는 데 익숙하다'의 뜻으로 to는 부정사 to가 아닌 전치사이다. 따라서 전치사 뒤에는 반드시 동명사를 써야 한다.

기출 응용문제　　　　p. 148

1 ⑤	2 not blaming me	3 ②
4 ②	5 ④	6 ②
7 to make → making	8 ①	

| 해설 |

1 동사 wish는 목적어로 부정사를 쓴다.

2 동명사를 부정할 때 not을 동명사 바로 앞에 쓴다. 따라서 not blaming me로 문장을 완성한다.

3 unless(=if ~ not)로 시작되었으니까 뒤에 not이 또 나오면 안 되고, stop은 '~하는 것을 멈추다'란 의미일 때 「stop+동명사」로 쓴다. 따라서, '사람들이 그곳에 쓰레기 버리는 것을 멈추지 않으면'은 unless people stop throwing trash there가 된다.

4 ① '어제 그녀를 만나야 할 것을 기억한다'란 말은 상식적으로 맞지 않는다. 따라서 '만났던 것을 기억한다'의 의미인 동명사 seeing을 써야 한다. ③ mind는 동명사를 목적어로 쓴다. ④ want는 부정사를 목적어로 쓴다. ⑤ enjoy는 동명사만을 목적어로 취한다.

5 ④는 '(주어가) ~하고 있는 중이다'라는 진행형이다. 진행형인 be+V-ing에서 V-ing는 현재분사로 분류된다.

6 cannot help 다음에는 동명사를 쓴다.

7 be interested in에서 in이 전치사이므로 to make는 동명사형인 making으로 써야 한다.

중간·기말고사 100점 100승　　　　p. 150

1 like going	2 ②	3 ①	4 ①
5 Walking alone at night			
6 him not being honest			
7 ②	8 ④	9 ③	10 ⑤
11 ②	12 ③	13 her screaming	
14 me[my] getting			
15 ③ to try → trying		16 ③	
17 prevented / playing			
18 prevented (또는 kept) / from		19 ②	
20 ①	21 ③	22 ⑤	23 ③

| 해설 |

1 「feel like+동명사」를 쓴다.

2 동사 like 뒤에 쓰인 traveling은 동명사이다. ②는 전치사의 목적어로 쓰인 passing이 동명사이고 나머지는 모두 현재분사이다.

3 '~을 학수고대하다'의 의미로 look forward to를 쓴다. 여기서 to는 전치사이므로 to 뒤에 동명사(going)를 사용한 ①번이 올바르다.

4 remember 뒤에 동명사는 이미 한 행동이나 행위를 나타낸다. 따라서 that 절 뒤에 이미 동작을 행한 과거시제 locked를 쓴 ①이 올바르다.

5 문장 맨 앞에 동명사를 써서 Walking alone at night의 어순으로 써야 한다.

6 동명사를 부정할 때 not을 동명사 바로 앞에 쓴다. him은 동명사의 의미상 주어이므로 him not being honest의 어순으로 써야 한다.

7 「look forward to+(동)명사」는 '~을 고대하다', 「devote one's life to+(동)명사」는 '~에 일생을 바치다'는 의미이다.

8 ⓐ는 이미 동작을 행한 것이므로 동명사를 쓰고, ⓑ는 '~하려고 했지만 하지 못했다'의 의미를 설명하고 있으므로 to부정사를 쓴다.

9 동명사의 의미상 주어로 소유격이나 목적격을 쓸 수 있다.

10 ⑤ 전치사 about 뒤에 쓰인 going은 동명사이고, 나머지는 모두 현재분사이다.

11 cannot help 뒤에는 동명사가 와야 하므로 be worried about에서 be는 동명사 형태(being)가 되어야 한다.

12 ① mind 뒤에는 동명사를 쓴다. ② finish 뒤에도 동명사를 쓴다. ④ can't afford+to부정사를 쓴다. ⑤ decide는 부정사를 목적어로 취한다.

13 동사 screamed를 동명사로 쓰고 주어 she를 동명사의 의미상 주어인 소유격으로 바꿔 동명사 바로 앞에 쓴다.

14 get을 동명사 getting으로 바꾸고 주어 I를 동명사의 의미상 주어인 소유격이나 목적격으로 바꿔 동명사 바로 앞에 쓴다.

15 전치사 in 뒤에 동명사를 쓴다. 따라서 ③의 to try를 trying 으로 고쳐야 한다.

16 '이전에 봤던 것을 기억한다'는 의미이므로 동명사로 쓰고, 동사 avoid는 목적어로 동명사를 쓴다.

17 「prevent A from B(동명사)」는 'A로 하여금 B하는 것을 막다/못하게 하다'의 뜻이다. 따라서 빈칸은 과거시제인 prevented를 쓰고 '테니스를 치다'의 의미인 play를 동명 사형인 playing으로 쓴다.

18 '폭설로 인해 비행기가 출발하지 못했다'는 의미이므로 prevented 또는 kept를 쓰고 전치사 from을 쓴다. 관용 표현이므로 전치사 from을 다른 전치사로 쓰면 안 된다.

19 spent 뒤에는 동명사, be busy 뒤에도 동명사, expect 는 목적어로 부정사를 쓴다.

20 전치사 다음에 동사가 오면 반드시 동명사를 써야 한다.

21 '~에 익숙하다'의 의미로 be accustomed to+V-ing 또 는 be(=get) used to+V-ing를 쓴다.

22 '과거에 그녀를 사랑했던 것을 지금 후회한다'라는 의미이므 로 '(과거에) ~하지 말았어야 했는데 사실은 했다'를 의미 하는 should not have+p.p.를 표현을 이용한 ⑤가 적절 하다.

23 can't help 뒤에는 동명사를 쓴다.

중간 · 기말고사 평가대비 단답형 주관식   p. 154

A 1 The company is looking forward to working with you again.
    2 On hearing the announcement, all the reporters started to transmit the news.
    3 Being polite to parents is a must.
    4 My sister left without finishing her dinner.

B 1 in watching   2 for helping
    3 on taking   4 at drawing

C 1 his[him] graduating   2 Yu-na Kim being
    3 watching   4 their[them] being

D 1 remember to borrow   2 stopped to talk
    3 forget meeting   4 forget visiting

| 해설 |

A 1 전치사 to 뒤에는 동명사 working을 써야 한다. 2 전치사 on 뒤에는 동명사 hearing을 써야 한다. 3 문장의 주어로 쓸 때 동명사 Being을 써야 한다 4 전치사 without 뒤에도 동명사 finishing을 써야 한다.

B 1 동사 watch를 동명사 watching으로 고쳐 be interested in watching으로 문장을 완성한다. 2 동사 helped를 동명 사 helping으로 고쳐 thanked us for helping으로 문장을 완성한다. 3 동사 take를 동명사형인 taking으로 고쳐 insisted on taking으로 문장을 완성한다. 4 동사 draw를 동명사 drawing으로 고쳐 be not good at drawing으로 문장을 완성한다.

C 1 전치사 뒤에는 동명사를 써야 하므로 동사 graduate를 graduating으로 고치고 주어 he를 의미상 주어인 소유격 (his) 또는 목적격(him)으로 고쳐 동명사 바로 앞에 쓴다. 2 전치사 뒤에는 동명사를 써야 하므로 동사 is를 being으 로 고치고 고유명사인 사람 이름은 동명사 바로 앞에 그대 로 사용하여 의미상 주어로 쓴다. 3 과거에 했던 행위를 나 타내므로 동사 remembers 뒤에 동명사를 쓴다. 4 전치사 뒤에는 동명사를 써야 하므로 동사 be를 being으로 고치고 주어 they를 의미상 주어인 소유격 또는 목적격으로 고쳐 동 명사 바로 앞에 쓴다.

D 1 '책을 빌려야 하는 것을 기억한다'란 뜻으로 앞으로 해야 할 일이나 행위를 나타내므로 부정사를 사용한 remember to borrow로 문장을 완성한다. 2 '~하기 위하여 멈췄다'의 의 미이므로 부정사를 이용한 stopped to talk로 문장을 완성 한다. 3 만났던 일은 과거에 이미 경험한 일이므로 동명사 meeting을 이용한 forget meeting으로 문장을 완성한다. 4 방문한 것은 과거에 이미 경험한 일이나 행동이므로 동명 사 visiting을 이용한 forget visiting으로 문장을 완성한다.

실전 서술형 평가문제 A   p. 156

모범답안

1 I try to avoid using the car when I can walk somewhere.
2 Mark (has) stopped going to soccer practice because he has broken his leg.
3 Jason won't mind working this weekend.
4 I look forward to seeing you again.
5 Did you remember to take the rubbish out before you left the house?

실전 서술형 평가문제 B   p. 157

모범답안

1 I stopped smoking.
2 I want to be(=become) an English teacher. 또는 I want to teach English.
3 I enjoy waterskiing (in the summer).
4 I finished cleaning the room.
5 I plan to travel to Paris[France / the Eiffel Tower].

모범답안

1 tried knocking on the door
2 forget meeting the famous actress
3 forgot to set the alarm
4 forget to go out to see movies (with some friends)
5 remembers to play tennis
6 forget to have dinner with Tom

Chapter 06 분사

1-1 분사의 종류와 역할
p. 161

Challenge 1

01 rising   02 smiling   03 sitting
04 painted   05 made   06 fallen
07 talking

Challenge 2

01 Do you know the girl sitting next to Susan?
02 The man sleeping under the tree is my father.
03 The girl injured in the accident was taken to the hospital.
04 The murderer arrested by the police officer last week died in jail.

1-2 보어자리에서 명사의 동작을 설명하는 분사
p. 163

Challenge 1

01 beating / 목적격 보어   02 crying / 주격 보어
03 standing / 명사 수식   04 standing / 주격 보어
05 cleaning / 목적격 보어   06 knocked / 목적격 보어
07 spoken / 명사 수식

Challenge 2

01 lying in front of the door
02 repaired by them
03 had her car stolen
04 called in the classroom

1-3 감정을 나타내는 분사 / 현재분사와 동명사의 구별
p. 165

Challenge 1

01 interesting   02 interested   03 surprised
04 surprising   05 shocking   06 shocked

Challenge 2

01 exciting / excited
02 frightening / frightened

Challenge 3

01 동   02 동   03 분   04 분

2-1 분사구문 만들기
p. 167

Challenge 1

01 Walking in the park
02 Admitting what he says
03 Turning to the right at the corner
04 driving to my office

Challenge 2

01 If you turn to the left
02 Because(=As) she was poor
03 Although(=Though) I admit what you say
04 After she picked up the phone

Challenge 1

01 with tears flowing　　02 with the door locked
03 with the cell phone ringing all the time

Challenge 2

01 Having finished the project
02 Having a slight cold
03 Having lived in Spain
04 Hearing the news
05 Having met him before

2-3 being과 having been의 생략 / 의미상 주어

p. 171

Challenge 1

01 Being excited / Excited
02 Having been educated / Educated

Challenge 2

01 It being fine
02 The train being crowded

Challenge 3

01 Written　　02 Located　　03 Graduating

이것이 시험에 출제되는 영문법이다!　p. 172

Ex1 (b)　　Ex2 (d)　　Ex3 (b)　　Ex4 Not
Ex5 (c)
Ex6 There being nobody around, she hurried home.
Ex7 (d)　　Ex8 (c)

| 해설 |

Ex1 cross의 동작 주체는 a black cat이다. 스스로 동작이 가능한 주체이므로 현재분사 crossing을 쓴다.
Ex2 얼굴에 페인트가 묻은 채로 일을 하는 것이므로 with 뒤에 있는 명사 face는 페인트칠을 할 수 있는 주체가 되지 못하고 페인트칠을 당하는 대상이 된다. 따라서 과거분사 painted를 쓴다.
Ex3 감정을 주는 주체가 it 즉 a movie이다. 따라서 현재분사 amazing을 써야 한다.
Ex4 분사구문의 부정은 분사 바로 앞에 not을 쓴다.
Ex5 문장 맨 앞의 분사를 구분하는 문제는 주어의 행동 유무에 따라 결정된다. 주어 즉, the painting은 스스로 행동이

가능한 생물체가 아닌 동작의 대상이 되므로 과거분사인 stolen으로 써야 한다.
Ex6 주어가 서로 다르기 때문에 주어를 각각 따로 써 주어야 한다. 특히 유도부사 there가 포함된 경우 분사 앞에 there가 온다.
Ex7 목적격 보어 자리의 분사는 목적어가 주체냐 객체냐에 따라 분사의 형태가 결정된다. 목적어가 동작이 가능하지 않은 객체인 picture이므로 과거분사 taken을 써야 한다.
Ex8 코트를 입었는데도 여전히 추운 것을 보니 '~임에도 불구하고'라는 뜻의 접속사 though가 적절하다.

기출 응용문제　p. 174

1 ③ listen to → listening to　2 ⑤　　　3 ⑤
4 crossed　　5 ②　　　6 ②　　　7 ②
8 ③
9 Not having slept for two days, she is very tired now.

| 해설 |

1 동시 동작을 나타내는 표현으로 listen을 listening으로 고쳐야 한다. 그렇지 않으면 sat과 listen의 동사가 2개 등장하는 틀린 문장이 된다.
2 ⑤는 동명사로 쓰였고 나머지는 모두 분사구문이다.
3 시간을 나타내는 접속사 when이 적절하다.
4 「with+명사+분사」에서 명사 legs가 스스로 동작을 하는 주체가 될 수 없으므로 과거분사 crossed를 써야 한다.
5 운전하는 동작의 주체가 the man이므로 현재분사 driving the taxi가 올바르다.
6 bowed와 put이 과거로 시제가 동일하므로 bowed는 bowing이 되어야 한다. 또한 부사절과 주절의 주어(she)가 같으므로 분사구문의 의미상 주어는 생략한다.
7 주절과 주어가 같으므로 부사절의 주어도 you를 쓴다. leaving은 현재 말하는 시점과 같으므로 현재시제인 leave로 고쳐 쓴다.
8 첫 번째 문장에는 동시 동작을 나타내는 현재분사 reaching을 쓰고 두 번째 문장에는 빈칸 앞에 있는 명사 dress가 만들어지는 대상이므로 과거분사인 made를 쓴다.
9 접속사는 생략한다. 잠을 자지 못한 것은 피곤한 현재의 상태보다 더 이전의 일이므로 완료 분사구문인 「having+p.p.」를 이용하여 Not having slept for two days, she~로 문장을 완성한다. 분사구문의 부정은 분사구문 바로 앞에 not을 써 주기만 하면 된다.

1 ③   2 made   3 ④

4 Turning   5 Not having   6 ⑤   7 ③

8 When we arrived

9 Because(=As) I didn't have

10 ②   11 ③   12 ①   13 ③

14 arriving   15 Because he was poor

16 If you take this bus

17 When I walked along the street   18 ③

19 disappointing / disappointed

20 shocking / shocked

21 can't read the book written

22 Frankly speaking

23 Generally speaking   24 Judging from

25 ⑤   26 ④   27 ④

| 해설 |

1 '일반적으로 말해서'라는 의미는 generally speaking으로 쓴다.

2 「관계대명사+be동사」를 생략하고 과거분사가 직접 명사를 수식할 수 있다. 여기서 명사 watch는 행위가 불가능한 사물이므로 과거분사 made를 쓴다.

3 숙제를 끝낸 시점이 더 과거이므로 완료 분사구문 Having finished를 써야 한다.

4 접속사와 동일한 주어를 생략하고, 주어 you가 행동이 가능한 주체이므로 turn을 현재분사형인 turning으로 바꾼다.

5 접속사와 동일한 주어를 생략하고, have를 현재분사형인 having으로 고친다. 분사구문의 부정은 바로 앞에 not을 써주기만 하면 된다.

6 puppy는 잠을 자는 주체이므로 과거분사(slept) 대신 현재분사를 써야 한다. 따라서 The puppy sleeping in the house is very cute.로 써야 한다.

7 사람은 감정을 줄 수도 있고 감정을 받을 수도 있지만 ③에서는 영화를 보고 실망감을 받게 된 것이므로 disappointing을 disappointed로 써야 한다.

8 시간의 접속사 when을 쓰고, 주어가 같기 때문에 생략했으므로 주어도 we를 그대로 쓴다. 시제 arriving은 주절의 found와 같은 과거시제임을 내포하고 있으므로 과거시제인 arrived로 고쳐 쓰기만 하면 된다.

9 이유의 접속사 because 또는 as를 쓰고 주어가 같기 때문에 생략했으므로 주어 I를 그대로 쓴다. 시제 not having 또한 주절의 시제 couldn't buy와 같은 과거시제임을 내포하고 있으므로 과거시제인 didn't have로 고쳐 쓰기만 하면 된다.

10 해변으로 나간 것보다 아침을 먹은 것이 시간적으로 앞선 과거이므로 완료 분사구문인 Having eaten을 쓰고, (b)는 동시 동작인 '~하면서'의 의미이므로 현재분사 watching으로 써야 한다. 마찬가지로 watch라는 동작의 주체는 행

동이 가능한 He이므로 현재분사형(watching)을 쓴 것이다.

11 ③에서 밑줄 친 taking은 수동의 표현인 taken으로 바꾸어야 한다. names는 동작이 불가능한 대상이므로 과거분사를 써야 한다.

12 주어진 문장은 문장 맨 앞 즉, 주어 자리에 쓴 동명사이다. ①은 주절과 분리되는 분사구문이고 나머지는 모두 동명사이다.

13 콘서트라는 대상은 감정을 주는 대상이므로 현재분사, 주어 I는 콘서트를 보고 감정을 받은 사람이므로 과거분사를 쓴다.

14 접속사를 생략하고 현재분사 arriving으로 고쳐 쓸 수 있다. 비행기를 행위의 주체로 보고 과거분사가 아닌 현재분사를 쓴 것이다.

15 '가난했기 때문에'라는 의미이므로 접속사 because를 쓴다. 주어가 같고 시제가 같기 때문에 was를 being으로 고쳐 분사구문을 만든 것이다. 따라서 Because he was poor로 부사절을 완성한다.

16 '이 버스를 탄다면'이라는 의미이므로 접속사 if를 쓴다. 주어가 같고 시제가 같으므로 take를 taking으로 고쳐 분사구문을 만든 것이다. 따라서 If you take this bus로 부사절을 완성한다.

17 '길을 따라 걸었을 때'라는 의미이므로 접속사 when을 쓴다. 주어가 같고, 시제가 같기 때문에 walked를 walking으로 고쳐 분사구문을 만든 것이다. 따라서 When I walked along the street로 부사절을 완성한다.

18 ③은 동사 finished의 목적어로 쓰인 동명사이고, 나머지는 모두 분사로 쓰였다.

19 축구팀의 성적이 감정을 주는 주체이므로 현재분사를, we는 사람으로 감정을 받는 대상이므로 과거분사를 쓴다.

20 영화는 감정을 주는 주체이므로 현재분사를, I는 감정을 받는 대상이므로 과거분사를 써야 한다.

21 분사구문으로 과거분사 written이 명사 the book을 수식할 수 있도록 I can't read the book written in Japanese.로 문장을 쓴다.

22 솔직히 말해서=Frankly speaking

23 일반적으로 말해서=Generally speaking

24 ~로 판단하건대=Judging from

25 '죽어가고 있는'이라는 의미를 나타내기 위해 dead를 dying으로 고쳐야 한다.

26 killing은 동시 동작을 나타내는 분사이다. 동작이 연속적으로 일어날 수 있도록 접속사 and를 쓰고 a spaceship을 대신하는 대명사 it, 그리고 동사는 과거시제(killed)를 쓴다.

27 「have+목적어+p.p.」의 어순으로 쓰는 것이 적절하다.

A   1   written in English is my father's
    2   leaving in the early morning
    3   fallen under the tree
B   1   While he bathed   2   Though they knew
    3   If you are hungry
    4   Although Kevin was born
C   1   Because[As] I had no money
    2   Turning to the right
    3   written in French   4   dancing in the hall
D   1   Generally speaking   2   The night coming
    3   Not having met   4   Judging from
    5   with her arms folded

| 해설 |

A 1 written이 명사 the book을 수식할 수 있도록 주어와 be동사를 생략하고 the book 뒤에 그대로 붙여 쓴다. 2 주어 it을 생략하고 동사 leaves를 현재분사인 leaving으로 고쳐 명사 the train을 수식하는 분사로 만든다. 명사 the train이 행위의 주체이므로 과거분사가 아닌 현재분사로 고쳐야 한다. 3 주어와 have를 생략하고 과거분사 fallen이 명사 leaves를 수식할 수 있도록 뒤에 위치시킨다. leaves 는 떨어져 있는 상태를 나타내므로 현재분사가 아닌 과거분사 fallen을 써야 한다.

B 1 bathing은 주절의 주어와 시제가 같기 때문에 주어 he 를 그대로 쓰고 동사는 과거시제인 bathed로 쓴다. 2 knowing은 주절의 주어와 시제가 같기 때문에 주어 they 를 그대로 쓰고 동사는 과거시제인 knew로 고쳐 쓴다. 3 주어와 동사가 생략되었다. 따라서 주절과 동일한 주어라 생략되었던 you를 그대로 쓰고, 형용사(hungry)가 보어가 될 수 있도록 알맞은 be동사 are를 써주면 된다. 4 born은 주절의 주어와 시제가 같기 때문에 생략하고 Being born의 분사구문에서 Being을 생략한 형태이다. 따라서 주어 Kevin을 쓰고 동사도 과거시제로 일치시켜 was born으로 쓴다.

C 1 '돈이 없었기 때문에'라는 이유를 나타내므로 접속사 because 또는 as를 쓰고 주어와 시제가 동일하여 had가 having으로 만들어진 것이므로 주어 I를 그대로 쓰고 시제 도 동일한 had를 써서 Because[As] I had no money로 부사절을 만든다. 2 주어가 같으므로 접속사와 주어를 생략 한다. 주어 you는 행동을 스스로 할 수 있는 생물체이므로 turn을 현재분사형인 turning으로 고쳐 쓰기만 하면 된다. 3 「관계사+be동사」를 생략해서 짧게 줄여 쓴다. 따라서 written이 명사 letter를 수식하는 분사가 만들어진다. 4 「관계사+be동사」를 생략한다. 따라서 dancing이 명사 girls를 수식하는 분사가 만들어진다.

D 1 '일반적으로 말하면'의 뜻인 비인칭 독립 분사구문의 generally speaking을 쓴다. 2 come을 분사형인 coming 으로 쓰고 주절과 주어가 다르므로 the night를 분사 coming 앞에 써 준다. 3 만나지 못했던 것은 주소를 알지 못하는 것 보다 더 과거의 일이므로 meet을 완료 분사구문인 having met으로 쓰고 부정의 의미를 담고 있으므로 not을 having met 앞에 써 준다. 4 judging from은 비인칭 독립 분사구 문으로 쓰이는 숙어 표현이다. 5 '(목적어가) ~한 채로'의 의미로 「with+명사+분사」를 쓴다. 목적어로 her arms를 쓰고 arms가 스스로 행위를 할 수 있는 주체가 아니므로 fold는 과거분사형인 folded로 쓴다. 따라서 with her arms folded로 문장을 완성한다.

실전 서술형 평가문제 A   p. 182

모범답안

1   Feeling very tired   2   Listening to music
3   Not eating breakfast

실전 서술형 평가문제 B   p. 183

모범답안

1   disappointing / disappointed
2   embarrassing / embarrassed
3   depressing / depressed
4   fascinated / fascinating
5   exciting / exciting / excited

실전 서술형 평가문제 C   p. 184

모범답안

1   Kelly always listens to music with her eyes closed.
2   Susan sobbed loudly with tears running down her cheeks.
3   Nancy stood by the window with her arms folded.
4   Tom was watching TV with his wife eating popcorn.

1-1 셀 수 있는 명사
p. 187

Challenge 1

01 are   02 a car   03 an accident
04 men   05 C   06 C
07 classes

Challenge 2

01 get   02 were   03 has
04 were   05 is   06 exists

1-2 셀 수 없는 명사
p. 189

Challenge 1

01 CN   02 UN   03 UN
04 UN   05 UN

Challenge 2

01 pictures   02 meat   03 friends
04 questions   05 advice   06 coffee
07 honesty

1-3 셀 수 있는 명사와 셀 수 없는 명사
p. 191

Challenge 1

01 the paper   02 noise   03 a hair
04 hair   05 room   06 papers
07 a light   08 light
09 very good weather

Challenge 2

01 luggage   02 a paper   03 advice
04 hair   05 time

1-4 셀 수 없는 명사를 세는 방법
p. 193

Challenge 1

01 a sheet of paper   02 a cup of coffee
03 a carton of milk   04 a bottle of beer
05 two glasses of water   06 two loaves of bread

Challenge 2

01 a cup of coffee   02 two pieces of meat
03 a bottle of water   04 three pounds of pork
05 eight glasses of water

1-5 주의해야 할 명사의 수
p. 195

Challenge 1

01 belongings   02 clothes   03 is
04 are   05 was   06 Arms
07 hands   08 friends   09 was

Challenge 2

01 two pairs of sneakers   02 a pair of glasses
03 three pairs of jeans   04 a new pair of pants

1-6 명사의 격
p. 197

Challenge 1

01 friends'   02 child's   03 children's
04 man's   05 men's

Challenge 2

01 tomorrow's meeting   02 dollars' worth
03 pounds' weight   04 two weeks' holiday

Challenge 3

01 The cover of the book
02 the legs of the desk   03 Some friends of mine
04 This iPhone of my brother's
05 seven hours' sleep

2-1 부정관사 a와 an의 쓰임
p. 199

Challenge 1

01 a   02 some   03 a   04 an
05 some   06 some   07 an

Challenge 2

01 ①   02 ③   03 ④   04 ②
05 ⑥   06 ⑤

2-2 정관사 the의 쓰임
p. 201

Challenge 1

01 some / a / The / the
02 some / a / a / a / The / The / the
03 some / a / a / the / The / the / the / the

Challenge 2

01 a → the   02 the → a   03 an → the
04 an → the   05 a → the

2-3 관사를 쓰지 않는 경우
p. 203

Challenge 1

01 a   02 the   03 a   04 X
05 X   06 X   07 X   08 X

Challenge 2

01 by the e-mail의 the 삭제
02 the lunch의 the 삭제
03 the wonderful dinner의 the를 a로 고침
04 the college의 the 삭제
05 a physics의 a 삭제
06 a rich의 a를 the로 고침

이것이 시험에 출제되는 영문법이다!
p. 204

Ex1 (c)   Ex2 (b)   Ex3 (b)
Ex4 furnitures → furniture   Ex5 (c)   Ex6 (b)
Ex7 (b)   Ex8 (c)

| 해설 |

Ex1 news는 단수 취급하여 단수형 동사 was를 쓴다.
Ex2 「수사+명사」가 형용사처럼 명사를 수식할 때는 수사 뒤의 명사를 복수형으로 쓰지 않는다.
Ex3 noise는 셀 수 없는 명사이므로 단수 동사 is를 쓴다.
Ex4 furniture는 셀 수 없는 명사라 –s를 붙일 수 없다.
Ex5 bread는 셀 수 없는 명사이므로 -(e)s를 붙일 수 없고 단위명사 piece에 -s를 붙여 pieces로 쓴다.
Ex6 시간을 나타내는 명사의 소유격은 비록 무생물이지만 -'s 또는 '(어퍼스트로피)로 나타낸다.
Ex7 주어진 문장에서 부정관사 an은 same의 뜻으로 (b)와 의미가 같다. (a)는 '약간의, 얼마간'의 의미이다.
Ex8 식사를 나타내는 명사 앞에는 관사를 쓰지 않는다.

기출 응용문제
p. 206

1 ③   2 poor people   3 ④
4 ⑤   5 ①, ②   6 ①   7 ②
8 ②

| 해설 |

1 「수사+명사」가 형용사처럼 사용되어 하이픈(−)으로 연결된 경우에는 수사 뒤의 명사를 복수형으로 쓰지 않는다. 따라서 ③이 올바르다. ① rice는 물질명사라 -s를 붙일 수 없고 ② 불운은 관사 없이 bad luck이라고 써야 한다. ④ '학생들의 질문에 답했다'에서 학생들의 질문은 the students' questions이 되어야 하고 ⑤ '종이 두 장'은 물질명사 paper에 -s를 붙일 수 없다.
2 「the+형용사」는 복수 보통명사로, '~한 사람들'의 뜻이다. 따라서 the poor는 poor people과 같은 뜻이다.
3 운동 경기 앞에는 정관사를 쓰지 않는다.
4 '조각'을 나타내는 pieces가 올바르다.
5 ①의 bread는 셀 수 없는 명사이므로 three loaves / pieces of bread로 쓴다. ② milk는 셀 수 없으므로 단위를 나타내는 명사 glass를 복수로 써야 한다.
6 셀 수 없는 명사는 제아무리 많아도 단수 취급한다. 따라서 are를 is로 써야 한다.
7 물질명사를 세는 단위명사는 그 물질에 따라서 각각 다르므로 잘 익혀 두어야 한다. a loaf of는 빵 덩어리를 세는 단위이며, 종이를 셀 때는 주로 a sheet of나 a piece of를 사용한다.
8 ②에 쓰인 부정관사가 'the same'의 뜻이다.

중간·기말고사 100점 100승
p. 208

1 ③   2 ⑤   3 (C)
4 (E)   5 (D)   6 (A)   7 (B)
8 ③   9 a   10 x   11 a
12 an   13 x   14 ④   15 ②
16 ⑤   17 of mine   18 ⑤
19 many rains → much rain   20 shake hands
21 ①   22 the handicapped
23 cup   24 sheets   25 tube
26 loaf   27 piece   28 ①

| 해설 |

1 ③의 형용사 honest의 첫 음이 모음으로 소리나므로 부정관사 an을 쓴다. 나머지는 모두 a를 쓴다.
2 shake hands(악수하다), make friends(친구를 사귀다)처럼 상호관계를 나타내는 경우 복수 명사를 써야 한다.
8 물질명사를 세는 단위는 그 물질에 따라 각각 달리 쓰이므로, 잘 익혀 두어야 한다. ③ '석 잔의 물'이라고 할 때 단위명사 glass에 -s를 써야 한다.

14 watch TV는 관용적으로 관사 없이 쓰고, go to bed와 같이 사물 등이 본래의 목적으로 쓰일 때도 관사 없이 쓴다.

15 ②처럼 신체 일부를 지칭할 때는 정관사 the를 써야 한다.

16 ⑤ a/an이 수식하는 명사는 소유격과 함께 쓸 수 없기 때문에 「of+소유대명사」나 「명사의 소유격」의 이중 소유격을 이용하여 a friend of mine으로 쓴다.

17 some의 수식을 받는 명사는 소유격과 함께 쓸 수 없으므로 '내 친구들 중 몇 명'은 some friends of mine으로 쓴다.

18 listen to music은 정관사 없이 쓴다.

19 rain은 셀 수 없는 명사이므로 복수형을 만들 수 없고 수를 나타내는 형용사 many와도 함께 쓸 수 없다. 따라서 much rain으로 바꿔야 한다.

20 '악수하다'는 반드시 복수형을 이용하여 shake hands로 써야 한다.

21 handicapped people을 「the+형용사」로 쓴 the handicapped가 올바르다.

22 they는 복수 명사를 대신하는 대명사로, 앞서 나온 the handicapped를 가리킨다.

28 the homeless는 복수 보통명사인 homeless people과 같다. 따라서 복수 명사로 취급하여 동사도 복수형인 need를 써야 한다.

중간·기말고사 평가대비 단답형 주관식   p. 211

A 1 a your friend → your friend / a friend of yours
  2 moneys → money
  3 cup of teas → cups of tea
  4 the desk's legs → the legs of the desk
B 1 T-shirt → a T-shirt, T-shirt → The T-shirt
  2 go to church → go to the church
  3 by an e-mail → by e-mail
C 1 the   2 the   3 x   4 the

| 해설 |

A 1 부정관사 a는 소유격과 나란히 쓸 수 없다. 따라서 a를 빼거나 a friend of yours로 고쳐야 한다. 2 money는 셀 수 없는 명사이므로 -s를 붙여 복수형을 쓰지 않는다. 3 tea는 셀 수 없는 명사이므로 단위를 나타내는 cup을 이용하여 two cups of tea로 써야 한다. 4 사물의 소유격은 of를 사용한다.

B 1 첫 번째 문장에 나온 T-shirt에는 '하나'라는 의미로 부정관사 a를 써야 한다. 앞서 나온 명사를 다시 언급할 때 뒤에 나오는 명사에는 정관사 the를 붙인다. 2 건물 본래의 목적이 아닌 다른 목적으로 '그 교회를 간다'라고 말할 경우 정관사 the를 쓴다. 3 통신수단을 나타내는 by 다음에는 관사를 쓰지 않는다.

3 1 상대방도 알고 있는 것을 가리킬 때 정관사 the를 쓴다. 2 신체 일부를 가리킬 때에도 정관사 the를 쓴다. 3 관직, 신분을 나타내는 명사 앞에는 관사를 쓰지 않는다. 4 최상급

앞에는 정관사 the를 붙인다.

실전 서술형 평가문제 A   p. 212

모범답안

1 Q: Is there any bread on the table?
  A: Yes, there is some bread.
2 Q: Is there any rice on the table?
  A: No, there isn't any rice.
3 Q: Are there any apples on the table?
  A: Yes, there are some apples.
4 Q: Is there any butter on the table?
  A: Yes, there is some butter.
5 Q: Is there any paper on the table?
  A: No, there isn't any paper.

실전 서술형 평가문제 B   p. 213

모범답안

1 time	2 times	3 papers
4 paper	5 paper	6 lights
7 light	8 hair / hair	9 hairs

실전 서술형 평가문제 C   p. 214

모범답안

1 She has a carton of milk.
2 There are three slices/pieces of pizza (in this picture).
3 She needs two pieces/sheets of paper.
4 I bought two loaves of meat (yesterday).

Chapter 08 대명사

1-1 it의 용법(1) p. 217

Challenge 1

01 a car
02 to solve the problem
03 some cheese
04 to go on a trip to Europe
05 he advised me to persuade her
06 they were all shouting

Challenge 2

01 It is impossible to understand the problem.
02 It is foolish behaving like that.
03 It is certain that travel broadens our mind.
04 I think it better to make use of solar energy.
05 I believe it good his taking care of orphans.

1-2 it의 용법(2) / 지시대명사 p. 219

Challenge 1

01 It was Ted that I met at the library this morning.
02 It was at the library that I met Ted this morning.
03 It was this morning that I met Ted at the library.

Challenge 2

01 she didn't answer the letter
02 Do your best
03 let's go to the movies
04 play

Challenge 3

01 those
02 that
03 those
04 those

1-3 재귀대명사 p. 221

Challenge 1

01 myself
02 yourself
03 yourselves
04 himself
05 herself
06 itself
07 ourselves
08 themselves

Challenge 2

01 himself
02 ourselves / √
03 myself / √
04 herself
05 themselves
06 itself / √

Challenge 3

01 each other
02 themselves
03 each other
04 themselves
05 each other

2-1 one / ones p. 223

Challenge 1

01 one
02 it
03 one's
04 one
05 ones
06 one

Challenge 2

01 one
02 one
03 ones
04 ones

Challenge 3

01 it
02 it
03 one
04 them
05 ones
06 It

2-2 -thing, -body, -one p. 225

Challenge 1

01 somewhere
02 anything
03 someone
04 anything
05 nothing
06 No one

Challenge 2

01 anything
02 something
03 nothing / somewhere / anywhere
04 somebody
05 anybody

Challenge 3

01 The bus was completely empty. There wasn't anybody on it.
02 The teacher didn't say anything about the result of the exam.

2-3 all, every, each, both p. 227

Challenge 1

01 has
02 student
03 are
04 was
05 are

Challenge 2

01 Every waiter speaks excellent English.

02 All the workers start at 8 a.m.
03 All the children want some pizza.
04 Every boy always plays soccer after school.

2-4 another, other, the other, the others

p. 229

Challenge 1

01 the other   02 another   03 Another
04 another   05 another   06 the other

Challenge 2

01 Other   02 other   03 others
04 The others   05 the others   06 others

2-5 자주 쓰이는 부정대명사

p. 231

Challenge 1

01 The other   02 others   03 others
04 Another   05 another / the other
06 the others   07 the other
08 another / the other   09 others
10 others   11 The others   12 Others
13 The others   14 another

이것이 시험에 출제되는 영문법이다!

p. 232

Ex1 (b)   Ex2 (d)   Ex3 (b)   Ex4 (c)
Ex5 (d)   Ex6 (b)   Ex7 (b)   Ex8 (a)

| 해설 |

Ex1 종류는 같지만 대상이 다른 사전이므로 대명사 one을 쓴다. 특정한 것이 아니므로 one이 올바르다.
Ex2 단수 명사 performance를 지칭하므로 대명사 that으로 처리한다.
Ex3 주어가 셀 수 없는 명사이므로 단수 동사인 is를 쓴다.
Ex4 each 뒤에는 반드시 단수 명사(book)를 써야 한다.
Ex5 주어가 she이므로 재귀대명사는 herself를 쓴다.
Ex6 긍정문에는 something을 쓴다.
Ex7 정해지지 않은 다른 한 명은 another로 쓴다. 학생이 두 명밖에 없다는 단서가 있다면 the other가 정답이 된다.
Ex8 여행객 수가 정해져 있지 않기 때문에 others를 써야 한다.

기출 응용문제

p. 234

1 looking at herself   2 ②   3 ④
4 ④   5 ⑤   6 ③   7 ③

| 해설 |

1 거울 속의 자기 자신을 보고 있으므로 she의 재귀대명사인 herself를 이용하여 looking at herself로 문장을 완성한다.
2 특정한 연필을 지칭하는 것이 아니므로 대명사 one을 쓴다.
3 It ~ that 강조구문이다. 따라서 빈칸에는 대명사 It을 쓴다.
4 100달러와 10달러 지폐를 제외한 나머지 정해진 모든 지폐에 미국 대통령 사진이 있다는 의미이므로 the other를 이용하여 the other bills로 쓴다.
5 ones는 앞에 나온 명사 thoughts를 대신하는 부정대명사이다.
6 불특정한 사람[것]들 중 일부는 some, 또 다른 일부는 others 또는 other+복수 명사로 쓴다.
7 복수 명사 ears를 대신할 때는 those를 쓴다. 두 번째 문장은 '~하는 사람들'이란 뜻의 those who~ 구문이다. 따라서 공통으로 들어갈 말은 those이다.

중간·기말고사 100점 100승

p. 236

1 ④	2 ③	3 ⑤	4 ④
5 ⑤	6 ①		
7 Ⓐ play Ⓑ work		8 ⑤	9 ④
10 ②	11 It is	12 ④	
13 another	14 Some	15 the other	
16 the others		17 one	18 ②
19 ②	20 ①	21 ④	22 ②
23 ②	24 ①	25 Every	
26 Each	27 All		

| 해설 |

1 '그녀에게 미안한 것이 없다'라는 부정의 의미이므로 nothing 이 올바르다.
2 '한 계좌에서 다른 계좌로 이체한다'라는 의미이므로 one과 another를 쓴다. 정해지지 않은 명사를 대신하므로 the other(s)는 쓸 수 없다.
3 보기와 같이 가목적어 it으로 쓰인 것은 ⑤이다. ①은 It ~ that 강조용법, ②는 대명사, ③은 가주어, ④는 비인칭 주어 it이다.
4 Each는 단수형 동사(has)를 쓴다.
5 some과 other/others는 함께 어울린다. 정해지지 않은 명사이므로 other kids로 써야 한다.
6 ①의 herself는 '자신이 직접'이란 의미의 강조용법이다. 강조용법은 문장에서 강조하는 역할만을 담당하므로 생략해도 의미에 영향을 끼치지 않는다.
7 this는 후자인 play, that은 공간적으로 떨어진 전자를 가리키므로 work가 된다.
8 단수 명사 the cost of living(생활비)을 대신하므로 that을 쓴다.
9 ④는 Which team will win the game doesn't matter.를 가주어 It을 사용하여 It doesn't matter which team will

win the game.으로 전환한 문장이다. ①③ 강조용법, ② 비인칭 it, ⑤ 상황의 it이다.

10 Some ~ (and) others ~는 '불특정한 여러 개[명] 중에서 일부는 ~하고 다른 일부는 ~하다'라는 뜻이므로, 빈칸에는 others가 알맞다.

11 주어인 the question이 부정사 to answer의 목적어로 자리가 이동되었으므로 비어있는 주어 자리에는 가주어와 동사가 필요하다. 따라서 It is로 문장을 완성한다.

12 '둘 다, 양쪽'의 뜻인 both가 올바르다.

13 A is one thing, B is another는 'A와 B는 별개의 것이다'라는 의미이다.

14 정해지지 않은 것[사람] 중에서 몇몇은 some, 나머지는 others를 쓴다.

15 정해진 둘 중에 하나는 one, 나머지 하나는 정관사 the를 사용하여 the other로 쓴다.

16 정해진 사람 중 몇몇은 some, 나머지는 정관사 the를 사용하여 the others를 쓴다.

17 특정한 명사를 가리키지 않을 때는 one을 사용한다.

18 동사는 It ~ that으로 강조하지 않고 동사 앞에 do / does / did를 사용하여 강조한다.

19 ②에서 ourselves는 동사의 목적어로 쓰였고, 나머지는 모두 강조의 용법으로 쓰였다.

20 여러 개[사람] 중에서 일부를 제외한 나머지 전체는 the others를 쓴다.

21 상대방에게 권유하는 의문문에는 something을 사용한다.

22 정해진 두 개 중 하나는 one, 나머지는 정관사 the를 사용하여 the other를 쓴다.

23 ①⑤의 재귀대명사는 동사의 목적어, ③은 전치사의 목적어이다. ④의 by oneself는 '혼자서'라는 뜻의 숙어 표현이다. ②의 재귀대명사는 강조하기 위하여 쓰였으므로 생략할 수 있다.

24 앞에 나온 특정한 명사를 대신하는 대명사 it과, 가주어로 쓰인 it이므로 공통 단어는 it이다.

중간ㆍ기말고사 평가대비 단답형 주관식   p. 240

A 1 anyone   2 something
   3 anything   4 someone
B 1 those   2 they / you
   3 It   4 it
C 1 One / the other 2 Some / others
D 1 We think it strange that she should leave
     without telling us.
   2 My parents see it crazy to wear a miniskirt
     in cold winter.
   3 Western people believe it unlucky to break
     a mirror.
E 1 taught myself   2 blamed herself
   3 help yourselves 4 enjoy themselves

| 해설 |

A 1 부정문에서 사람을 가리킬 때 anyone 또는 anybody를 쓴다. 2 긍정문에서 사람이 아닌 물건 등을 가리킬 때 something을 쓴다. 3 사물이나 대상을 가리킬 때 부정문에서 anything을 사용한다. 4 긍정문에서 정해지지 않은 사람을 나타내는 부정대명사는 someone 또는 somebody이다.

B 1 명사 ears를 대신하는 복수 명사는 those이다. 2 동사 (speak)가 복수형이므로 주어는 they 또는 you가 가능하다. 3 날씨를 나타내는 비인칭 대명사 it이 필요하다. 4 가목적어 it을 쓴다.

C 1 정해진 두 명의 친구 중 한 명은 one, 나머지 다른 한 명은 정관사 the를 이용하여 the other로 쓴다. 2 정해지지 않은 사람들 중 몇몇은 some, 다른 사람들은 others로 쓴다. 정해지지 않은 수이므로 정관사 the를 쓰지 않는다.

D 1 목적어 that she should leave without telling us 자리에 it을 쓰고 모두 뒤로 보낸다. 2 목적어 to wear a miniskirt in cold winter 자리에 it을 쓰고 모두 뒤로 보낸다. 3 목적어 to break a mirror 자리에 it을 쓰고 모두 뒤로 보낸다.

E 1 주어가 I, 시제는 과거이므로 taught myself로 문장을 완성한다. 2 주어가 여성 단수 명사이고 시제는 과거이므로 blamed herself로 문장을 완성한다. 3 '마음껏 드세요'라는 의미의 help yourselves로 문장을 완성한다. 4 주어가 they, 시제는 현재이므로 enjoy themselves로 문장을 완성한다.

실전 서술형 평가문제 A   p. 242

모범답안

1 The population of Australia is much smaller than that of Japan.

2 The water in this lake is cleaner than that of that lake.

3 The ears of a rabbit are longer than those of a human.

4 Jason's manners aren't often much better than those of a child.

5 The climate of Korea is like that of Italy.

실전 서술형 평가문제 B   p. 243

모범답안

1 One is a doctor and the other is a teacher.

2 The other colors(=The others) are red, blue, and black.

3 The other students(=The others) went outside and played soccer.

모범답안

1 It was Scott that(=who) broke the glasses yesterday.

2 It was the glasses that Scott broke yesterday.

3 It was yesterday that Scott broke the glasses.

Chapter 09 형용사   p. 245~270

1-1 형용사의 역할   p. 247

Challenge 1

01 한정적   02 서술적   03 한정적
04 서술적   05 서술적

Challenge 2

01 live   02 alive   03 drunken   04 asleep
05 alike

Challenge 3

01 She is taller than her elder sister.
02 Tennis is an outdoor game.
03 I think the drunken drivers are very dangerous.
04 My main concern now is to take care of my parents.

1-2 형용사의 다양한 쓰임   p. 249

Challenge 1

01 어떤, 특정한   02 나쁜   03 아픈
04 작고한   05 늦은   06 오른쪽의   07 옳은

Challenge 2

01 anything particular   02 something nice
03 to drink something hot
04 anything cold to drink
05 nothing white   06 anything wrong

Challenge 3

01 the blind   02 handicapped people

2-1 many, much, a lot of, lots of   p. 251

Challenge 1

01 Was there much yellow dust in Seoul yesterday?
02 Did you prepare much food for Thanksgiving?
03 This year I didn't invite many people. I just invited my immediate family.

Challenge 2

01 How many chickens does he raise?
02 How much pizza does she want?

Challenge 3

01 a lot of   02 too much   03 too many
04 a lot of

2-2 some, any, no, none   p. 253

Challenge 1

01 some / any   02 any   03 any
04 some   05 some   06 no   07 any
08 no   09 None   10 none

Challenge 2

01 There isn't any sugar in your coffee.
02 Kevin doesn't have any free time.
03 My sister is married, but she has no children.
04 I couldn't make an omelette because there were no eggs.

2-3 (a) few, (a) little
p. 255

Challenge 1

01 a few   02 few
03 a little   04 a little / a few
05 a few / Few   06 little / a few
07 a little

Challenge 2

01 very few   02 very little   03 very little
04 very little   05 Very few   06 Very few

Challenge 3

01 I don't have many books in my schoolbag.
02 There isn't much milk in the bottle.

3-1 형용사 역할을 하는 분사
p. 257

Challenge 1

01 broken vase   02 reading a book
03 written in easy English

Challenge 2

01 shocking / shocked
02 embarrassed
03 interesting / interested
04 boring / bored

이것이 시험에 출제되는 영문법이다!
p. 258

Ex1 (c)   Ex2 (d)
Ex3 something hot to drink   Ex4 (c)   Ex5 (a)
Ex6 (d)   Ex7 exciting   Ex8 boring

| 해설 |

Ex1 사람이 감정을 받는 것이 아닌, '새 직업에 관한 이야기' 가 감정을 주는 것이므로 interesting을 쓴다.
Ex2 much는 셀 수 없는 명사 앞에만 사용한다.
Ex3 something과 같은 부정대명사가 부정사와 함께 쓰일 때는 「something+형용사+to부정사」 순으로 쓴다.
Ex4 the rich 또는 rich people과 the poor 또는 poor people로 써야 한다.
Ex5 셀 수 있는 명사(enemies) 앞에는 few를 쓰고, 셀 수 없는 명사(energy) 앞에는 little을 써야 한다.
Ex6 하이픈(-)이 숫자와 결합하여 명사를 꾸밀 경우 복수형으로 쓰지 않는다.
Ex7 축구 경기 자체는 감정을 주는 대상일 뿐 감정을 받는 생

물체가 되지 못한다. 따라서 현재분사 exciting으로 빈칸을 완성한다.
Ex8 남에게 지루한 감정을 전달하는 사람이므로 boring을 써야 한다.

기출 응용문제
p. 260

1 ①   2 ②   3 ②   4 ⓓ
5 ②   6 ⑤   7 ⑤
8 sleep → asleep

| 해설 |

1 four years old가 하이픈(-)으로 연결되어 명사를 수식하는 형용사 기능을 할 경우 복수형(years)으로 쓰지 않는다.
2 의미상 주어 of you 앞에는 일반 형용사 important를 쓰지 않고 foolish, wise와 같이 사람의 성질이나 성격을 나타내는 형용사를 쓴다.
3 something과 같은 부정대명사가 부정사와 함께 쓰일 때는 「something+형용사+to부정사」 순으로 쓴다.
4 -thing으로 끝나는 부정대명사는 형용사가 앞에서 직접 수식하지 않고 뒤에서 수식한다. 따라서 ⓓ의 unimportant를 something 뒤에 위치시킨다.
5 '시험을 통과한 학생이 거의 없다'는 의미이므로 few를 쓴다. 셀 수 있는 명사 students 앞에 오는 부정의 의미를 지닌 수량 형용사는 few이다.
6 셀 수 있는 명사 buildings 앞에 오는 부정의 의미를 지닌 수량 형용사는 few이다.
7 you가 감정을 받는 대상이므로 annoying을 과거분사형인 annoyed로 쓴다.
8 연결동사 fell 뒤에 보어로 형용사 asleep을 써야 한다. sleep은 동사이다.

중간·기말고사 100점 100승
p. 262

1 ③   2 ④   3 ⑤   4 ④
5 ②   6 little → few
7 any → some 또는 several
8 breaking → broken   9 ①   10 ④
11 ⑤   12 ②   13 ②   14 ④
15 ②   16 big   17 ②
18 the unemployed   19 ⑤
20 frightening / frightened
21 shocking / shocked   22 ⑤   23 ⑤

| 해설 |

1 exciting은 '흥분시키는'이라는 뜻으로 능동적인 뜻을 나타낸다. 이에 비해 excited는 '흥분한'이라는 뜻의 과거분사형 형용사로, 주어가 감정의 주체(주로 사람)가 된다.
2 time은 셀 수 없는 명사이므로 many를 쓸 수 없다. time에

복수형 -s를 붙일 때는 '횟수'를 나타내는 two times, three times일 때 가능하다.

3 일반적으로 형용사는 앞에서 명사를 수식하지만, -thing, -body, -one으로 끝나는 명사를 수식할 때는 형용사가 뒤에 위치한다. 그러므로 ⑤는 Christina has something different.가 되어야 한다.

4 셀 수 없는 명사(water)이고 긍정의 의미이므로 (a)는 a little을 쓴다. (b) 역시 셀 수 없는 명사이지만 부정의 의미이므로 little을 쓴다.

5 ① 행동 가능한 명사(woman)이므로 현재분사 talking을 쓴다. ③ 행동 가능한 명사(people)이므로 현재분사 waiting을 쓴다. ④ 행동 가능한 명사(people)일지라도 초대를 받은 대상이 되므로 과거분사 invited로 쓴다. ⑤ goods(상품)는 행동할 수 있는 대상이 아니므로 과거분사 made를 쓴다.

6 셀 수 있는 명사 앞에는 little이 아닌 few를 쓴다.

7 긍정문에서는 any 대신 some이나 several을 쓴다.

8 '부서진 창문들'이란 뜻으로 창문은 행동을 주체적으로 할 수 없는 대상이므로 과거분사인 broken을 써야 한다.

9 긍정문이고 셀 수 없는 명사(sugar) 앞이므로 some이나 a little이 올 수 있고, salt도 셀 수 없는 명사이므로 a little이 올 수 있다.

10 seem 뒤에는 보어로 형용사를 쓰고 명사(difficulty)는 쓰지 않는다.

11 ⑤를 제외한 나머지는 형용사 뒤에서 수식하는데 -thing으로 끝나는 명사나 대명사를 형용사가 수식할 때 명사 뒤에 위치한다. 그러나 ⑤와 같이 일반 형용사는 명사 앞에서 수식한다.

12 kind는 소녀를 꾸미는 일반 형용사이고 나머지는 모두 '~인 사람들'의 뜻인 복수 보통명사 「the+형용사/분사」이다.

13 셀 수 없는 명사(meat) 앞에는 a little을 쓴다.

14 재미있는 감정을 주는 주체는 컴퓨터이므로 현재분사형인 interesting을 써야 한다. 사물은 감정을 받을 수 없으므로 과거분사형을 쓸 수 없다.

15 셀 수 있는 명사 앞에 오면서 '(너무) 많은'의 뜻을 지닌 too many가 올바르다.

16 모자를 쓸 수 있을 만큼 충분히 크지 않다면, 머리가 모자에 비해 크다는 의미이므로 '머리가 너무 큰'이란 뜻의 too big이 올바르다.

17 무언가를 나타내는 대명사는 something이지만, 의문문에서는 anything을 쓴다. -thing으로 끝나는 단어는 형용사가 뒤에서 수식하므로 ②가 올바른 문장이다.

18 unemployed people과 the unemployed는 같은 뜻이다.

19 셀 수 없는 명사 advice 앞에는 a little을 써야 한다.

20 woman이 감정을 주는 주체이므로 frightening을 쓰고 children이 감정을 받는 대상이므로 frightened로 쓴다.

21 news가 감정을 주는 주체이므로 shocking을 쓰고 citizens는 감정을 받는 대상이므로 shocked로 쓴다.

22 ⑤의 a few는 가지고 쓸 연필이 있다는 긍정의 의미이므로 서로 의미가 다르다.

23 ⑤의 right은 '바로'의 의미이다.

중간·기말고사 평가대비 단답형 주관식   p. 266

A 1 exciting   2 exciting
   3 excited   4 depressing
   5 depressed   6 depressed
B 1 few   2 few   3 little   4 little
C 1 the injured   2 something hot to drink

해설

A 1 시애틀에 가는 것이 흥미진진한 경험이므로 현재분사 exciting을 쓴다. 2 '새로운 장소'가 흥미진진한 감정을 주는 주체이므로 현재분사 exciting을 쓴다. 3 사람(Laura)이 감정을 받는 것이므로 과거분사 excited를 쓴다. 4 날씨가 우울한 감정을 주는 주체이므로 현재분사 depressing을 쓴다. 5 '추운 날씨가 나를 우울하게 만든다.'라는 의미로 감정을 받는 건 목적어(me)이므로 목적격 보어로 과거분사 depressed를 쓴다. 6 '날씨로 인해 우울해 하는 건 바보 같은 일이다'라는 의미로 감정을 받는 것이므로 과거분사인 depressed를 쓴다.

B 1~2 셀 수 있는 명사 앞에서 '거의 없는'이란 부정의 뜻인 few가 알맞다. 3~4 셀 수 없는 명사 time과 chance 앞에서 '거의 없는'이란 부정의 뜻인 little을 쓴다.

C 1 '부상자들'이란 의미로 the injured 또는 injured people을 쓸 수 있다. 2 something을 부정사와 함께 쓸 경우의 어순은 「something+형용사+to부정사」이다.

실전 서술형 평가문제 A   p. 267

모범답안

1 Is there any bread on the table? / there's some bread (on the table)

2 Are there any pineapples on the table? / there aren't any pineapples (on the table)

3 Are there any kiwis on the table? / there are some kiwis (on the table)

4 Is there any cheese on the table? / there isn't any cheese (on the table)

5 Is there any orange juice? / there is some orange juice

실전 서술형 평가문제 B

p. 268

모범답안

1 How many eggs does he eat? / He eats five eggs.
2 How many slices of bread does he eat? / He eats seven slices of bread.
3 How much butter and cheese does he put on the bread? / He puts a lot of butter and cheese on the bread.
4 How many doughnuts does he eat? / He eats four doughnuts.
5 How much coffee does he drink? / He drinks some coffee.
6 How much money does he spend on breakfast? / He spends a lot of money (on breakfast).

실전 서술형 평가문제 D

p. 270

모범답안

1 The strange scream was frightening. / The children were frightened.
2 The news was shocking. / The citizens were shocked.
3 politics is very interesting. / Julia is very interested in politics.
4 Her story was amazing. / Everyone was amazed.

실전 서술형 평가문제 C

p. 269

모범답안 (Answers will vary. Sample answers.)

1 I don't eat many eggs. 또는 I eat (a) few eggs. 또는 I eat a lot of eggs.
2 I eat a lot of ice cream. 또는 I eat (a) little ice cream. 또는 I don't eat much ice cream.
3 I don't eat many potatoes. 또는 I eat (a) few potatoes. 또는 I eat a lot of potatoes.
4 I don't eat much meat. 또는 I eat (a) little meat. 또는 I eat a lot of meat.
5 I eat a lot of chocolate. 또는 I don't eat much chocolate. 또는 I eat (a) little chocolate.
6 I don't eat many bananas. 또는 I eat a lot of bananas. 또는 I eat (a) few bananas.
7 I drink a lot of coffee. 또는 I don't drink much coffee. 또는 I drink (a) little coffee.
8 I don't eat much fruit. 또는 I eat a lot of fruit. 또는 I eat (a) little fruit.

중학영문법 3-A

한국에서 유일한 중학영문법 알짜 3제

 정답 및 해설

3-A

한국에서 유일한

중학영문법

알짜 3000제

📖 단어장

IamBooks

중학교 3학년 영문법

3-A

한국에서 유일한

중학영문법

알짜 3000제

단어장

과학적 암기 비법인 쪽지 접기 메모리를 활용하세요.

(반드시 읽고 단어 암기장을 활용하세요!)

1. 단어와 한글 뜻을 보면서 단어를 암기합니다.
2. 맨 왼쪽 ①번을 접어서 영단어가 보이지 않게 합니다. 세 번째 칸의 한글 뜻을 보면서 영어 단어를 다시 쓰되, 이번에는 맨 밑에서부터 반대로 적어 올라갑니다.
3. 다시 ②번 선을 접어 한글 뜻 부분을 안보이게 합니다.
4. 자신이 적은 영단어 뜻을 보면서 마지막 칸에 다시 한글 뜻을 적는데, 이번에는 중간부터 아래 위로 하나씩 올라갔다 내려갔다 하면서 써봅니다. (또는 한글만 보고 소리내어 영단어를 말하면서 최종 확인을 합니다.)
5. 어휘를 암기한 후, 원어민이 녹음한 MP3 파일을 들으면서 빈칸에 영단어 또는 숙어 표현을 적고, 자신이 받아 적은 단어의 뜻을 다시 한글로 적어 봅니다.

   (MP3 파일 다운 : www.iambooks.co.kr)

> ①
> 단어 암기 후 이 부분을 접어
> 한글만 보고 다시 영어로 쓰세요.

Chapter **01** 시제				
001	take place	발생하다, 열리다		
002	study	ⓥ 공부하다		
003	live	ⓥ 살다		
004	teach	ⓥ 가르치다		
005	speak	ⓥ 말하다		
006	work	ⓝ 직장, 회사		

> ② 다시 이 부분을 접고
> 자신이 적은 영단어를 보고 아래서부터
> 위로 한글 뜻을 써보세요.

001	island	ⓝ 섬		
002	semester	ⓝ 학기		
003	certificate	ⓝ 증명서		
004	come along	생기다, 나타나다		
005	apologize	ⓥ 사과(변명)하다		
006	the Atlantic Ocean	대서양		
007	penicillin	ⓝ 페니실린		
008	washing machine	세탁기		
009	insurance company	보험회사		
010	movie theater	영화관		
011	chopsticks	ⓝ 젓가락		
012	take a shower	샤워하다		
013	turn off	끄다, 잠그다		
014	these days	요즈음, 요새		
015	improve	ⓥ 향상시키다, 증진하다		
016	satisfied	ⓐ 만족한		
017	electricity	ⓝ 전기		
018	count the minutes	손꼽아 기다리다		
019	postage	ⓝ 우편 요금, 우송료		
020	comfortable	ⓐ 편안한, 안락한		
021	succeed	ⓥ 성공하다		
022	get married	결혼하다		
023	be about to	막 ~하려고 하다		
024	ex-boyfriend	예전 남자 친구		
025	all day	하루 종일		

녹음된 문장을 듣고 빈칸에 단어 또는 표현을 쓰고, 그 뜻도 써보세요.

001 Jeju-do is the largest _____ in South Korea. 뜻 _____

002 The winter _____ starts next week. 뜻 _____

003 When you finish the course, a _____ will be sent to you. 뜻 _____

004 If another job _____ _____ this fall, I will take it. 뜻 _____

005 Until he _____ about the accident, I will not talk to him. 뜻 _____

006 The Amazon River flows into ___ _____ _____. 뜻 _____

007 Did Marie and Pierre Curie discover _____? 뜻 _____

008 Today most women have _____ _____. 뜻 _____

009 Did you use to work at an _____ _____? 뜻 _____

010 There used to be four _____ _____ in town. 뜻 _____

011 Scott is used to using _____, but it was difficult at the beginning. 뜻 _____

012 Lucy is _____ ___ _____ now. 뜻 _____

013 The water is boiling. Could you _____ it _____? 뜻 _____

014 I'm taking yoga lessons _____ _____. 뜻 _____

015 Eun-seon is trying to _____ her Japanese this year. 뜻 _____

016 Bob is always complaining. He is never _____. 뜻 _____

017 I was studying when the _____ went off. 뜻 _____

018 I'll be _____ ____ _____ till I see you this Friday. 뜻 _____

019 Right now she is weighing it to see how much _____ it needs. 뜻 _____

020 These shoes are very _____. 뜻 _____

021 She will _____ because she works hard. 뜻 _____

022 They're going to _____ _____ next week. 뜻 _____

023 Please don't make a noise! The movie ___ _____ ___ start. 뜻 _____

024 She is meeting her _____ this Sunday. 뜻 _____

025 We were going to play tennis yesterday, but it rained _____ _____. 뜻 _____

026	doorknob	ⓝ (문의) 손잡이		
027	head for	~으로 향하다		
028	object	ⓝ 물체, 목적, 대상		
029	participate in	~에 참가하다		
030	telephone	ⓥ 전화를 걸다		
031	departure	ⓝ 출발		
032	go up	들어가다, 들어서다		
033	population	ⓝ 인구		
034	put out	(불을) 끄다		
035	predator	ⓝ 포식(육식)동물, 약탈자		
036	greenhouse effect	온실효과		
037	ancient	ⓐ 고대의, 오래된		
038	get in touch with	~와 연락[접촉]하다		
039	trip	ⓝ 여행		
040	arrange	ⓥ 준비[배열]하다		
041	footstep	ⓝ 발소리		
042	invitation	ⓝ 초대		
043	crawl	ⓥ 기어가다		
044	prepare for	~을 위해 준비하다		
045	go on holiday	휴가를 가다		
046	impressed	ⓐ 감명을 받은		
047	husband	ⓝ 남편		
048	throw	ⓥ 던지다, 팽개치다		
049	hand	ⓥ (직접) 건네주다		
050	office	ⓝ 사무실		

녹음된 문장을 듣고 빈칸에 단어 또는 표현을 쓰고, 그 뜻도 써보세요.

026 The door is closed. Kelly has her hand on the _____. 뜻 _____

027 Susan is putting on her coat and _____ ____ the door. 뜻 _____

028 Every _____ falls at the same speed. 뜻 _____

029 He visited Korea to _____ ___ a house-building project. 뜻 _____

030 I was about to leave when you _____ me. 뜻 _____

031 I will cancel my _____ if it rains tomorrow. 뜻 _____

032 As the boat was _____ ____ the river, I felt something was lost. 뜻 _____

033 The _____ of the world is rising very fast. 뜻 _____

034 Last night firemen _____ _____ a small fire in a bedroom. 뜻 _____

035 We stayed in the car, because there were a lot of _____ close by. 뜻 _____

036 The Earth is getting warmer because of the _____ ____. 뜻 _____

037 This _____ temple will be 1,000 years old next year. 뜻 _____

038 She wants to _____ ___ _____ _____ Mike. 뜻 _____

039 The family is planning an overseas _____. 뜻 _____

040 Kevin's wife _____ a surprise birthday party for him. 뜻 _____

041 I was walking along the street when I heard _____ behind me. 뜻 _____

042 I won't accept his _____. 뜻 _____

043 She often _____ under her bed. 뜻 _____

044 He is _____ ____ the meeting on Wednesday at 9:00. 뜻 _____

045 If you feel tired, you must ___ ___ _____. 뜻 _____

046 We were _____ with his life story. 뜻 _____

047 She first met her _____ in 2006. 뜻 _____

048 You are always _____ your socks everywhere. 뜻 _____

049 I just _____ the box to the postal worker. 뜻 _____

050 I was about to leave when she came into the _____. 뜻 _____

001	purse	ⓝ (여성용) 지갑	
002	be in trouble	어려움[곤경]에 처하다	
003	already	ⓐⓓ 이미, 벌써	
004	movie actor	영화 배우	
005	station	(철도의) 정거장, 역	
006	cast	ⓝ 깁스	
007	company	ⓝ 회사, 동료, 교제	
008	freshman	ⓝ 신입생, 1학년생	
009	bill	ⓝ 고지서, 청구서	
010	beach volleyball	비치 발리볼	
011	photographer	ⓝ 사진가	
012	news anchor	뉴스 진행자	
013	delicious	ⓐ 맛있는, 맛좋은	
014	break out	(전쟁 등 안 좋은 일이) 발생하다	
015	in fact	사실은, 실은	
016	graduate from	~를 졸업하다	
017	take a vacation	휴가를 얻다	
018	right now	지금은, 지금 당장	
019	wait for	~를 기다리다	
020	so far	지금까지	
021	many times	여러 번, 자주	
022	painting	ⓝ 그림	
023	be on a diet	다이어트 중이다	
024	go out for a walk	산책하러 나가다	
025	get divorced	이혼하다, 파경을 맞다	

녹음된 문장을 듣고 빈칸에 단어 또는 표현을 쓰고, 그 뜻도 써보세요.

001 Julia is looking for her _____. She can't find it.   뜻 _____

002 Tom has lost his cell phone. He __ __ _____ now.   뜻 _____

003 I've _____ searched the Internet but found nothing.   뜻 _____

004 Have you ever met a _____ _____?   뜻 _____

005 He has just arrived at the _____.   뜻 _____

006 Jane can't walk because her leg is in a _____.   뜻 _____

007 She has worked in this _____ since 2005.   뜻 _____

008 I have met her since I was a _____ in high school.   뜻 _____

009 Our phone _____ has risen since we bought a cell phone.   뜻 _____

010 She hasn't played _____ _____ since last summer.   뜻 _____

011 Laura has been a _____ for ten years.   뜻 _____

012 She was a _____ _____ for 5 years.   뜻 _____

013 I have never eaten such a _____ food.   뜻 _____

014 My history teacher told us the Korean War _____ __ in 1950.   뜻 _____

015 ___ _____, I was in Seattle last year.   뜻 _____

016 Maria _____ _____ high school in 1999.   뜻 _____

017 Have you _____ __ _____ recently?   뜻 _____

018 Bob and Sunny are in their car _____ ____.   뜻 _____

019 We've been _____ ____ the bus for 20 minutes.   뜻 _____

020 She has read 50 pages ___ _____.   뜻 _____

021 Lisa has talked to Jason on the phone _____ _____.   뜻 _____

022 He has painted more than fifty _____.   뜻 _____

023 She had _____ __ __ _____ for three months.   뜻 _____

024 After I had finished my homework, I ____ ___ ___ __ _____.   뜻 _____

025 They had lived together for 15 years when they ___ _____.   뜻 _____

026	take off	이륙하다, 날아오르다		
027	hometown	ⓝ 고향		
028	fare	ⓝ 요금, 통행료		
029	at last	마침내, 결국		
030	a few days	며칠		
031	back	ⓝ 등		
032	show up	(예정된 곳에) 나타나다		
033	catch a cold	감기 걸리다		
034	dental clinic	치과 (병원)		
035	teenager	ⓝ 십대		
036	strength	ⓝ 강점, 장점, 능력		
037	by the time	그때까지		
038	boring	ⓐ 지루한		
039	harbor	ⓝ 항구, 피난처		
040	amusement park	놀이 공원		
041	little	ⓐ 어린		
042	fashion designer	패션 디자이너		
043	talent	ⓝ 재능, 소질, 수완		
044	go fishing	낚시하러 가다		
045	be in hospital	입원하다		
046	economy	ⓝ 경제, 절약		
047	accident	ⓝ 사고		
048	newspaper	ⓝ 신문		
049	realize	ⓥ 깨닫다, 실감[이해]하다		
050	break into	침입하다		

녹음된 문장을 듣고 빈칸에 단어 또는 표현을 쓰고, 그 뜻도 써보세요.

026   When I arrived at the airport, the plane had _____ ____.   뜻 _____

027   You went back to your _____ after many years.   뜻 _____

028   Last week the bus _____ was 80 cents. Now it is 90.   뜻 _____

029   ___ _____ the bus came. I had been waiting for 30 minutes.   뜻 _____

030   I hadn't been feeling well for ____ _____ _____.   뜻 _____

031   She had been sitting for 3 hours, so her _____ started to hurt.   뜻 _____

032   Sunny didn't _____ ___ until 2 o'clock.   뜻 _____

033   He _____ __ _____ because he had been singing in the rain.   뜻 _____

034   I am at the _____ _____ now. I have been waiting for 35 minutes.   뜻 _____

035   Julia has hated her brother since she was a _____.   뜻 _____

036   We have proved our _____ to the whole world.   뜻 _____

037   ___ _____ _____ the concert began, they had been standing in a line.   뜻 _____

038   This is the most _____ movie that I have ever seen.   뜻 _____

039   I decided to get up early before the ship entered the _____.   뜻 _____

040   Have you ever been to the _____ _____?   뜻 _____

041   Since I was _____, I have been interested in clothes and fashion.   뜻 _____

042   My friends say that I will make a good _____ _____.   뜻 _____

043   I like clothes, but that doesn't mean that I have _____ in design.   뜻 _____

044   Jacob often had _____ _____ before he moved to Seoul.   뜻 _____

045   She has _____ ___ _____ since July.   뜻 _____

046   It's a book about the Korean _____.   뜻 _____

047   My brother hasn't had any _____ since he bought a new car.   뜻 _____

048   She has been working for a _____ since 2005.   뜻 _____

049   I _____ my briefcase was still on my desk.   뜻 _____

050   Somebody had _____ _____ the office during the night.   뜻 _____

001	foreign language	외국어		
002	customer	ⓝ 고객, 단골, 거래처		
003	cancer	ⓝ 암		
004	needs	ⓝ 요구, 필요, 의무		
005	any minute	지금 당장이라도, 금방이라도		
006	outdoors	야외에서		
007	warm-hearted	ⓐ 마음이 따뜻한		
008	traffic policeman	교통경찰관		
009	musician	ⓝ 음악가, 연주가		
010	humid	ⓐ 습기 있는, 눅눅한		
011	natural	ⓐ 당연한, 타고난, 자연의		
012	plug	ⓥ 막다, 틀어막다		
013	shut	ⓥ 닫다, 잠그다		
014	hand in	제출하다		
015	scholarship	ⓝ 장학금		
016	offer	ⓥ 제안[제의, 제공]하다		
017	through	㉄ ~동안, 내내, ~을 통과하여		
018	book	ⓥ 예약하다		
019	raw	ⓐ 날것의, 덜 익은		
020	be up to	~에 달려있다		
021	reveal	ⓥ 드러내다, 폭로하다		
022	promise	ⓝ 약속, 서약, 계약		
023	seriously	㉕ 심하게, 진지하게		
024	government	ⓝ 정부		
025	for a while	한동안, 잠시 (동안)		

녹음된 문장을 듣고 빈칸에 단어 또는 표현을 쓰고, 그 뜻도 써보세요.

001   Can you speak any _____ _____?   뜻 _____

002   _____ can use the computers for free.   뜻 _____

003   Children can have _____.   뜻 _____

004   Customers' _____ can change daily.   뜻 _____

005   Look at those dark clouds. It could start raining _____ _____.   뜻 _____

006   It's summer now. My friends and I can play tennis _____.   뜻 _____

007   She must be _____ like her mother.   뜻 _____

008   He is a _____ _____.   뜻 _____

009   She may become a great _____.   뜻 _____

010   It may be hot and _____ all weekend.   뜻 _____

011   It is _____ that she should get angry with him.   뜻 _____

012   You should _____ your nose. Here comes the smelly boy.   뜻 _____

013   Would you _____ the door, please?   뜻 _____

014   May I _____ ___ my homework tomorrow, please?   뜻 _____

015   Could I have a _____ application?   뜻 _____

016   Your friend looks thirsty. _____ her something to drink.   뜻 _____

017   You must drive slowly _____ the school zone.   뜻 _____

018   To get a cheap ticket, you have to _____ in advance.   뜻 _____

019   Many vegetables can be eaten _____. You don't have to cook them.   뜻 _____

020   You don't have to answer the phone. It ____ ____ ____ you.   뜻 _____

021   It is probable that the secretary _____ the secret.   뜻 _____

022   She must have forgotten the _____.   뜻 _____

023   The driver got _____ hurt in a car crash.   뜻 _____

024   _____ should have done more to help homeless people.   뜻 _____

025   She must have gone to China. I haven't seen her ____ __ _____.   뜻 _____

026	reserve	ⓥ 예약해 두다, 보존하다	
027	cut down	줄이다	
028	shave	ⓥ 면도하다, 깎다	
029	register	ⓥ 등록[기록]하다	
030	necessary	ⓐ 필요한	
031	safety rule	안전수칙	
032	forbidden	ⓐ 금지된	
033	settler	ⓝ 이주자	
034	somewhere	ⓐⓓ 어딘가에	
035	reception desk	(호텔의) 접수처, 프런트	
036	journalist	ⓝ 저널리스트, 기자	
037	thanks to	~덕분에	
038	make sure	확인하다	
039	name after	~의 이름을 따서 명명하다	
040	carry on	유지해 나가다	
041	crop	ⓝ 농작물	
042	medicine	ⓝ 의약품	
043	chemical	ⓝ 화학 물질	
044	snakebite	ⓝ 뱀에 물린 상처	
045	starve	ⓥ 굶주리다, 배고프다	
046	global	ⓐ 세계의, 지구의	
047	advertise	ⓥ 광고하다	
048	translate	ⓥ 번역하다	
049	deliver	ⓥ 배달[전달]하다	
050	exact	ⓐ 정확한	

녹음된 문장을 듣고 빈칸에 단어 또는 표현을 쓰고, 그 뜻도 써보세요.

026 We should have _____ a table. 뜻 _____

027 You had better _____ _____ on your smoking. 뜻 _____

028 You should _____ your beard before your job interview. 뜻 _____

029 You must _____ your motorcycle to take part in the race. 뜻 _____

030 It is _____ for us to study English. 뜻 _____

031 You had better obey the _____ _____. 뜻 _____

032 You may not enter the _____ areas of the temple. 뜻 _____

033 American _____ had a hard time moving west. 뜻 _____

034 I must have dropped my cellular phone _____. 뜻 _____

035 You must leave your key at the _____ _____ when you go out. 뜻 _____

036 I would rather be a school teacher than a _____. 뜻 _____

037 We received a free dinner, _____ ___ our new friend. 뜻 _____

038 Did you _____ _____ he was not a Dane? 뜻 _____

039 He's _____ _____ our brave king. 뜻 _____

040 You have to _____ ___ with the work about the farm. 뜻 _____

041 The topsoil is needed for growing _____. 뜻 _____

042 Weeds were often used as _____, too. 뜻 _____

043 Some of the old weed cures have _____ that are useful. 뜻 _____

044 It was used for centuries as a cure for _____. 뜻 _____

045 When do we eat? I'm _____. 뜻 _____

046 English is a _____ language. 뜻 _____

047 Braniff Airlines wanted to _____ its nice seats. 뜻 _____

048 Its advertisement was _____ from English to Spanish. 뜻 _____

049 The meaning of an advertisement is _____ by the exact words. 뜻 _____

050 I don't know the _____ date when he came. 뜻 _____

001	volleyball	ⓝ 배구		
002	once a month	한 달에 한 번		
003	speed of light	빛의 속도		
004	function	ⓝ 기능, 직능, 의식		
005	goal	ⓝ 목표, 목적		
006	overwork	ⓥ 과로하다		
007	eyesight	ⓝ 시력, 시야		
008	washing machine	세탁기		
009	refuse	ⓥ 거절하다, 거부하다		
010	police station	경찰서		
011	gorgeous	ⓐ 멋진, 호화스러운		
012	manage to	그럭저럭 ~하다		
013	duplicator	ⓝ 복사기		
014	shut up	입을 다물다, 닥치다		
015	meditation	ⓝ 명상, 묵상		
016	full moon	보름달		
017	immediately	ⓐⓓ 즉각, 곧, 즉시로		
018	context	ⓝ 문맥		
019	fall in love with	~와 사랑에 빠지다		
020	right	ⓝ 권리		
021	conference	ⓝ 회의, 학회		
022	discussion	ⓝ 토론		
023	relaxation	ⓝ 기분전환, 풀림, 이완		
024	infection	ⓝ 감염, 병균		
025	take part in	~에 참여[참가]하다		

녹음된 문장을 듣고 빈칸에 단어 또는 표현을 쓰고, 그 뜻도 써보세요.

001 To play _____ at the beach is always exciting. 뜻 _____

002 To visit my parents _____ __ _____ is a joy in my life. 뜻 _____

003 It is impossible to travel faster than the _____ __ _____. 뜻 _____

004 The _____ of the heart is to pump blood. 뜻 _____

005 The _____ of the meeting is to reach a decision. 뜻 _____

006 Not to _____ is good for your health. 뜻 _____

007 Jane has bad _____. Her wish is to see things clearly. 뜻 _____

008 Can you show me how to use this _____ _____? 뜻 _____

009 She tried to give him his medicine, but he _____ to open his mouth. 뜻 _____

010 Please tell me how to get to the _____ _____. 뜻 _____

011 It was a _____ day, so we decided to go for a walk. 뜻 _____

012 We should _____ __ get to the airport in time. 뜻 _____

013 Can you show me how to use this _____? 뜻 _____

014 She told me to _____ ____ at once. 뜻 _____

015 Doing _____ helps calm us down. 뜻 _____

016 We watched the _____ _____ rise yesterday. 뜻 _____

017 The police forced the crowd to leave the building _____. 뜻 _____

018 You can guess the meaning of the words from the _____. 뜻 _____

019 He is the first man to _____ __ _____ _____ me. 뜻 _____

020 People have a _____ to enjoy a happy life. 뜻 _____

021 The _____ is going to be held in Moscow next week. 뜻 _____

022 Our teacher sometimes uses videos for _____. 뜻 _____

023 I play tennis twice a week for exercise and _____. 뜻 _____

024 Jennifer used some medicine to cure an _____ on her arm. 뜻 _____

025 I'm going to _____ _____ ___ volunteer work. 뜻 _____

16

026	pronounce	ⓥ 발음하다		
027	at midnight	한밤중에		
028	haunted house	흉가		
029	rude	ⓐ 무례한, 교양 없는		
030	opportunity	ⓝ 기회		
031	lose weight	살을 빼다		
032	remodel	ⓥ 개조하다, 리모델링하다		
033	endure	ⓥ 참다, 견디다, 지탱하다		
034	absent	ⓐ 결석의, 부재의		
035	ignore	ⓥ 무시하다		
036	social	ⓐ 사회적인, 사교적인		
037	to make matters worse	설상가상으로		
038	to be frank with you	솔직히 말하면		
039	candidate	ⓝ 지원자, 후보자		
040	impolite	ⓐ 버릇 없는, 무례한		
041	be supposed to	~하기로 되어 있다		
042	bodyguard	ⓝ 보디가드, 경호원		
043	wage	ⓝ 급료, 임금		
044	consume	ⓥ 소비하다, 소모하다		
045	lord	ⓝ 주인, 지배자, 왕		
046	article	ⓝ 기사, 물품		
047	revolt	ⓝ 반란		
048	classify	ⓥ 분류하다		
049	product	ⓝ 제품, 생산품		
050	communication	ⓝ 의사소통		

녹음된 문장을 듣고 빈칸에 단어 또는 표현을 쓰고, 그 뜻도 써보세요.

026 Some of these words are not easy to _____.　　뜻 _____

027 ___ _____ I awoke to see a woman standing near the door.　　뜻 _____

028 He went to the _____ _____, never to come back.　　뜻 _____

029 He cannot be a gentleman to say such a _____ thing.　　뜻 _____

030 You would be foolish to miss the _____ again.　　뜻 _____

031 To _____ _____, you had better take up some sport.　　뜻 _____

032 The building was too old to be _____ again.　　뜻 _____

033 My dad is strong enough to _____ the difficult situation.　　뜻 _____

034 I am sorry to have been _____ yesterday.　　뜻 _____

035 She seems to _____ his advice all the time.　　뜻 _____

036 It's not easy for shy people to meet others at _____ events.　　뜻 _____

037 ___ _____ _____ _____, it began to rain hard.　　뜻 _____

038 ___ ___ _____ _____ _____, she is not honest.　　뜻 _____

039 It is necessary to choose the best _____ for the job.　　뜻 _____

040 It is _____ of him to leave without saying goodbye.　　뜻 _____

041 You _____ _____ ___ teach me how to ride a bicycle.　　뜻 _____

042 The president has a team of _____ to protect him.　　뜻 _____

043 We are to get a 10 percent _____ increase in January.　　뜻 _____

044 People are the only creatures that _____ without producing.　　뜻 _____

045 Yet they are _____ of all the animals.　　뜻 _____

046 Jessica collects information and writes _____ for newspapers.　　뜻 _____

047 The general was shocked to hear the news of a _____.　　뜻 _____

048 It's a human trait to try to _____ the things we find in the world.　　뜻 _____

049 Selling the _____ is the most important goal.　　뜻 _____

050 The more _____ develops, the smaller the world becomes.　　뜻 _____

001	health	ⓝ 건강	
002	field	ⓝ 분야, 벌판, 경기장	
003	novel	ⓝ 소설	
004	as long as	~하는 한, ~이기만 하면	
005	suggest	ⓥ 제안하다, 암시하다	
006	regret	ⓥ 후회하다, 뉘우치다	
007	disturb	ⓥ 방해하다, 혼란시키다	
008	be proud of	~을 자랑스러워하다	
009	activity	ⓝ 활동	
010	keep a diary	일기를 쓰다	
011	have a picnic	소풍[피크닉]을 가다	
012	reliable	ⓐ 믿을 수 있는	
013	be ashamed of	~을 부끄러워하다	
014	be worried about	~을 걱정하다	
015	insist on	~을 주장[요구]하다	
016	deny	ⓥ 부인[거절]하다	
017	steal	ⓥ 훔치다, 몰래 가지다	
018	give up	포기하다	
019	consider	ⓥ 고려하다, 생각하다	
020	over and over	여러 번 되풀이하여	
021	inform	ⓥ 알리다, 통지하다	
022	hit	ⓥ 때리다, 치다, 맞히다	
023	look forward to ⓥ + ing	~을 학수고대하다	
024	recycle	ⓥ 재활용하다	
025	worthwhile	ⓐ 가치 있는	

녹음된 문장을 듣고 빈칸에 단어 또는 표현을 쓰고, 그 뜻도 써보세요.

001 Eating too much is bad for _____. 뜻 _____

002 English is necessary in many _____. 뜻 _____

003 My hobby is reading _____. 뜻 _____

004 ___ _____ ___ we live, our heart never stops beating. 뜻 _____

005 Nancy _____ going to the movies. 뜻 _____

006 She _____ not playing the game more seriously. 뜻 _____

007 He enjoyed not being _____ at home. 뜻 _____

008 I ___ _____ ___ never being late for school. 뜻 _____

009 My favorite _____ is doing yoga. 뜻 _____

010 _____ ___ _____ teaches children how to write clearly. 뜻 _____

011 It was a gorgeous day, so I suggested _____ ___ _____. 뜻 _____

012 My car isn't very _____. It keeps breaking down. 뜻 _____

013 I ____ _____ ___ being scolded in front of my friends. 뜻 _____

014 I ____ _____ ____ being late for the concert. 뜻 _____

015 Bob _____ ___ paying the restaurant bill. 뜻 _____

016 They _____ stealing the money. 뜻 _____

017 They decided to _____ the money. 뜻 _____

018 Sunny _____ ___ dating the ugly boy. 뜻 _____

019 Have you ever _____ studying abroad? 뜻 _____

020 He kept asking me the same question _____ _____ _____. 뜻 _____

021 We regret to _____ you that we're unable to offer you the job. 뜻 _____

022 I'll never forget her _____ me. 뜻 _____

023 I'm _____ _____ ___ _____ you again. 뜻 _____

024 By _____ paper and bottles, we can protect the environment. 뜻 _____

025 It is _____ to read a newspaper everyday. 뜻 _____

026	disease	ⓝ (질)병, 퇴폐, 타락	
027	the moment~	~하자마자, ~하는 바로 그 순간	
028	competition	ⓝ 경쟁, 경기	
029	communicate	ⓥ 의사소통하다	
030	blame	ⓥ 비난하다, 책임지우다	
031	trash	ⓝ 쓰레기, 폐물	
032	language barrier	언어장벽	
033	make friends	친구를 사귀다	
034	scream	ⓥ 비명을 지르다	
035	distinctly	ⓐ 뚜렷하게, 정말로	
036	complain about	~에 대해 불평하다	
037	difference	ⓝ 차이(점), 특이점	
038	population	ⓝ 인구, 주민	
039	go bowling	볼링 치러 가다	
040	watchmaker	ⓝ 시계 기술자(제작자)	
041	donate	ⓥ 기부[기증]하다	
042	earthquake	ⓝ 지진	
043	tremor	ⓝ 떨림, 전율	
044	announcement	ⓝ 발표, 공표, 성명(서)	
045	rubbish	ⓝ 쓰레기	
046	set the alarm	알람을 맞추다	
047	by accident	우연히	
048	exhibition	ⓝ 전시회, 박람회	
049	portrait	ⓝ 초상화	
050	countryside	ⓝ 농촌, 시골	

녹음된 문장을 듣고 빈칸에 단어 또는 표현을 쓰고, 그 뜻도 써보세요.

026 Once you get the _____, it is no use taking medicine. 뜻 _____

027 _____ _____ I saw him, I fell in love with him. 뜻 _____

028 In business, _____ controls the market. 뜻 _____

029 She had no trouble _____. 뜻 _____

030 Thank you for not _____ me in that kind of situation. 뜻 _____

031 You should stop throwing _____ there. 뜻 _____

032 We couldn't communicate because of the _____ _____. 뜻 _____

033 Many people are interested in _____ _____ with foreigners. 뜻 _____

034 I heard her _____ in the dark room. 뜻 _____

035 I _____ remember looking at the door. 뜻 _____

036 Kelly _____ _____ him not being honest with her. 뜻 _____

037 Bill, tell us the _____ between these. 뜻 _____

038 The _____ of the world is rising very fast. 뜻 _____

039 After Mike finished working, he _____ _____ with his friends. 뜻 _____

040 In the end I had to have it done by a _____. 뜻 _____

041 He couldn't help _____ after he saw the situation of the poor. 뜻 _____

042 My mother is very afraid of _____. 뜻 _____

043 She can feel the _____ that nobody else seems to notice. 뜻 _____

044 On hearing the _____, they started to transmit the news. 뜻 _____

045 Did you take the _____ out before you left the house? 뜻 _____

046 Jessica forgot to _____ ____ _____ on Wednesday. 뜻 _____

047 When they came on to the ship, the rope was cut ____ _____. 뜻 _____

048 I went to the French Art _____ at the National Museum. 뜻 _____

049 Vincent van Gogh was famous for painting _____. 뜻 _____

050 He spent the rest of his life alone in a studio in the _____. 뜻 _____

001	destroyed	ⓐ 파괴된	
002	rural	ⓐ 시골의, 농업의	
003	fallen	ⓐ 떨어진, 쓰러진	
004	flood waters	홍수로 불어난 물	
005	face	ⓝ 얼굴	
006	admire	ⓥ 감탄하다	
007	be covered with	~로 덮여 있다	
008	etiquette	ⓝ 예의, 에티켓	
009	injured	ⓐ 부상당한	
010	murderer	ⓝ 살인자	
011	water	ⓥ ~에 물을 뿌리다	
012	bark	ⓥ 짖다	
013	doorbell	ⓝ 초인종	
014	parking lot	주차장	
015	satisfied	ⓐ 만족한	
016	audience	ⓝ 관중, 청중	
017	frightened	ⓐ 겁이 난, 무서워하는	
018	waiting room	대기실, 대합실	
019	walking stick	지팡이	
020	embarrassed	ⓐ 창피한, 난처한	
021	service station	주유소	
022	stomachache	ⓝ 위통, 복통	
023	admit	ⓥ 인정하다, 허락하다	
024	dial	ⓥ (번호를) 돌리다	
025	cheek	ⓝ 뺨	

녹음된 문장을 듣고 빈칸에 단어 또는 표현을 쓰고, 그 뜻도 써보세요.

001 I visited the _____ city soon after the war.　　뜻 _____

002 People living in the city don't know _____ pleasures.　　뜻 _____

003 Look at the leaves that have _____ on the ground.　　뜻 _____

004 The rising _____ _____ soon covered the street.　　뜻 _____

005 Her smiling _____ made everyone happy.　　뜻 _____

006 Everyone _____ the pictures painted by him.　　뜻 _____

007 The garden _____ _____ _____ fallen leaves.　　뜻 _____

008 The students talking loudly in the back seats have no _____.　　뜻 _____

009 The girl _____ in the accident was taken to the hospital.　　뜻 _____

010 The _____ arrested by the police officer last week died in jail.　　뜻 _____

011 Julia was _____ the flowers in the garden.　　뜻 _____

012 The dog kept _____ all night.　　뜻 _____

013 We heard the _____ ringing.　　뜻 _____

014 She had her car stolen in that _____ ____.　　뜻 _____

015 I'm not _____ with my job.　　뜻 _____

016 All the _____ was excited about the concert.　　뜻 _____

017 The children were _____ by the strange noise.　　뜻 _____

018 Kevin is waiting for you in the _____ _____.　　뜻 _____

019 The old woman was walking with a _____ _____.　　뜻 _____

020 When she saw me, she got so _____.　　뜻 _____

021 If you turn around, you will see a _____ _____.　　뜻 _____

022 Eating too much, he had a _____.　　뜻 _____

023 Though I _____ what you say, I don't like the way you say it.　　뜻 _____

024 Picking up the phone, she _____ his number.　　뜻 _____

025 Lisa smiled with tears running down her _____.　　뜻 _____

24

026	recognize	ⓥ 알아보다, 인지하다	
027	fluently	ⓐ 유창하게	
028	pale	ⓐ 창백한	
029	behavior	ⓝ 행동, 행실	
030	be over	끝나다	
031	put off	미루다, 연기하다	
032	frankly speaking	솔직히 말하면	
033	generally speaking	일반적으로 말해	
034	shout	ⓥ 소리 지르다, 외치다	
035	silent	ⓐ 조용한, 말 없는	
036	beginner	ⓝ 초보자	
037	indulgent	ⓐ 관대한, 엄하지 않은	
038	make sure	반드시 ~하다	
039	goods	ⓝ 상품	
040	seashore	ⓝ 해변, 해안, 바닷가	
041	noodle	ⓝ 국수, 면류	
042	experience	ⓝ 경험	
043	judging from	~로 판단하건대	
044	diabetes	ⓝ 당뇨병	
045	heart disease	심장병	
046	drowned	ⓐ 익사한	
047	undertake	ⓥ (떠)맡다, 착수하다	
048	rub	ⓥ 문지르다	
049	depend on	~에 의존하다	
050	survey	ⓝ 조사 (자료)	

녹음된 문장을 듣고 빈칸에 단어 또는 표현을 쓰고, 그 뜻을 써보세요.

026 Not having seen my uncle for a long time, I didn't _____ him. 뜻 _____

027 Having lived in Spain when he was young, he speaks Spanish _____. 뜻 _____

028 When she heard the news, she turned _____. 뜻 _____

029 Surprised at his _____, she could not say a word. 뜻 _____

030 When the class _____ _____, the students left quickly. 뜻 _____

031 The weather was getting worse, so the departure was _____ _____. 뜻 _____

032 _____ _____, she doesn't love me. 뜻 _____

033 _____ _____, women live longer than men. 뜻 _____

034 As I was excited about the news, I _____ with joy. 뜻 _____

035 Having been given the letter, she kept _____ for a long time. 뜻 _____

036 Written in simple English, this book is good for _____. 뜻 _____

037 Korean parents seem to be very _____ toward their children. 뜻 _____

038 _____ _____ that you haven't left anything behind. 뜻 _____

039 The _____ made by the company are famous for their quality. 뜻 _____

040 It was pleasant to walk along the _____ early in the morning. 뜻 _____

041 These _____ were made into instant ramen in 1958. 뜻 _____

042 Working as a reporter was a wonderful _____. 뜻 _____

043 _____ _____ his appearance, he looks like a thief. 뜻 _____

044 I have a girlfriend suffering from _____. 뜻 _____

045 The life guard cured the old lady dying from _____ _____. 뜻 _____

046 While he bathed in the river, he was _____. 뜻 _____

047 Though knowing the difficulty, they _____ the work. 뜻 _____

048 _____ your muscles with lotion. 뜻 _____

049 Your health _____ ___ how much you take care of it. 뜻 _____

050 The following _____ is about your eating and exercise habits. 뜻 _____

001	take care of	~을 돌보다		
002	fault	ⓝ 잘못, 실책(수), 결점		
003	investigate	ⓥ 수사[조사]하다		
004	graze	ⓥ (가축이) 풀을 뜯어먹다		
005	vote	ⓥ 투표하다		
006	criminal	ⓝ 범인, 범죄자		
007	clergy	ⓝ 성직자들		
008	huge	ⓐ 거대한, 막대한		
009	consist of	~로 구성되다		
010	contentment	ⓝ 만족		
011	vegetarian	ⓝ 채식주의자		
012	nutritionist	ⓝ 영양사, 영양학자		
013	statistics	ⓝ 통계학		
014	make friends	친구하다, 친해지다(with)		
015	belongings	ⓝ 재산, 소유물, 소지품		
016	sharp	ⓐ 날카로운, 뾰족한		
017	depressing	ⓐ 침울하게 만드는		
018	shake hands	악수하다		
019	latest	ⓐ 최신의		
020	region	ⓝ 지역, 영역, 분야		
021	basement	ⓝ 지하실		
022	document	ⓝ 문서, 서류		
023	tax	ⓝ 세금		
024	deeply	ⓐ 깊이		
025	plenty of	많은		

녹음된 문장을 듣고 빈칸에 단어 또는 표현을 쓰고, 그 뜻도 써보세요.

001 He _____ ___ the cows, chickens and sheep.   뜻 _____

002 It wasn't your _____. It was an accident.   뜻 _____

003 The police are _____ the murder case.   뜻 _____

004 Cattle are _____ in the field.   뜻 _____

005 People over 18 have a right to _____ in this country.   뜻 _____

006 A policeman is coming close to the _____.   뜻 _____

007 The _____ were present at the meeting.   뜻 _____

008 The crowd at the baseball game was _____.   뜻 _____

009 Water _____ ___ oxygen and hydrogen.   뜻 _____

010 Happiness consists in _____.   뜻 _____

011 A _____ is a person who doesn't eat meat.   뜻 _____

012 _____ recommend drinking eight glasses of water.   뜻 _____

013 _____ is a very difficult subject.   뜻 _____

014 She easily _____ _____ with the old.   뜻 _____

015 My _____ are still in the car.   뜻 _____

016 Be careful! These scissors are very _____.   뜻 _____

017 The news we heard was very _____.   뜻 _____

018 I _____ _____ with the movie star yesterday.   뜻 _____

019 This iPhone of my brother's is the company's _____ model.   뜻 _____

020 The wine from this _____ tastes good.   뜻 _____

021 The building has a _____. Sunny keeps her bike there.   뜻 _____

022 I will send the _____ by e-mail.   뜻 _____

023 Do you think the rich should pay more _____ to help the poor?   뜻 _____

024 The audience in the stadium was _____ moved at the concert.   뜻 _____

025 There are _____ _____ chairs.   뜻 _____

026	unfortunate	ⓐ 운이 없는, 불행한		
027	seize	ⓥ (붙)잡다, 붙들다		
028	source	ⓝ 원천, 출처, 근원		
029	bow	ⓥ 머리를 숙이다		
030	physicist	ⓝ 물리학자		
031	handicapped	ⓐ 신체적 장애가 있는		
032	unanimously	ⓐⓓ 만장일치로		
033	play	ⓝ 연극		
034	admire	ⓥ ~에 감탄[칭찬]하다		
035	artificial	ⓐ 인공의, 인조의		
036	awkward	ⓐ 서투른, 어색한		
037	mobile	ⓐ 이동할 수 있는		
038	supply	ⓥ 공급하다		
039	aptitude	ⓝ 적성, 재능		
040	discipline	ⓝ 훈련, 규율		
041	enroll	ⓥ 등록하다		
042	establish	ⓥ 확립[설치]하다		
043	quantity	ⓝ 양, 분량, 질량		
044	satellite	ⓝ 인공위성		
045	adjust	ⓥ 맞추다, 조정하다		
046	gym suit	체육복		
047	measure	ⓥ 재다, 측정하다		
048	protein	ⓝ 단백질		
049	destination	ⓝ 목적지, 행선지		
050	protest	ⓝ 항의		

녹음된 문장을 듣고 빈칸에 단어 또는 표현을 쓰고, 그 뜻도 써보세요.

026 We were very _____. We had bad luck. 뜻 _____

027 She _____ me by the collar. 뜻 _____

028 Sunshine is a _____ of vitamin D. 뜻 _____

029 Korean people usually _____ when they meet. 뜻 _____

030 He is now the greatest _____ in the world. 뜻 _____

031 It is certain that even _____ people can succeed. 뜻 _____

032 The members _____ elected him president of FIFA. 뜻 _____

033 It was a very good _____ written by Shakespeare. 뜻 _____

034 Parents should _____ their children's good behavior. 뜻 _____

035 He is the scientist in the field of _____ intelligence. 뜻 _____

036 It's _____ expressing my feelings via e-mail. 뜻 _____

037 Three billion people have _____ phones. 뜻 _____

038 The information is being _____ by network cable. 뜻 _____

039 She really had an _____ in this field. 뜻 _____

040 _____ that is too strict will harm children. 뜻 _____

041 So many students _____ in that class. 뜻 _____

042 A famous private school plans to _____ its local campus. 뜻 _____

043 They produce the items in large _____. 뜻 _____

044 They put a _____ in orbit successfully. 뜻 _____

045 I asked him to _____ my starting time for work to 9 a.m. 뜻 _____

046 The sale of ____ _____ is increasing recently. 뜻 _____

047 You can _____ sugar by weighing it on the balance scale. 뜻 _____

048 Athletes should eat high quality _____ and low fat food. 뜻 _____

049 When you fly, your baggage is usually carried to your _____. 뜻 _____

050 She accepted the charge without any _____. 뜻 _____

001	handwriting	ⓝ 필적, 필체		
002	persuade	ⓥ 설득하다		
003	unify	ⓥ 통일하다, 단일화하다		
004	impossible	ⓐ 불가능한		
005	broaden	ⓥ 넓히다		
006	solar energy	태양 에너지		
007	orphan	ⓝ 고아		
008	warrior	ⓝ 전사, 무인		
009	authority	ⓝ 당국, 공공사업 기관		
010	distinguish	ⓥ 구별하다		
011	of oneself	저절로		
012	between ourselves	우리끼리 얘긴데		
013	for oneself	혼자 힘으로		
014	shave	ⓥ 면도하다, 깎다		
015	selfish	ⓐ 이기적인		
016	regulation	ⓝ 법규, 규칙, 규정		
017	laptop	ⓝ 휴대용 컴퓨터		
018	completely	ⓐⓓ 완전히, 전적으로		
019	noise pollution	소음 공해		
020	acquire	ⓥ 습득하다, 획득하다		
021	common	ⓐ 흔한, 평범한, 보통의		
022	development	ⓝ 발전, 성장, 개발		
023	one another	서로 서로		
024	associate	ⓝ 동료, 친구, 조합원		
025	utilize	ⓥ 이용하다		

녹음된 문장을 듣고 빈칸에 단어 또는 표현을 쓰고, 그 뜻도 써보세요.

001 I found it impossible to read his _____. 뜻 _____

002 We found it useless _____ him. 뜻 _____

003 I think it possible that Korea will be _____ in 30 years. 뜻 _____

004 I tried to solve the problem, but it was _____. 뜻 _____

005 It is certain that travel _____ our mind. 뜻 _____

006 I think it better to make use of _____ _____. 뜻 _____

007 I believe it good his taking care of _____. 뜻 _____

008 Her appearance was that of a _____. 뜻 _____

009 Your opinion is quite different from that of the _____. 뜻 _____

010 It can be _____ from those of another company. 뜻 _____

011 That machine turns off ___ _____. 뜻 _____

012 _____ _____, I don't like her. 뜻 _____

013 I want to make it ___ _____. 뜻 _____

014 Steve cut himself while he was _____ this morning. 뜻 _____

015 Some people are very _____. They think only of themselves. 뜻 _____

016 One should obey the traffic _____. 뜻 _____

017 My _____ broke down, so I bought a new one this week. 뜻 _____

018 The bus was _____ empty. There wasn't anybody on it. 뜻 _____

019 Other types of pollution are water pollution and _____ _____. 뜻 _____

020 It is one thing to _____ knowledge; it is quite another to apply it. 뜻 _____

021 Other _____ last names are Smith, Wilson, and Jones. 뜻 _____

022 They believe that the _____ of technology leads to happiness. 뜻 _____

023 All the students helped _____ _____ prepare for the test. 뜻 _____

024 Mr. Schmidt is smarter than his _____. 뜻 _____

025 Some of them _____ airplanes for business. 뜻 _____

026	allowance	ⓝ 용돈		
027	afterlife	ⓝ 사후(의 삶)		
028	substance	ⓝ 물질		
029	goal	ⓝ 목표, 목적		
030	be tired of	~이 지겹다		
031	comprehension	ⓝ 이해, 이해력		
032	aggressive	ⓐ 공격적인		
033	agriculture	ⓝ 농업		
034	expansion	ⓝ 팽창, 확장		
035	diplomat	ⓝ 외교관		
036	pedestrian	ⓝ 보행자		
037	brutal	ⓐ 잔인한, 야만적인		
038	conservation	ⓝ (환경, 자연) 보존, 보호		
039	pessimistic	ⓐ 비관적인		
040	supervise	ⓥ 감독[관리]하다		
041	anxiety	ⓝ 걱정, 근심		
042	philosophy	ⓝ 철학		
043	extinct	ⓐ 멸종된, 사라진		
044	merit	ⓝ 뛰어남, 장점		
045	apparent	ⓐ 명백한, 뚜렷한		
046	inadequate	ⓐ 부적당한, 불충분한		
047	sympathize	ⓥ 동정[공감]하다		
048	contract	ⓝ 계약, 계약서		
049	symptom	ⓝ 증상		
050	contribute	ⓥ 기부[기여]하다, 공헌하다		

녹음된 문장을 듣고 빈칸에 단어 또는 표현을 쓰고, 그 뜻도 써보세요.

026 Some kids get an _____ for doing nothing. 뜻 _____

027 Nobody knows what the _____ will be like. 뜻 _____

028 The air is composed of two different kinds of _____. 뜻 _____

029 Each person has different _____ to achieve. 뜻 _____

030 I ___ _____ ___ it. I want something new. 뜻 _____

031 I have to take a test in listening _____. 뜻 _____

032 Some animals are naturally _____. 뜻 _____

033 _____ is about growing plants for food. 뜻 _____

034 We need more workers because of the _____. 뜻 _____

035 They live in France because their father is a _____. 뜻 _____

036 A car hit the _____ and injured two of them. 뜻 _____

037 He was the victim of a _____ murder. 뜻 _____

038 We know how important the _____ of wildlife is. 뜻 _____

039 Don't be so _____! Everything will be OK. 뜻 _____

040 The manager _____ the workers. 뜻 _____

041 She couldn't sleep because of _____. 뜻 _____

042 _____ is the study about the meaning of life. 뜻 _____

043 Dinosaurs became _____ millions of years ago. 뜻 _____

044 What are the _____ of this plan? 뜻 _____

045 It was _____ that she didn't like him. 뜻 _____

046 These shoes are _____ for cold weather. 뜻 _____

047 I _____ with you. I had a similar experience myself. 뜻 _____

048 I have a one-year _____ with the company. 뜻 _____

049 A sore throat is often a _____ of a cold. 뜻 _____

050 She _____ to a charity collection. 뜻 _____

001	near	prep ~근처에	
002	floor	n 층, 방바닥	
003	drunken	a 술취한, 만취한	
004	unconscious	a 의식을 잃은, 모르는	
005	wander	v 돌아다니다, 헤매다	
006	suspicious	a 수상쩍은, 의심스러운	
007	donate	v 기부[제공]하다	
008	address	n 주소	
009	environmental hormone	환경 호르몬	
010	embarrassed	a 당혹한	
011	expert	n 전문가	
012	particular	a 특별한, 특정한	
013	volunteer	n 자원봉사자, 지원자	
014	facility	n 시설, 기능	
015	immigrate	v 이주하다	
016	yellow dust	황사	
017	prepare	v 준비하다	
018	recipe	n 요리법, 조리법	
019	refrigerator	n 냉장고	
020	flickering	a 깜박거리는	
021	compose	v 작곡하다, 만들다	
022	tax	n 세금	
023	drown	v 익사하다, 익사시키다	
024	receive	v 받다, 접수하다	
025	export	v 수출하다	

녹음된 문장을 듣고 빈칸에 단어 또는 표현을 쓰고, 그 뜻도 써보세요.

001 There's an Italian restaurant _____ my house. 뜻 _____

002 What _____ are you going to? 뜻 _____

003 The _____ man was lying on the road. 뜻 _____

004 The police found an old man _____ on the bench. 뜻 _____

005 A drunken man was _____ in the parking lot. 뜻 _____

006 There's something _____ about that man. 뜻 _____

007 We should _____ money for the poor. 뜻 _____

008 I don't know her present _____. 뜻 _____

009 Certain plastic containers produce _____ _____. 뜻 _____

010 His ill manner made us _____. 뜻 _____

011 His late wife was an _____ in this field. 뜻 _____

012 I don't have anything _____ to tell you. 뜻 _____

013 Lots of _____ are trained to help handicapped people. 뜻 _____

014 Our city's subway system is equipped with _____ for the blind. 뜻 _____

015 A lot of people _____ to America. 뜻 _____

016 Was there a lot of _____ _____ in Seoul yesterday? 뜻 _____

017 Did you _____ much food for Thanksgiving? 뜻 _____

018 This _____ calls for a lot of garlic, so it's going to be delicious. 뜻 _____

019 There wasn't much food in the _____. 뜻 _____

020 There was a _____ light in the distance. 뜻 _____

021 Do you like symphonies _____ by Beethoven? 뜻 _____

022 Do you think the rich should pay more _____ to help poor people? 뜻 _____

023 A boy swimming in the river nearly _____. 뜻 _____

024 I _____ a letter written in English yesterday. 뜻 _____

025 Most of the goods made in this factory are _____. 뜻 _____

026	abandoned	ⓐ 버려진, 황폐한	
027	unemployed	ⓐ 실직한, 실업자의	
028	government	ⓝ 정부	
029	protein	ⓝ 단백질	
030	left-handed	ⓐ 왼손잡이의	
031	convenient	ⓐ 편리한	
032	ancestor	ⓝ 조상, 시조	
033	specialist	ⓝ 전문가	
034	timid	ⓐ 겁 많은, 소심한	
035	spokesperson	ⓝ 대변인	
036	academic	ⓐ 학문의	
037	inconvenient	ⓐ 불편한	
038	tragic	ⓐ 비극의	
039	amusement	ⓝ 재미, 오락	
040	recovery	ⓝ 회복	
041	capture	ⓥ 붙잡다, 포착[체포]하다	
042	infect	ⓥ 전염[감염]시키다	
043	engagement	ⓝ 약혼, 약속	
044	treatment	ⓝ 취급, 대우, 치료	
045	refund	ⓥ 환불하다	
046	satisfaction	ⓝ 만족, 만족감	
047	trend	ⓝ 유행, 추세, 경향	
048	institution	ⓝ 기관, 공공단체	
049	minority	ⓝ 소수	
050	entirely	ⓐⓓ 완전히, 전적으로	

녹음된 문장을 듣고 빈칸에 단어 또는 표현을 쓰고, 그 뜻도 써보세요.

026 The children approached the _____ house.   뜻 _____

027 Government decided to create more jobs for the _____. 뜻 _____

028 The homeless need more help from the _____.   뜻 _____

029 I eat a little meat every day because I want _____ in my diet. 뜻 _____

030 _____ people usually use their left hand more often. 뜻 _____

031 We should provide _____ services for disabled people. 뜻 _____

032 Few American Indians speak the language of their _____. 뜻 _____

033 My doctor referred me to a medical _____.   뜻 _____

034 The boy looks very weak and _____.   뜻 _____

035 He was the _____ for the company.   뜻 _____

036 The school is noted for its _____ excellence.   뜻 _____

037 Isn't it _____ living so far out of town?   뜻 _____

038 It is _____ that she died so young.   뜻 _____

039 We watched in _____ as children danced.   뜻 _____

040 He made a quick _____ after his illness.   뜻 _____

041 The police _____ the robbers.   뜻 _____

042 He _____ his classmates with his cold.   뜻 _____

043 He announced his _____ to Olivia.   뜻 _____

044 Their _____ of the animals was very cruel.   뜻 _____

045 We guarantee to _____ you your money in full.   뜻 _____

046 He looked at his work with _____.   뜻 _____

047 She tries to follow the latest _____ in fashion.   뜻 _____

048 Most of the schools are government _____.   뜻 _____

049 Only a _____ of the students speak English.   뜻 _____

050 She looks _____ different from her sister.   뜻 _____